A Course in Behavioral Economics

Erik Angner

George Mason University, USA

palgrave
macmillan

First published 2012 by
PALGRAVE MACMILLAN

Palgrave Macmillan in the UK is an imprint of Macmillan Publishers Limited, registered in England, company number 785998, of Houndmills, Basingstoke, Hampshire RG21 6XS.

Palgrave Macmillan in the US is a division of St Martin's Press LLC, 175 Fifth Avenue, New York, NY 10010.

Palgrave Macmillan is the global academic imprint of the above companies and has companies and representatives throughout the world.

Palgrave® and Macmillan® are registered trademarks in the United States, the United Kingdom, Europe and other countries.

ISBN 978–0–230–30454–3

This book is printed on paper suitable for recycling and made from fully managed and sustained forest sources. Logging, pulping and manufacturing processes are expected to conform to the environmental regulations of the country of origin.

A catalogue record for this book is available from the British Library.

A catalog record for this book is available from the Library of Congress.

To Iris

The master-piece of philosophy would be to develop the means which Providence employs to attain the ends it proposes over man, and to mark out accordingly a few lines of conduct which might make known to this unhappy biped individual the way in which he must walk within the thorny career of life, that he might guard against the whimsical caprices of this fatality to which they give twenty different names, without having as yet come to understand or define it.

The Marquis de Sade, *Justine*

Contents

Part III Choice under Risk and Uncertainty

Part IV Intertemporal Choice

Figures

Tables

Preface

As a Ph.D. student in economics, behavioral economics struck me as the most exciting field of study by far. Even with the benefit of some spectacular teachers, though, I felt that the existing literature failed to convey an adequate understanding of the nature and significance of the project, and how the many different concepts and theories described as "behavioral" were tied together. When as an assistant professor I was offered the opportunity to teach my own course, I discovered that there were very few texts occupying the niche between popular-science-style treatments, which do not contain enough substance for a university-level course, and original scientific papers, which are not easily readable and typically fail to provide sufficient background to be comprehensible to a novice reader.

This introduction to behavioral economics was written to be the book I wish I had had as a student, and the book that I want to use as a teacher. It aspires to situate behavioral economics in historical context, seeing it as the result of a coherent intellectual tradition; it offers more substance than popular books but more context than original articles; and it not only describes individual concepts and theories but also tries to show how they hang together. The book was designed to be used as a user-friendly, self-contained, freestanding textbook suitable for a one-semester course for advanced undergraduates, but can easily be used in conjunction with books or articles in a variety of higher-level courses.

In recognition of the fact that many students of behavioral economics come from outside traditional economics, the exposition was developed to appeal to advanced undergraduates across the social and behavioral sciences, humanities, business, public health, and so on. The book contains no advanced mathematics and presupposes no knowledge of standard economic theory. Thorough battle-testing at a medium-sized state university in the US over the course of several years has confirmed that the treatment is accessible to economics majors and non-majors alike.

Serious economics does not need to be intimidating, and this book aims to prove it. Abstract, formal material is introduced in a progressively more difficult manner, which serves to build confidence in students with limited previous exposure. A wealth of examples and exercises serve to make the underlying intuitions as clear as possible. In order to sustain the interest of readers with different backgrounds, and to illustrate the vast applicability of economic analysis, examples are drawn from economics, business, marketing, medicine, philosophy, public health, political science, public policy, and elsewhere. More open-ended problems encourage students to apply the ideas and theories presented here to decision problems they might come across outside the classroom.

The book is arranged in five main parts: (I) choice under certainty, (II) judgment under risk and uncertainty, (III) choice under risk and uncertainty, (IV) intertemporal choice, and (V) strategic interaction. Each part contains two chapters: an even-numbered one outlining standard neoclassical theory and an odd-numbered one discussing behavioral alternatives. The unique structure makes it easy for instructors to teach the book at a more advanced level, as they can easily assign even-numbered chapters as background reading and supplement the odd-numbered chapters with more advanced material of their choosing. Additional resources are available via the companion website http://www.palgrave.com/economics/angner.

The non-trivial amount of neoclassical theory in this book may warrant explanation. First, because behavioral economics was developed in response to neoclassical economics, large portions of behavioral economics can only be understood against this background. Second, while behavioral economists reject the standard theory as a *descriptive* theory, they typically accept it as a *normative* theory. Third, much of behavioral economics is a modification or extension of neoclassical theory. Finally, to assess the relative merits of neoclassical and behavioral economics, it is necessary to understand both. Just as the study of a foreign language teaches students a great deal about their native tongue, so the study of behavioral economics will teach them a lot about standard economics.

As a textbook rather than an encyclopedia, this book does not aspire to completeness but explores a selection of the most important ideas in behavioral economics and their interrelations. Many fascinating ideas, developments, and avenues of research have deliberately been omitted. No doubt every behavioral economist will disagree with some of my decisions about the things that were left out. But I think most will agree about the things that were left in. The material presented in this book is, on the whole, uncontroversially part of the canon, and as such should be familiar to anyone who wishes to have a basic grasp of behavioral economics.

Like standard introductory textbooks, this book does not aim to review the empirical case offered in favor of the theories it presents. As a result, the exposition is uncluttered by extensive discussion of data, standards of evidence, empirical (including experimental) methodology, and statistical techniques. Instead, theories are illustrated with stories intended to elicit the intuition underlying the theory and to demonstrate that it is not entirely implausible. In this respect, the present book is no different from any of the widely used introductions to microeconomics, to take one example.

For readers who wish to continue their study of behavioral economics, or who want to know more about its methodology, history, and philosophy, every chapter ends with a further reading section, which offers a selection of citation classics, review articles, and advanced textbooks. While this may be the first book in behavioral economics for many readers, my hope is that it will not be the last.

Erik Angner

Acknowledgments

This book draws on many different sources of inspiration. I am particularly grateful to the teachers who set me off on this path (among them Cristina Bicchieri, Robyn Dawes, Baruch Fischhoff, George Loewenstein, Philip Reny, and Alvin Roth), whether or not they approve of the place to which it led, and to the students (too numerous to name) who keep me on the straight and narrow by catching errors in my work.

The manuscript was immensely improved by the encouragement and criticism offered by Aléta Bezuidenhout and Jaime Marshall at Palgrave Macmillan, and by Elizabeth Stone's meticulous handling of the production process. I thank friends, colleagues, and anonymous reviewers for helpful feedback on earlier drafts and Lillie Flowers and Jared Sutton for able copyediting. NBCUniversal Media, LLC, kindly granted permission to use an image from *Deal or No Deal*. The Board of Trustees of the University of Alabama System for the University of Alabama at Birmingham generously granted permission to reproduce the author photograph by Steven W. Wood. Original illustrations by Cody Taylor are used with the artist's kind permission. The epigraph appears in *Opus Sadicum* (de Sade, 1889 [1791], p. 7). Every effort has been made to trace copyright holders, but if any have been inadvertently overlooked we will be pleased to make the necessary arrangements at the first opportunity. I gratefully acknowledge support from a Quality Enhancement Plan Development Grant from the University of Alabama at Birmingham.

Most importantly, Elizabeth Blum's love and support every step along the way were essential to the completion of the project.

Further suggestions for improvement are most welcome via the companion website http://www.palgrave.com/economics/angner. As always, errors remain my own.

About the Author

Erik Angner is Associate Professor of Philosophy, Economics, and Public Policy at George Mason University. As a result of serious mission creep, he holds two PhDs – one in Economics and one in History and Philosophy of Science – both from the University of Pittsburgh. He is the author of *Hayek and Natural Law* as well as numerous journal articles and book chapters on behavioral and experimental economics, the economics of happiness, and the history, philosophy, and methodology of contemporary economics. He has taught behavioral economics at the undergraduate level since 2006.

Introduction

Chapter 1

Introduction

Economics: Neoclassical and behavioral

This is a book about **theories of decision**. To use the language of the epigraph, such theories are about the negotiation of "the thorny career of life": they tell us how we make, or how we should make, decisions. Not that the Marquis de Sade would have spoken in these terms, living as he did in the eighteenth century, but the theory of decision seems to be exactly what he had in mind when he imagined "the masterpiece of philosophy."

Developing an acceptable theory of decision would be an achievement. Most human activity – finance, science, medicine, arts, and life in general – can be understood as a matter of people making certain kinds of decisions. Consequently, an accurate theory of decision would cover a lot of ground. Maybe none of the theories we will discuss is the masterpiece of which de Sade thought so highly. Each theory can be, has been, and perhaps should be challenged on various grounds. However, decision theory has been an active area of research in recent decades, and it may have generated real progress.

Modern theories of decision (or **theories of choice** – I will use the terms interchangeably) say little about what goals people will or should pursue. Goals may be good or evil, mean-spirited or magnanimous, altruistic or egoistic, short-sighted or far-sighted; they may be Mother Teresa's or the Marquis de Sade's. Theories of decision simply take a set of goals as given. Provided a set of goals, however, the theories have much to say about how people will or should pursue those goals.

Theories of decision are variously presented as descriptive or normative. A **descriptive** theory describes how people *in fact* make decisions. A **normative** theory captures how people *should* make decisions. It is at least theoretically possible that people make the decisions that they should make. If so, one and the same theory can simultaneously be descriptively adequate and normatively correct. However, it is possible that people fail to act in the manner in which they should. If so, no one theory can be both descriptively adequate and normatively correct.

Exercise 1.1 Descriptive vs. normative   Which of the following claims are descriptive and which are normative? (Answers to this and other exercises can be found in the Appendix.)

(a) On average, people save less than 10 percent of their income for retirement.
(b) People do not save as much for retirement as they should.
(c) Very often, people regret not saving more for retirement.

It can be unclear whether a claim is descriptive or normative. "People save too little" is an example. Does this mean that people do not save as much as they should? If so, the claim is normative. Does this mean that people do not save as much as they wish they did? If so, the claim is descriptive.

Example 1.2 Poker Suppose that you are playing poker, and that you are playing to win. Would you benefit from having an adequate descriptive theory, a correct normative theory, or both?

A descriptive theory would give you information about the actions of the other players. A normative theory would tell you how you should behave in light of what you know about the nature of the game, the expected actions of the other players, and your ambition to win. All this information is obviously useful when playing poker: so you would benefit from having both kinds of theory.

Some theories of decision are described as **theories of rational choice**. In every-day speech, the word "rationality" is used loosely; frequently it is used simply as a mark of approval. For our purposes, a theory of rational decision is best seen as a **definition** of rationality, that is, as specifying what it means to be rational. Every theory of rational decision serves to divide decisions into two classes: rational and irrational. Rational decisions are those that are in accordance with the theory; irrational decisions are those that are not. A theory of rational choice can be thought of as descriptive or normative (or both). To say that a theory of rational decision is descriptive is to say that people in fact act rationally. To say that a theory of rational decision is normative is to say that people should act rationally. To say that a theory of rational decision is simultaneously descriptive and normative is to say that people act and should act rationally. Typically, the term **rational-choice theory** is reserved for theories that are (or that are thought to be) normatively correct, whether or not they are simultaneously descriptively adequate.

For generations now, economics has been dominated by an intellectual tradition broadly referred to as **neoclassical economics**. If you have studied economics but do not know whether or not you were taught in the neoclassical tradition, it is almost certain that you were. Neoclassical economics is characterized by its commitment to a theory of rational choice that is simultaneously presented as descriptively adequate and normatively correct. This approach presupposes that people by and large act in the manner that they should. Neoclassical economists do not need to assume that all people act rationally all the time, but they insist that deviations from perfect rationality are so small or so unsystematic as to be negligible. Because of its historical dominance, I will refer to neoclassical economics as standard economics, and to neoclassical economic theory as standard theory.

This is an introduction to **behavioral economics**: the attempt to increase the explanatory and predictive power of economic theory by providing it with more psychologically plausible foundations, where "psychologically plausible" means consistent with the best available psychology. Behavioral economists share neoclassical economists' conception of **economics** as the study of people's decisions under conditions of scarcity and of the results of those decisions for society. But behavioral economists reject the idea that people by and large behave in the manner that they should. While behavioral economists certainly do not deny that some people act rationally some of the time, they believe that the deviations from rationality are large enough, systematic enough, and consequently predictable enough, to warrant the development of new descriptive theories of decision. If this is right, a descriptively adequate theory cannot at the same time be normatively correct, and a normatively correct theory cannot at the same time be descriptively adequate.

1.2 The origins of behavioral economics

Behavioral economics can be said to have a short history but a long past. Only in the last few decades has it emerged as an independent subdiscipline of economics. By now, top departments of economics have behavioral economists on their staff. Behavioral economics gets published in mainstream journals. Traditional economists incorporate insights from behavioral economics into their work. In 2002, Daniel Kahneman (one of the most famous behavioral economists) won the Nobel Memorial Prize "for having integrated insights from psychological research into economic science, especially concerning human judgment and decision-making under uncertainty." In spite of its short history, however, efforts to provide economics with plausible psychological foundations go back a long way.

The establishment of modern economics is marked by the publication in 1776 of Adam Smith's *Wealth of Nations*. Classical economists such as Smith are often accused of having a particularly simple-minded (and false) picture of human nature, according to which people everywhere and always, in hyper-rational fashion, pursue their narrowly construed self-interest. This accusation, however, is unfounded. Smith did not think people were rational:

> How many people ruin themselves by laying out money on trinkets of frivolous utility? What pleases these lovers of toys is not so much the utility, as the aptness of the machines which are fitted to promote it. All their pockets are stuffed with little conveniences ... of which the whole utility is certainly not worth the fatigue of bearing the burden.

Smith wrote these words 200 years before the era of pocket calculators, camera phones, iPads, and GPS-enabled watches. Nor did Smith think people were selfish: "[There] are evidently some principles in [man's] nature, which interest him in the fortune of others, and render their happiness necessary to him, though he derives nothing from it except the pleasure of seeing it." In fact, Smith and the other classical economists had a conception of human nature that was remarkably multi-faceted; indeed, they did not draw a sharp line between psychology and economics the way we do.

Early neoclassical economics was built on the foundation of **hedonic psychology**: an account of individual behavior according to which individuals seek to maximize pleasure and minimize pain. In W. Stanley Jevons' words: "Pleasure and pain are undoubtedly the ultimate objects of the Calculus of Economics. To satisfy our wants to the utmost with the least effort ... in other words, to *maximise pleasure*, is the problem of Economics." The early neoclassical economists were inspired by the philosopher Jeremy Bentham, who wrote: "Nature has placed mankind under the governance of two sovereign masters, *pain* and *pleasure* ... They govern us in all we do, in all we say, in all we think." Because it was assumed that individuals have direct access to their conscious experience, some economists defended the principles of hedonic psychology on the basis of their introspective self-evidence alone.

After World War II, however, many economists were disappointed with the meager results of early neoclassicism in terms of generating theories with predictive power and so came to doubt that introspection worked. Similar developments took place in other fields: behaviorism in psychology, verificationism in philosophy, and operationalism in physics can all be seen as expressions of the same intellectual trend. Postwar neoclassical economists aimed to improve the predictive power of their theories by focusing on what can be publicly observed rather than on what must be experienced. Instead of taking a theory about pleasure and pain as their foundation, they took a theory of preference. The main difference in the latter is that people's feelings of pleasure and pain are unobservable, whereas their choices can be directly observed. On the assumption that choices reflect personal preferences, we can have direct observable evidence about what people prefer. Thus, postwar neoclassical economists hoped to completely rid economics of its ties to psychology – hedonic and otherwise.

In spite of the relative hegemony of neoclassical economics during the second half of the twentieth century, many economists felt that their discipline would benefit from closer ties to psychology and other neighboring fields. What really made a difference, however, was the cognitive revolution. In the 1950s and 1960s, researchers in psychology, computer science, linguistics, anthropology, and elsewhere rejected the demands that science focus on the observable and that all methods be public. Instead, these figures advocated a "science of cognition" or **cognitive science**. The cognitive scientists were skeptical of naive reliance on introspection, but nevertheless felt that a scientific psychology must refer to things "in the head," including beliefs and desires, symbols, rules, and images. Behavioral economics is a product of the cognitive revolution. Like cognitive scientists, behavioral economists – though skeptical of the theories and methods of the early neoclassical period – are comfortable talking about beliefs, desires, rules of thumb, and other things "in the head." Below, we will see how these commitments get played out in practice.

1.3 Methods

Before we explore in earnest the concepts and theories developed by behavioral economists in the last few decades, I want to discuss the data that behavioral economists use to test their theories and the methods they use to generate such data.

Some of the earliest and most influential papers in behavioral economics relied on participants' responses to hypothetical choices. In such studies, participants were asked to imagine that they found themselves in a given choice situation and to indicate what decision they would make under those conditions. Here is one such question: "Which of the following would you prefer? A: 50% chance to win 1,000, 50% chance to win nothing; B: 450 for sure." Other early papers relied on readers' intuitions about how people might behave under given conditions. Thus, they offered scenarios such as: "Mr S. admires a $125 cashmere sweater at the department store. He declines to buy it, feeling that it is too extravagant. Later that month he receives the same sweater from his wife for a birthday present. He is very happy. Mr and Mrs S. have only joint bank accounts." These thought experiments were apparently inspired in part by the author's observations of the behavior of fellow economists, who argued that people were always rational but at times behaved irrationally in their own lives.

More recently, hypothetical choice studies were almost completely displaced by **laboratory experiments** in which laboratory participants make real choices involving real money. Such experiments have been run for decades. In the early 1970s, for example, two psychologists ran experiments at a Las Vegas casino, where a croupier served as experimenter, professional gamblers served as participants, and winnings and losses were paid in real money. More frequently, behavioral economists use college undergraduates or other easily accessible participants. When behavioral economists engage in experimental studies, they can be hard to distinguish from neoclassical experimental economists, that is, neoclassical economists who use experiments to explore how people make decisions. Experimentalists agree that decisions performed by laboratory subjects must be real, and that actual winnings must be paid out.

Behavioral economists, during the last decade or so, have increasingly relied on data gathered "in the field." In one famous **field study**, researchers studied the behavior of New York City cab drivers by using data from "trip sheets" – forms that drivers use to record the time passengers are picked up and dropped off as well as the amount of the fares – and from the cabs' meters, which automatically record the fares. Researchers in this study simply observed how participants behaved under different conditions. In **field experiments**, researchers randomly assign participants to test and control groups, and then note how (if at all) the behavior of individuals in the two groups differs.

To some extent, behavioral economists use what psychologists call **process measures**, that is, methods that provide hints about cognitive and emotional processes underlying decision-making. Some rely on **process-tracing** software to assess what information people use when making decisions in games. Others use brain scans, typically using functional Magnetic Resonance Imaging (fMRI), which allows researchers to examine, albeit crudely, which parts of an individual's brain are activated in response to a task or decision. Imaging methods have already been applied to a diversity of economic tasks, including decision-making under risk and uncertainty, intertemporal choice, buying and selling behavior, and strategic behavior in games. Even more exotic neuroscience methods are sometimes employed. One recent study explored what happens when you use a tool called Transcranial Magnetic Stimulation to disable a part of participants' brains. The increasing use of methods borrowed from neuroscience is, not coincidentally, connected to the rise of **neuroeconomics**, which integrates economics with neuroscience.

The use of multiple methods to generate evidence raises interesting methodological problems. This is particularly true when evidence from different sources points in slightly different directions. Sometimes, however, evidence from multiple sources points in the same direction. When this is true, behavioral economists have more confidence in their conclusions. It can be argued that part of the reason why behavioral economics has turned into such a vibrant field is that it successfully integrates evidence of multiple kinds, generated by a variety of methods.

1.4 Looking ahead

As stated in the Preface, this book is arranged in five main parts: (I) choice under certainty, (II) judgment under risk and uncertainty, (III) choice under risk and uncertainty, (IV) intertemporal choice, and (V) strategic interaction. Each part contains two chapters: an even-numbered one outlining standard neoclassical theory and an odd-numbered one discussing behavioral alternatives. As suggested in Section 1.1, the ultimate goal of behavioral economics is to generate novel insights into people's decisions under conditions of scarcity and the results of those decisions for society. Behavioral and neoclassical economists alike try to attain this goal by building abstract, formal theories. In this book we will explore increasingly general theories, both neoclassical and behavioral.

Studying behavioral economics is a non-trivial enterprise. For one thing, the level of abstraction can pose an initial challenge. But as we will see below, it is the very fact that economics is so abstract that makes it so very useful: the more abstract the theory, the wider its potential application. Some readers may be prone to putting down a book like this as soon as they notice that it contains mathematics. Please do not. There is no advanced math in the book, and **numeracy** – the ability with or knowledge of numbers – is incredibly important, even to people who think of themselves as practically oriented.

Exercise 1.3 Numeracy　In a recent study on financial decision-making, people's answers to three quick mathematics questions were strong predictors of their wealth: households where both spouses answered all three questions correctly were *more than eight times* as wealthy as households where neither spouse answered any question correctly. So if you have ever struggled with math, be glad that you did. You can try answering the three questions for yourself:

(a) If the chance of getting a disease is 10 percent, how many people out of 1000 would be expected to get the disease?
(b) If five people all have the winning numbers in the lottery, and the prize is 2 million dollars, how much will each of them get?
(c) Let us say you have $200 in a savings account. The account earns 10 percent interest per year. How much would you have in the account at the end of two years?

To underscore the usefulness of behavioral economics, the book discusses a variety of applications. Among other things, you will learn how to choose a wingman or wingwoman, how to design a marketing scheme that works, how not to fall for such marketing schemes, how to compute the probability that your love interest is seeing somebody else, how to sell tires, and how to beat anyone at rock-paper-scissors. Ultimately, behavioral economics sheds light on human beings – the way they really are, as opposed to the way great thinkers of the past have thought they should be – and on the nature of the human condition.

Further reading

Angner and Loewenstein (2012) offers a longer discussion of the nature, historical origin, and methods of behavioral economics as compared with neoclassical economics. The *Wealth of Nations* is Smith (1976 [1776]); the quotes in the history section are from Smith (2002 [1759], p. 211) and Smith (2002 [1759], p. 11), Jevons (1965 [1871], p. 37), and Bentham (1996 [1789], p. 11). The sample questions in the methods section come from Kahneman and Tversky (1979, p. 264) and Thaler (1985, p. 199). The psychologists who went to Vegas are Lichtenstein and Slovic (1973). The study of NYC cabdrivers is Camerer et al. (1997), and that which disabled parts of participants' brains Knoch et al. (2006). Camerer et al. (2005) provides a widely cited overview of neuroeconomics. The study on financial decision-making is Smith et al. (2010); the three numeracy questions were adapted from the University of Michigan Health and Retirement Study.

Part I

Choice under Certainty

Chapter 2
Rational Choice under Certainty

Introduction

As promised, we begin by discussing the theory of rational choice. This theory forms the foundation of virtually all modern economics and is one of the first things you would learn in a graduate-level microeconomics class. As a theory of rational choice (see Section 1.1), the theory specifies what it means to make rational decisions – in short, what it means to be rational.

In this chapter, we consider **choice under certainty**. The phrase "under certainty" simply means that there is no doubt as to which outcome will result from a given act. For example, if the staff at your local gelato place is minimally competent, so that you actually get vanilla every time you order vanilla and stracciatella every time you order stracciatella, you are making a choice under certainty. (We will discuss other kinds of choice in future chapters.) Before discussing what it means to make rational choices under conditions of certainty, however, we need to talk about what preferences are and what it means to have rational preferences.

The theory of rational choice under certainty is an **axiomatic** theory. This means that the theory consists of a set of **axioms**: basic propositions that cannot be proven using the resources offered by the theory, and which will simply have to be taken for granted. When studying the theory, the first thing we want to do is examine the axioms. As we go along, we will also introduce new terms by means of definitions. Axioms and definitions have to be memorized. Having introduced the axioms and definitions, we can prove many interesting claims. Thus, much of what we will do below involves proving new propositions on the basis of axioms and definitions.

2.2 Preferences

The concept of **preference** is fundamental in modern economics, neoclassical and behavioral. Formally speaking, a preference is a **relation**. The following are examples of relations: "Alf is older than Betsy," "France is bigger than Norway," and "Bill is worried he may not do as well on the exam as Jennifer." Notice that each of these sentences expresses a relationship between two entities (things, individuals). Thus, "Alf is older than Betsy" expresses a relationship between Alf and Betsy, namely, that the former is older than the latter. Because these examples express a relation between two entities, they are called **binary** relations. The following relation is not binary: "Mom stands between Bill and Bob." This relation is **ternary**, because it involves three different entities, in this case, people.

For convenience, we often use small letters to denote entities or individuals. We may use a to denote Alf and b to denote Betsy. Similarly, we often use capital letters to denote relations. We may use R to denote the relation "is older than." If so, we can write aRb for "Alf is older than Betsy." Sometimes we write Rab. Notice that the order of the terms matters: aRb is not the same thing as bRa. The first says that Alf is older than Betsy and the second that Betsy is older than Alf. Similarly, Rab is not the same thing as Rba.

Exercise 2.1 Relations   Assume that f denotes France and n denotes Norway, and that B means "is bigger than."

(a) How would you write that France is bigger than Norway?
(b) How would you write that Norway is bigger than France?
(c) How would you write that Norway is bigger than Norway?

In order to speak clearly about relations, we need to specify what sort of entities may be related to one another. When talking about who is older than whom, we may be talking about people. When talking about what is bigger than what, we may be talking about countries, houses, people, dogs, or many other things. Sometimes it matters what sort of entities we have in mind. When we want to be careful, which is most of the time, we define a **universe** U. The universe is the set of all things that can be related to one another. Suppose we are talking about Donald Duck's nephews Huey, Dewey, and Louie. If so, that is our universe. The convention is to list all members of the universe separated by commas and enclosed in curly brackets, like so: {Huey, Dewey, Louie}. Here, the order does not matter. So, the same universe can be written like this: {Louie, Dewey, Huey}. Thus: U = {Huey, Dewey, Louie} = {Louie, Dewey, Huey}.

Exercise 2.2 The universe   Suppose we are talking about all countries that are members of the United Nations. How would that be written?

A universe may have infinitely many members, in which case simple enumeration is inconvenient. This is true, for instance, when you consider the time at which you entered the space where you are reading this. There are infinitely many points in time between 11:59 am and 12:01 pm, for example, as there are between 11:59:59 am and 12:00:01 pm. In such cases, we need to find another way to describe the universe.

One relation we can talk about is this one: "is at least as good as." For example, we might want to say that "coffee is at least as good as tea." The "at least as good as" relation is often expressed using this symbol: $\succeq$. If c denotes coffee and t denotes tea, we can write the sentence as $c \succeq t$. This is the **(weak) preference relation**. People may have, and often will have his or their own preference relations. If we wish to specify whose preferences we are talking about, we use subscripts to denote individuals. If we want to say that for Alf coffee is at least as good as tea, and that for Betsy tea is at least as good as coffee, we say that $c \succeq_{Alf} t$ and $t \succeq_{Betsy} c$, or that $c \succeq_A t$ and $t \succeq_B c$.

Exercise 2.3 Preferences   Suppose d denotes "enjoying a cool drink on a hot day" and r denotes "getting roasted over an open fire."

(a) How would you state your preference over these two options?
(b) How would you express a masochist's preference over these two options?

In economics, we are typically interested in people's preferences over **consumption bundles**, which are collections of goods. You face a choice of commodity bundles when choosing between the #1 Big Burger meal and the #2 Chicken Burger meal at your local hamburger restaurant. In order to represent commodity bundles, we think of them as collections of individual goods along the following lines: three apples and two bananas, or two units of guns and five units of butter. When talking about

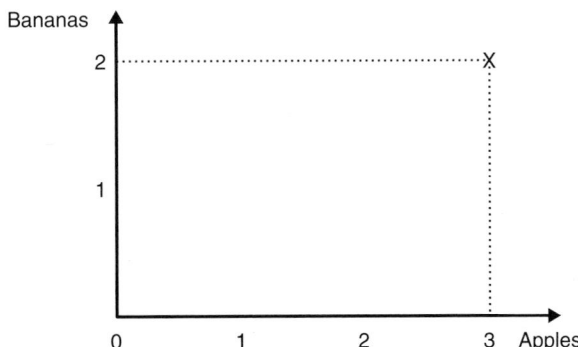

Figure 2.1 Set of alternatives

preference relations, the universe can also be referred to as the **set of alternatives**. If bundles contain no more than two goods, it can be convenient to represent the set of alternatives on a plane, as in Figure 2.1. When bundles contain more than two goods, it is typically more useful to write $\langle 3,2 \rangle$ for three apples and two bananas; $\langle 6,3,9 \rangle$ for six apples, three bananas, and nine citrus fruits; and so on.

2.3   Rational preferences

We begin building our theory of rational choice by specifying what it means for a preference relation to be rational. A **rational** preference relation is a preference relation that is transitive and complete.

A relation R is **transitive** just in case the following condition holds: for all x, y, and z in the universe, if x bears relation R to y, and if y bears relation R to z, then x must bear relation R to z. Suppose the universe is the set of all the Marx brothers. If so, "is taller than" is a transitive relation: if Zeppo is taller than Groucho, and Groucho is taller than Harpo, Zeppo must be taller than Harpo (Figure 2.2).

Example 2.4 *30 Rock*   Consider the following exchange from the TV show *30 Rock*. Tracy, Grizz, and Dot Com are playing computer games. Tracy always beats Grizz and Dot Com. When Kenneth beats Tracy but gets beaten by Grizz, Tracy grows suspicious.

> *Tracy:*   "How were you beating Kenneth, Grizz?"
> *Grizz:*   "I don't know."
> *Tracy:*   "If Kenneth could beat me and you can beat Kenneth, then by the transitive property, you should beat me too! Have you been letting me win?"
> *Dot Com:* "Just at some things."
> *Tracy:*   "Things? Plural?"

Now you are the first kid on the block who understands *30 Rock*. You also know that the show has a former economics or philosophy student on its staff.

If the universe consists of all people, examples of intransitive relations include "is in love with." Just because Sam is in love with Pat, and Pat is in love with Robin, it is not necessarily the case that Sam is in love with Robin. Sam *may* be in love with

Figure 2.2 The Marx brothers. Illustrations by Cody Taylor

Robin. But Sam may have no particular feelings about Robin, or Sam may resent Robin for attracting Pat's attention. It may also be the case that Robin is in love with Sam. This kind of intransitivity is central to the play *No Exit*, by the French existentialist philosopher Jean-Paul Sartre. In the play, which takes place in a prison cell, a young woman craves the affection of a man who desires the respect of an older woman, who in turn is in love with the young woman. Hence the most famous line of the play is: "Hell is other people." To show that a relation is intransitive, it is sufficient to identify three members of the universe such that the first is related to the second, and the second is related to the third, but the first is not related to the third.

Formally speaking, a preference relation $\succeq$ is transitive just in case the following is true:

Axiom 2.5 Transitivity of $\succeq$ *If* $x \succeq y$ *and* $y \succeq z$, *then* $x \succeq z$ *(for all* x, y, z*)*.

There are other ways of expressing the same thing. We might write: If $x \succeq y \succeq z$, then $x \succeq z$ (for all x, y, z). Using standard logic symbols, we might write: $x \succeq y$ & $y \succeq z \rightarrow x \succeq z$ (for all x, y, z). See the text box on page 16 for a useful list of logical symbols. Either way, transitivity says that if you prefer coffee to tea, and tea to root beer, you must prefer coffee to root beer; that is, you cannot prefer coffee to tea and tea to root beer while failing to prefer coffee to root beer.

A relation R is **complete** just in case the following condition holds: for any x and y in the universe, either x bears relation R to y, or y bears relation R to x (or both). If the universe consists of all people – past, present, and future – then "is at least as tall as" is a complete relation. You may not know how tall Caesar and Brutus were, but you do know this: either Caesar was at least as tall as Brutus, or Brutus was at least as tall as Caesar (or both, in case they were equally tall).

Given the universe of all people, examples of incomplete relations include "is in love with." For any two randomly selected people – your landlord and the current President of the US, for example – it is not necessarily the case that either one is in love with the other. Your landlord may have a crush on the President, or the other way around. But this need not be the case, and it frequently will not be. To show that a relation is incomplete, then, it is sufficient to identify two objects in the universe such that the relation does not hold either way.

Formally speaking, a preference relation $\succeq$ is complete just in case the following is true:

Axiom 2.6 Completeness of $\succeq$ *Either* $x \succeq y$ *or* $y \succeq x$ *(or both) (for all* x, y).

Completeness means that you must prefer tea to coffee or coffee to tea (or both); though your preference can go both ways, you cannot fail to have a preference between the two. The use of the phrase "(or both)" in the formula above is, strictly speaking, redundant: we use the "inclusive or," which is equivalent to "and/or" in everyday language. Using standard logical symbols, we might write: $x \succeq y \vee y \succeq x$ (for all x, y). If both $x \succeq y$ and $y \succeq x$, we say that there is a tie (see Section 2.4).

The following exercise serves to illustrate the concepts of transitivity and completeness.

Exercise 2.7   Assuming the universe is the set of all people – past, present, and future – are the following relations transitive? Are they complete?

(a) "is the mother of"
(b) "is an ancestor of"
(c) "is the sister of"
(d) "detests"
(e) "weighs more than"
(f) "has the same first name as"
(g) "is taller than"

When answering questions such as these, ambiguity can be a problem. A word like "sister" is ambiguous, which means that answers might depend on how it is used. As soon as the word is defined, however, the questions have determinate answers.

Exercise 2.8   Assuming the universe is the set of all natural numbers, meaning that $U = \{1, 2, 3, 4, \ldots\}$, are the following relations transitive? Are they complete?

(a) "is at least as great as" ($\geq$)
(b) "is equal to" ($=$)
(c) "is strictly greater than" ($>$)
(d) "is divisible by" ($|$)

Exercise 2.9 Preferences and the universe   Use your understanding of transitivity and completeness to answer the following questions:

(a) If the universe is {apple, banana, starvation}, what does the transitivity of the preference relation entail?
(b) If the universe is {apple, banana}, what does the completeness of the preference relation entail?

> **Logical symbols**
>
> Here is a list of the most common logical symbols:
>
> | | |
> |---|---|
> | $x \,\&\, y$ | x and y |
> | $x \lor y$ | x or y |
> | $x \to y$ | if x then y; x only if y |
> | $x \leftrightarrow y$ | x if and only if y; x just in case y |
> | $\neg p$ | not p |

As the last exercise suggests, the completeness of the preference relation implies that it is **reflexive**, meaning that $x \succcurlyeq x$ (for all x).

The choice of a universe might determine whether a relation is transitive or intransitive, complete or incomplete. If the universe were U = {Romeo, Juliet}, the relation "is in love with" would be complete, since for any two members of the universe, either the one is in love with the other, or the other is in love with the one. (This assumes that Romeo and Juliet are both in love with themselves, which might perhaps not be true.) Perhaps more surprisingly, the relation would also be transitive: whenever $x \succcurlyeq y$ and $y \succcurlyeq z$, it is in fact the case that $x \succcurlyeq z$.

The assumption that the weak preference relation is rational (transitive and complete) might seem fairly modest. Yet, in combination with a couple of definitions, this assumption is in effect everything necessary to build a theory of choice under certainty. This is a wonderful illustration of how science works: based on a small number of assumptions, we will build an extensive theory, whose predictions will then be confronted with actual evidence. The rest of this chapter spells out the implications of the assumption that the weak preference relation is rational.

2.4 Indifference and strict preference

As the previous section shows, the (weak) preference relation admits ties. When two options are tied, we say that the first option is **as good as** the second or that the agent is **indifferent** between the two options. That is, a person is indifferent between two options just in case, to her, the first option is at least as good as the second and the second is at least as good as the first. We use the symbol $\sim$ to denote indifference. Formally speaking:

Definition 2.10 Definition of indifference *$x \sim y$ if and only if $x \succcurlyeq y$ and $y \succcurlyeq x$.*

Using logical symbols, we might write: $x \sim y \Leftrightarrow x \succcurlyeq y \,\&\, y \succcurlyeq x$.

Assuming that the "at least as good as" relation is rational, the indifference relation is both reflexive and transitive. It is also **symmetric**: if x is as good as y, then y is as good as x. These results are not just intuitively plausible; they can be established by means of **proofs**. (See the text box on page 19 for more about proofs.) Properties of the indifference relation are established by the following proposition.

Proposition 2.11 Properties of indifference *The following conditions hold:*

(i) $x \sim x$ *(for all x)*
(ii) $x \sim y \rightarrow y \sim x$ *(for all x, y)*
(iii) $x \sim y \& y \sim z \rightarrow x \sim z$ *(for all x, y, z)*

Proof. Each part of the proposition requires a separate proof:

(i) 1. $x \succcurlyeq x$ by Axiom 2.6
     2. $x \succcurlyeq x \& x \succcurlyeq x$ from (1), by logic
     $\therefore x \sim x$ from (2), by Definition 2.10

(ii) 1. $x \sim y$ by assumption
      2. $x \succcurlyeq y \& y \succcurlyeq x$ from (1), by Definition 2.10
      3. $y \succcurlyeq x \& x \succcurlyeq y$ from (2), by logic
      4. $y \sim x$ from (3), by Definition 2.10
      $\therefore x \sim y \rightarrow y \sim x$ from (1)–(4), by logic

(iii) 1. $x \sim y \& y \sim z$ by assumption
       2. $x \succcurlyeq y \& y \succcurlyeq x$ from (1), by Definition 2.10
       3. $y \succcurlyeq z \& z \succcurlyeq y$ from (1), by Definition 2.10
       4. $x \succcurlyeq z$ from (2) and (3), by Axiom 2.5
       5. $z \succcurlyeq x$ from (2) and (3), by Axiom 2.5
       6. $x \sim z$ from (4) and (5), by Definition 2.10
       $\therefore x \sim y \& y \sim z \rightarrow x \sim z$ from (1)–(6), by logic

These are the complete proofs. In what follows, I will often outline the general shape of the proof rather than presenting the whole thing.   □

The indifference relation is not complete. To show this, it is enough to give a single counterexample. Any rational preference relation according to which the agent is not indifferent between all options will do (see, for instance, Figure 2.3).

Exercise 2.12 Prove the following principle: $x \succcurlyeq y \& y \sim z \rightarrow x \succcurlyeq z$.

If you have difficulty completing the proof, refer to the text box on page 19 for hints.

When a first option is at least as good as a second, but the second is not at least as good as the first, we say that the first option **is better than** the second or that the agent **strictly** or **strongly** prefers the first over the second. We use the symbol $\succ$ to denote **strict** or **strong preference**. Formally speaking:

Definition 2.13 Definition of strict preference $x \succ y$ *if and only if $x \succcurlyeq y$ and it is not the case that $y \succcurlyeq x$.*

Using logical notation, that is to say: $x \succ y \Leftrightarrow x \succcurlyeq y \& \neg y \succcurlyeq x$. For clarity, sometimes the "is at least as good as" relation will be called **weak preference**.

Assuming (still) that the weak preference relation is rational, it is possible to prove logically that the relation will have certain properties. The following proposition establishes some of them.

Proposition 2.14 Properties of strict preference   *The following conditions hold:*

(i) $x \succ y \,\&\, y \succ z \rightarrow x \succ z$ *(for all x, y, z)*
(ii) $x \succ y \rightarrow \neg y \succ x$ *(for all x, y)*
(iii) *not* $x \succ x$ *(for all x)*

Proof. (i) Suppose that $x \succ y \,\&\, y \succ z$. In order to establish that $x \succ z$, Definition 2.13 tells us that we need to show that $x \succeq z$ and that it is not the case that $z \succeq x$. The first part is Exercise 2.15. The second part goes as follows: suppose for a **proof by contradiction** that $z \succeq x$. From the first assumption and the definition of strict preference, it follows that $x \succeq y$. From the second assumption and Axiom 2.5, it follows that $z \succeq y$. But from the first assumption and the definition of strict preference, it also follows that $\neg z \succeq y$. We have derived a contradiction, so the second assumption must be false, and therefore $\neg z \succeq x$.

(ii) Begin by assuming $x \succ y$. Then, for a proof by contradiction, assume that $y \succ x$. Given the first assumption, Definition 2.13 implies that $x \succeq y$. Given the second assumption, the same definition implies that $\neg x \succeq y$. But this is a contradiction, so the second assumption must be false, and therefore $\neg y \succ x$.

(iii) See Exercise 2.16.   □

Proposition 2.14(i) says that the strict preference relation is transitive; 2.14(ii) that it is **anti-symmetric**; and 2.14(iii) that it is **irreflexive**.

Exercise 2.15   Using the definitions and propositions discussed so far, complete the first part of the proof of Proposition 2.14(i).

Notice that the proofs of Proposition 2.14(i) and (ii) involve constructing proofs by contradiction. Such proofs are also called **indirect proofs**. This mode of reasoning might look weird, but it is actually quite common in mathematics, science, and everyday thinking. For example, when mathematicians prove that $\sqrt{2}$ is an irrational number, they can proceed by assuming (for a proof by contradiction) that $\sqrt{2}$ is a rational number (meaning that $\sqrt{2}$ can be expressed as a fraction p/q of natural numbers p and q) and then use this assumption to derive a contradiction. In future exercises, you will see just how useful proofs by contradiction can be.

Exercise 2.16   Prove Proposition 2.14(iii). Prove it by contradiction, by first assuming that there is an x such that $x \succ x$.

Exercise 2.17   Prove the following principle: $x \succ y \,\&\, y \succeq z \rightarrow x \succ z$ (for all x, y, z). Notice that this proof has two parts. First, prove that $x \succeq z$; second, prove that $\neg z \succeq x$.

Exercise 2.18   Establish the following important and intuitive principles. (For the record, some of them are logically equivalent.)

(a) If $x \succ y$ then $x \succeq y$
(b) If $x \succ y$ then $\neg y \succeq x$
(c) If $\neg x \succ y$ then $y \succeq x$
(d) If $x \succeq y$ then $\neg y \succ x$

(e) If $\neg x \succcurlyeq y$ then $y \succ x$
(f) If $x \succ y$ then $\neg x \sim y$
(g) If $x \sim y$ then $\neg x \succ y$
(h) If $\neg x \sim y$ then either $x \succ y$ or $y \succ x$

In your various proofs, it is acceptable to rely on propositions already established (see text box below). The following exercises show how useful this can be.

Exercise 2.19   Prove that if $x \sim y$ and $y \sim z$ then $\neg x \succ z$.

Exercise 2.20 Negative transitivity   Prove the following two principles:

(a) If $\neg x \succcurlyeq y$ and $\neg y \succcurlyeq z$, then $\neg x \succcurlyeq z$
(b) If $\neg x \succ y$ and $\neg y \succ z$, then $\neg x \succ z$

The last two exercises illustrate some potentially problematic implications of the theory that we have studied in this chapter. Both are classics.

How to do proofs

The aim of a **proof** of a proposition is to establish the truth of the proposition with logical or mathematical certainty (see the proofs of Proposition 2.11(i)–(iii) for examples). A proof is a sequence of propositions, presented on separate lines of the page. The last line of the proof is the proposition you intend to establish, that is, the conclusion; the lines that come before it establish its truth. The conclusion is typically preceded by the symbol $\therefore$. All other lines are numbered using Arabic numerals. The basic rule is that each proposition in the proof must follow logically from (a) a proposition on a line above it, (b) an axiom of the theory, (c) a definition that has been properly introduced, and/or (d) a proposition that has already been established by means of another proof. Once a proof is concluded, logicians like to write "QED" – Latin for "quad erat demonstrandum," meaning "that which was to be shown" – or by the little box $\square$.

There are some useful hints, or rules of thumb, that you may want to follow when constructing proofs. **Hint one**: if you want to establish a proposition of the form $x \rightarrow y$, you typically want to begin by assuming what is to the left of the arrow; that is, the first line will read "1. x by assumption." Then, your goal is to derive y, which would permit you to complete the proof. If you want to establish a proposition of the form $x \leftrightarrow y$, you need to do it both ways: first, prove that $x \rightarrow y$, second, that $y \rightarrow x$. **Hint two**: if you want to establish a proposition of the form $\neg p$, you typically want to begin by assuming the opposite of what you want to prove for a proof by contradiction; that is, the first line would read "1. p by assumption for a proof by contradiction." Then, your goal is to derive a contradiction, that is, a claim of the form $q \ \& \ \neg q$, which would permit you to complete the proof.

Exercise 2.21 Vacations Suppose that you are offered two vacation packages, one to California and one to Florida, and that you are perfectly indifferent between the two. Let us call the Florida package f and the California package c. So $f \sim c$. Now, somebody improves the Florida package by adding an apple to it. You like apples, so the enhanced Florida package f^+ improves the original Florida package, meaning that $f^+ \succ f$. Assuming that you are rational, how do you feel about the enhanced Florida package f^+ compared to the California package c? Prove it.

Exercise 2.22 Tea cups Imagine that there are 1000 cups of tea lined up in front of you. The cups are identical except for one difference: the cup to the far left (c_1) contains one grain of sugar, the second from the left (c_2) contains two grains of sugar, the third from the left (c_3) contains three grains of sugar, and so on. Since you cannot tell the difference between any two adjacent cups, you are indifferent between c_n and c_{n+1} for all n between 1 and 999 inclusive. Assuming that your preference relation is rational, what is your preference between the cup to the far left (c_1) and the one to the far right (c_{1000})?

Remember that you can rely on your findings from Exercise 2.18 when answering these questions.

2.5 Preference orderings

The preference relation is often referred to as a **preference ordering**. This is so because a rational preference relation allows us to order all alternatives in a list, with the best at the top and the worst at the bottom. Figure 2.3 shows an example of a preference ordering.

A rational preference ordering is simple. Completeness ensures that each person will have exactly one list, because completeness entails that each element can be compared to all other elements. Transitivity ensures that the list will be linear, because transitivity entails that the strict preference relation will never have cycles, as when $x \succ y$, $y \succ z$, and $z \succ x$. Here are two helpful exercises about cycling preferences.

Exercise 2.23 Cycling preferences Using the definitions and propositions discussed so far, show that it is impossible for a rational strict preference relation to cycle. To do so, suppose (for the sake of the argument) that $x \succ y$ & $y \succ z$ & $z \succ x$ and show that this leads to a contradiction.

Heavenly Bliss

$\curlyvee$

Coke $\sim$ Pepsi

$\curlyvee$

Eternal Suffering

Figure 2.3 Preference ordering with tie

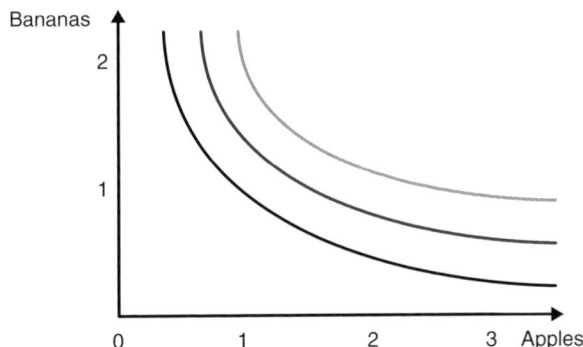

Figure 2.4 Indifference curves

Exercise 2.24 Cycling preferences, cont. By contrast, it is possible for the weak preference relation to cycle. This is to say that there may well be an x, y, and z such that $x \succcurlyeq y$ & $y \succcurlyeq z$ & $z \succcurlyeq x$. If this is so, what do we know about the agent's preferences over x, y, and z? Prove it.

In cases of indifference, the preference ordering will have ties. As you may have noticed, Figure 2.3 describes a preference ordering in which two items are equally good. Assuming that the universe is {Heavenly Bliss, Coke, Pepsi, Eternal Suffering}, this preference ordering is perfectly rational.

In economics, preference orderings are frequently represented using **indifference curves**, also called **indifference maps**. See Figure 2.4 for an example of a set of indifference curves. You can think of these as analogous to contour lines on a topographic map. By convention, each bundle on one of these curves is as good as every other bundle on the same curve. When two bundles are on different curves, one of the two bundles is strictly preferred to the other. Insofar as people prefer more of each good to less, bundles on curves to the top right will be strictly preferred to bundles on curves to the bottom left.

Exercise 2.25 Indifference curves Represent the following sets of indifference curves graphically.

(a) Suppose that an apple for you is always as good as two bananas.
(b) Suppose that one apple is always as good, as far as you are concerned, as a banana.
(c) Suppose that you do not care for tea without milk or for milk without tea. However, every time you have two units of tea and one unit of milk, you can make yourself a cup of tea with milk. You love tea with milk, and the more the better, as far as you are concerned.

2.6 Choice under certainty

To make a **choice under certainty** is to face a menu. A **menu** is a set of options such that you have to choose exactly one option from the set. This is to say that the menu has two properties. First, the items in the menu are **mutually exclusive**; that is, you can choose at most one of them at any given time. Second, the items in the menu are **exhaustive**; that is, you have to choose at least one of them.

Example 2.26 The menu If a restaurant offers two appetizers (soup and salad) and two entrées (chicken and beef) and you must choose one appetizer and one entrée, what is your set of alternatives?

Since there are four possible combinations, your set of alternatives is {soup-and-chicken, soup-and-beef, salad-and-chicken, salad-and-beef}.

Exercise 2.27 The menu, cont. If you can also choose to eat an appetizer only, or an entrée only, or nothing at all, what would the new menu be?

There is no assumption that a menu is small, or even finite, though we frequently assume that it is.

In economics, the menu is often referred to as the **budget set**. This is simply that part of the set of alternatives that you can afford given your budget, that is, your resources at hand. Suppose that you can afford at most three apples (if you buy no bananas) or two bananas (if you buy no apples). This would be the case, for instance, if you had $6 in your pocket and bananas cost $3 and apples $2. If so, your budget set – or your menu – is represented by the shaded area in Figure 2.5. Assuming that fruit is infinitely divisible, the menu is infinitely large. The line separating the items in your budget from the items outside of it is called the **budget line**.

Exercise 2.28 Budget sets Suppose that your budget is $12. Use a graph to answer the following questions:

(a) What is the budget set when apples cost $3 and bananas cost $4?
(b) What is the budget set when apples cost $6 and bananas cost $2?
(c) What is the budget set when apples always cost $2, the first banana costs $4, and every subsequent banana costs $2?

So what does it mean **to be rational**? To be rational, or **to make rational choices**, means (i) that you have a rational preference ordering, and (ii) that whenever you are faced with a menu, you choose the most preferred item, or (in the case of ties) one of

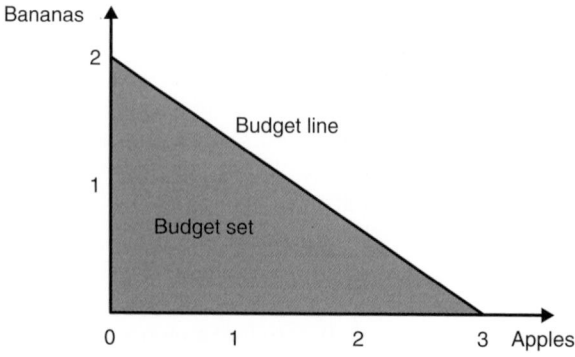

Figure 2.5 Budget set

the most preferred items. The second condition can also be expressed as follows: (ii′) that . . . you choose an item such that no other item in the menu is strictly preferred to it. Or like this: (ii″) that . . . you do not choose an item that is strictly less preferred to another item in the menu. *This is all we mean when we say that somebody is rational.* If you have the preferences of Figure 2.3 and are facing a menu offering Coke, Pepsi, and Eternal Suffering, the rational choice is to pick either the Coke or the Pepsi option. When there is no unique best choice, as in this case, the theory says that you have to choose one of the best options; it does not specify which one.

The rational decision can be determined if we know the agent's indifference curves and budget set. If you superimpose the former (from Figure 2.4) onto the latter (from Figure 2.5), you get a picture like Figure 2.6. The consumer will choose the bundle marked X, because it is the most highly preferred bundle in the budget set. As you can tell, there is no more highly preferred bundle in the budget set.

It is important to note what the theory of rationality does *not* say. The theory does not say why people prefer certain things to others, or why they choose so as to satisfy their preferences. It does not say that people prefer apples to bananas because they think that they will be happier, feel better, or be more satisfied, if they get apples than if they get bananas (although that may, in fact, be the case). This theory says nothing about feelings, emotions, moods, or any other subjectively experienced state. As far as this theory is concerned, the fact that you prefer a cool drink on a hot day to being roasted over an open fire is just a brute fact; it is not a fact that needs to be grounded in an account of what feels good or bad, pleasant or unpleasant, rewarding or aversive. Similarly, the theory does not say why people choose the most preferred item on the menu; as far as this theory is concerned, they just do.

Moreover, the theory does not say that people are selfish, in the sense that they care only about themselves; or that they are materialistic, in the sense that they care only about material goods; or that they are greedy, in the sense that they care only about money. The definition of rationality implies that a rational person is self-interested, in the sense that her choices reflect her own preference ordering rather than somebody else's. But this is not the same as being selfish: the rational individual may, for example, prefer dying for a just cause over getting rich by defrauding others. The theory in itself specifies only some formal properties of the preference

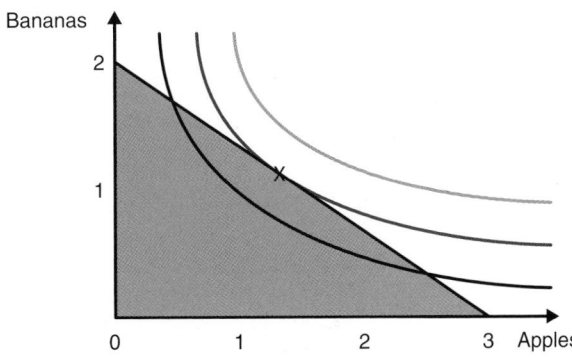

Figure 2.6 Consumer choice problem

relation; it does not say anything about the things people prefer. The theory is silent about whether or not they pursue respectable and moral ends: a rational person may prefer the destruction of the earth to the scratching of his little finger. Rational people may be weird, evil, sadistic, selfish, and morally repugnant, or saintly, inspiring, thoughtful, selfless, and morally admirable; they can act out of compulsion, habit, feeling, or as a result of machine-like computation. Their preferences cannot be intransitive or incomplete, and they cannot make choices that fail to reflect those preferences.

2.7 Utility

The notion of **utility**, which is central to modern economics, has generated a great deal of confusion. It is worth going slowly here. Suppose that you want to use numbers to express how much a person prefers something, how would you do it? One solution is obvious. Remember that a rational person's preferences allow us to arrange all alternatives in order of preference. Consider, for example, the preference ordering in Figure 2.3. The preference ordering has three "steps." In order to represent these preferences by numbers, we assign one number to each step, in such a way that higher steps are associated with higher numbers. See Figure 2.7 for an example.

A **utility function** associates a number with each member of the set of alternatives. In this case, we have associated the number 3 with Heavenly Bliss (HB). That number is called the utility of HB and is denoted $u(HB)$. In this case, $u(HB) = 3$. The number associated with Eternal Suffering (ES) is called the utility of ES and is written $u(ES)$. In this case, $u(ES) = 1$. If we use C to denote Coke and P to denote Pepsi, $u(C) = u(P) = 2$. Because we designed the utility function so that higher utilities correspond to more preferred items, we say that the utility function $u(\cdot)$ **represents** the preference relation $\succcurlyeq$.

As the example suggests, two conditions must hold in order for something to be a utility function. First, it must be a function (or a mapping) from the set of alternatives into the set of real numbers. This means that every alternative gets assigned exactly one number. If Figure 2.7 had empty spaces in the right-hand column, or if the figure had several numbers in the same cell, we would not have a proper utility function. While the utility function needs to assign some number to every alternative, it is acceptable (as the example shows) to assign the same number to several alternatives. Second, for something to be a utility function, it must assign larger numbers to more

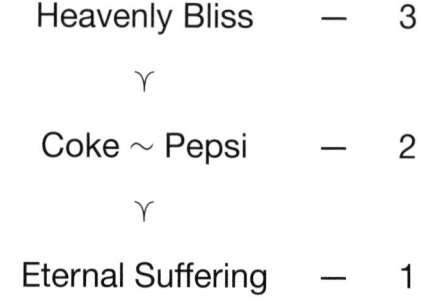

Heavenly Bliss   —   3

$\curlyvee$

Coke ~ Pepsi   —   2

$\curlyvee$

Eternal Suffering   —   1

Figure 2.7 Preference ordering with utility function

preferred alternatives; that is, if x is at least as good as y, the number assigned to x must be greater than or equal to the number assigned to y. To put it more formally:

Definition 2.29 Definition of u(·)   *A function $u(\cdot)$ from the set of alternatives into the set of real numbers is a utility function representing preference relation $\succcurlyeq$ just in case $x \succcurlyeq y \Leftrightarrow u(x) \geqslant u(y)$ (for all x and y).*

A function $u(\cdot)$ that satisfies this condition can be said to be an **index** or a **measure** of preference relation $\succcurlyeq$. Historically, the word "utility" has been used to refer to many different things, including the pleasure, happiness, and satisfaction of receiving, owning, or consuming something. Though most people (including economics professors) find it hard to stop speaking in this way, as though utility is somehow floating around "in your head," this usage is archaic. Utility is nothing but an index or measure of preference.

Given a rational preference relation, you may ask whether it is always possible to find a utility function that represents it. When the set of alternatives is finite, the answer is yes. The question is answered by means of a so-called **representation theorem**.

Proposition 2.30 Representation theorem   *If the set of alternatives is finite, then $\succcurlyeq$ is a rational preference relation just in case there exists a utility function representing $\succcurlyeq$.*

Proof. Omitted.   □

When the set of alternatives is infinite, representing preference relations gets more complicated. It remains true that if a utility function represents a preference relation, then the preference relation is rational. However, even if the preference relation is rational, it is not always possible to find a utility function that represents it.

As you may suspect, a utility function will associate strictly higher numbers with strictly preferred alternatives, and equal numbers to equally preferred alternatives. That is, the following proposition is true:

Proposition 2.31 Properties of u(·)   *Given a utility function $u(\cdot)$ representing preference relation $\succcurlyeq$, the following conditions hold:*

(i) $x \succ y \Leftrightarrow u(x) > u(y)$
(ii) $x \sim y \Leftrightarrow u(x) = u(y)$

Proof. (i) First, assume that $x \succ y$, so that $x \succcurlyeq y$ and $\neg y \succcurlyeq x$. Using Definition 2.29 twice, we can infer that $u(x) \geqslant u(y)$ and that not $u(y) \geqslant u(x)$. Simple math tells us that $u(x) > u(y)$. Second, assume that $u(x) > u(y)$, which implies that $u(x) \geqslant u(y)$ and that not $u(y) \geqslant u(x)$. Using Definition 2.29 twice, we can infer that $x \succcurlyeq y$ and $\neg y \succcurlyeq x$, which in turn implies that $x \succ y$.

(ii) See Exercise 2.32.   □

Recall (from the text box on page 19) that if you want to prove something of the form $A \Leftrightarrow B$, your proof must have two parts.

Exercise 2.32   Prove Proposition 2.31(ii).

It is easy to confirm that the proposition is true of the utility function from Figure 2.7.

One important point to note is that utility functions are not unique. The sequence of numbers $\langle 1, 2, 3 \rangle$ in Figure 2.7 could have been chosen very differently. The sequence $\langle 0, 1, 323 \rangle$ would have done as well, as would $\langle -1000, -2, 0 \rangle$ and $\langle -\pi, e, 1077 \rangle$. All these are utility functions, in that they associate higher numbers with more preferred options. As these examples show, it is important not to ascribe any significance to absolute numbers. To know that the utility I derive from listening to Justin Bieber is 2 tells you *absolutely nothing* about my preferences. But if you know that the utility I derive from listening to Arcade Fire is 4, you know something, namely, that I strictly prefer Arcade Fire to Justin Bieber. It is equally important not to ascribe any significance to ratios of utilities. Even if the utility of Arcade Fire is twice the utility of Justin Bieber, this does not mean that I like Arcade Fire "twice as much." The same preferences could be represented by the numbers 0 and 42, in which case the ratio would not even be well defined. In brief, for every given preference relation, there are many utility functions representing it. Utility as used in this chapter is often called **ordinal utility**, because all it does is allow you to order things.

How do utilities relate to indifference curves? A utility function in effect assigns one number to each indifference curve, as in Figure 2.8. This way, two bundles that fall on the same curve will be associated with the same utility, as they should be. Two bundles that fall on different curves will be associated with different utilities, again as they should be. Of course, higher numbers will correspond to curves that are more strongly preferred. For a person who likes apples and bananas, $u_1 < u_2 < u_3$.

How does utility relate to behavior? Remember that you choose rationally insofar as you choose the most preferred item (or one of the most preferred items) on the menu. The most preferred item on the menu will also be the item with the highest utility. So to choose the most preferred item is to choose the item with the highest utility. Now, **to maximize utility** is to choose the item with the highest utility. Thus, you choose rationally insofar as you maximize utility. Hence, *to maximize utility is to choose rationally*. Notice that you can maximize utility in this sense without necessarily going through any particular calculations; that is, you do not need to be able to solve mathematical maximization problems in order to maximize

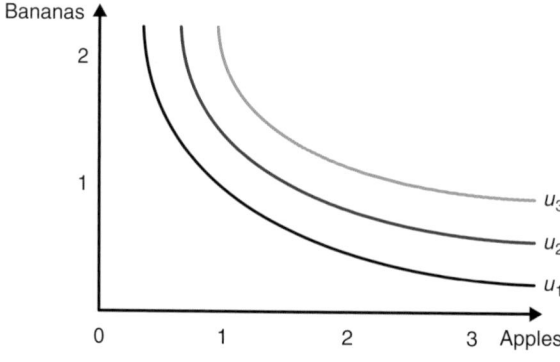

Figure 2.8 Indifference curves and utility

utility. Similarly, you can maximize utility without maximizing feelings of pleasure, satisfaction, contentment, happiness, or whatever; utility (like preference) still has nothing to do with subjectively experienced states of any kind. This is a source of endless confusion.

A final word about proofs

While the proofs discussed in this chapter may at first blush seem intimidating, notice that the basic principles are fairly simple. So far, we have introduced only two axioms, namely, the transitivity of the weak preference relation (Axiom 2.5 on page 14) and the completeness of the weak preference relation (Axiom 2.6 on page 15); three definitions, namely, the definition of indifference (Definition 2.10 on page 16), the definition of strict preference (Definition 2.13 on page 17), and the definition of utility (Definition 2.29 on page 25); and two hints (see text box on page 19). In order to complete a proof, there are only seven things that you need to know.

2.8 Discussion

The first thing to notice is how much mileage you can get out of a small number of relatively weak assumptions. Recall that we have made only two assumptions: that preferences are rational and that people choose so as to satisfy their preferences. As long as the two assumptions are true, and the set of alternatives is not too large, we can define the concept of utility and make sense of the idea of utility maximization. That is the whole theory. The second thing to notice is what the theory does not say. The theory does not say that people are selfish, materialistic, or greedy; it says nothing about why people prefer one thing over another; it does not presuppose that people solve mathematical maximization problems in their heads; and it makes no reference to things like pleasure, satisfaction, and happiness.

Though brief, this discussion sheds light on the nature of economics, as some economists see it. Nobel laureate Gary Becker defines the economic approach to behavior in terms of three features: "The combined assumptions of maximizing behavior, market equilibrium, and stable preferences, used relentlessly and unflinchingly, form the heart of the economic approach as I see it." Because this text is about individual choice, I have little to say about market equilibrium. However, what Becker has in mind when he talks about maximizing behavior and stable preferences should be eminently clear from what has already been said. In this analysis, preferences are **stable** in the sense that they are not permitted to change over time.

Is this a plausible theory of human behavior under conditions of certainty? To answer this question we need to separate the descriptive from the normative question. The first question is whether the theory is descriptively adequate, that is, whether people's choices *do as a matter of fact* reflect a rational preference ordering. This is the same as asking whether people maximize utility. Though both transitivity and completeness may seem obviously true of people's preferences, there are many cases in which they do not seem to hold: a person's preference relation over spouses, for example, is unlikely to be complete. The second question is whether the theory is normatively correct, that is, whether people's choices *should* reflect a rational preference ordering. This is the same as asking whether people *should* maximize utility. Though transitivity and completeness may seem rationally required, it can be argued that they are neither necessary nor sufficient for being rational.

Next, we explore what happens when the theory is confronted with data.

Additional exercises

Exercise 2.33   For each of the relations and properties in Table 2.1, use a check mark to identify whether or not the relation has the property.

Table 2.1   Properties of weak preference, indifference, and strong preference

	Property	Definition	$\succeq$	$\sim$	$\succ$
(a)	Transitivity	xRy & $yRz \rightarrow xRz$ (for all x, y, z)			
(b)	Completeness	$xRy \lor yRx$ (for all x, y)			
(c)	Reflexivity	xRx (for all x)			
(d)	Irreflexivity	$\neg xRx$ (for all x)			
(e)	Symmetry	$xRy \rightarrow yRx$ (for all x, y)			
(f)	Anti-symmetry	$xRy \rightarrow \neg yRx$ (for all x, y)			

Exercise 2.34   As part of your answer to the following questions, make sure to specify what the universe is.

(a) Give an example of a relation that is complete but not transitive.
(b) Give an example of a relation that is transitive but not complete.

Exercise 2.35 Irrationality   Explain (in words) why each of the two characters below is irrational according to the theory you have learned in this chapter.

(a) In the drama *Sophie's Choice*, the title character finds herself in a Nazi concentration camp and must choose which one of her children is to be put to death. She is not indifferent and cannot form a weak preference either way.
(b) An economics professor finds that he prefers a $10 bottle of wine to a $8 bottle, a $12 bottle to a $10 bottle, and so on; yet he does not prefer a $200 bottle to a $8 bottle.

Further reading

A nontechnical introduction to decision theory is Allingham (2002). More technical accounts can be found in Mas-Colell et al. (1995, Chapters 1–2). The Becker quote is from Becker (1976, p. 5).

Chapter 3

Decision-Making under Certainty

3.1 Introduction

The previous chapter showed how an extensive theory of choice under certainty can be built upon the foundation of a modest number of assumptions. Though the assumptions may seem weak, their implications can be challenged both on descriptive and normative grounds. In this chapter, we confront the theory with data. We explore some of the phenomena that behavioral economists argue are inconsistent with the theory of choice under certainty, as we know it. We focus on a couple of different phenomena, beginning with the failure to consider opportunity costs. Moreover, we will begin discussing what behavioral economists do when they discover phenomena that appear to be inconsistent with standard theory. In particular, we will discuss some of the building blocks of prominent behavioral alternatives, including prospect theory and the heuristics-and-biases program.

3.2 Opportunity costs

Imagine that you invest a small amount of money in real estate during a period when it strikes you as a safe and profitable investment. After you make the investment, the markets become unstable and you watch nervously as prices rise and fall. Finally, you sell your assets and realize that you have made a profit. "Wow," you say to yourself, "that turned out to be a great investment!" But when you boast to your friends, somebody points out that you could have earned even more money by investing in the stock market. At some level, you knew this. But you still feel that investing in real estate was a good choice: at least you did not lose any money. This is a case where you may have been acting irrationally because you failed to consider **opportunity costs**.

In order to analyze this kind of situation, let us stand back for a moment. An agent's decision problem can be represented using a **decision tree**: a graphical device showing what actions are available to some agent. Given that you only have two available actions – buying stocks and buying real estate – your decision problem can be represented as a decision tree (see Figure 3.1). Because this chapter is about choice under certainty, I will pretend that there is no uncertainty about the consequences that follow from each of these choices. (We will abandon this pretense in our discussion of choice under risk and uncertainty in Part III.)

Suppose that you are tempted to buy real estate. What is the cost of doing so? There would be an out-of-pocket or **explicit cost**: the seller of the property would want some money to give it up. The real cost, however, is what you forego when you buy the real estate. The opportunity cost – or **implicit cost** – of an alternative is the value of what you would have to forego if you choose it. In dollar terms, suppose that stocks will gain $1000 over the next year and that real estate will gain $900. If so, the opportunity costs of buying real estate is $1000 and the opportunity cost of buying stocks is $900. If you buy real estate, then, your economic profit will be $900 − $1000 = −$100$. If you buy stock, your economic profit would be $1000 − $900 = 100.

Figure 3.1   Simple decision tree

If there are more than two options, the opportunity cost is the value of the *most valuable* alternative option. Suppose that you can choose between stocks, real estate, and bonds, and that bonds will gain $150 over the next year. The opportunity cost of buying stocks would remain $900, and the economic profit would still be $100.

Exercise 3.1 Investment problem

(a) Draw a decision tree illustrating this decision problem.
(b) What is the opportunity cost of buying real estate?
(c) What is the opportunity cost of buying bonds?

Decision trees make it clear that you cannot choose one alternative without forego-ing another: whenever you choose to go down one branch of the tree, there is always another branch that you choose not to go down. When you vacation in Hawaii, you cannot at the same time vacation in Colorado; when you use your life savings to buy a Ferrari, you cannot at the same time use your life savings to buy a Porsche; when you spend an hour reading sociology, you cannot spend the same hour read-ing anthropology; when you are in a monogamous relationship with *this* person, you cannot at the same time be in a monogamous relationship with *that* person; and so on. Consequently, there is an opportunity cost associated with every available option in every decision problem.

For another example, imagine that you are considering going to the movies. On an ordinary evening, the decision that you are facing might look like Figure 3.2. Remember that the opportunity cost of going to the movies is the value of the most valuable option that you would forego if you went to the movies; that is, the oppor-tunity cost of going to the movies is the greatest utility you could get by going down one of the other branches of the decision tree, that is, the utility of the most valuable alternative use for some $10 and two hours of your time.

As a matter of notation, we write $a_1, a_2, \ldots, a_n$ to denote the n different acts available to you, $u(a_1), u(a_2), \ldots, u(a_n)$ to denote the utilities of those acts, and

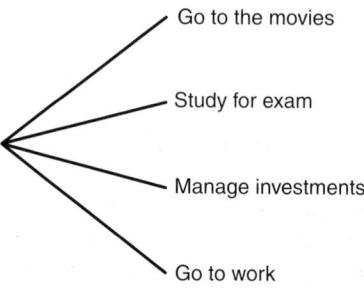

Figure 3.2   Everyday decision tree

$c(a_1), c(a_2), \ldots, c(a_n)$ to denote the opportunity costs of those acts. The opportunity cost $c(a_i)$ of act a_i can then be defined as follows:

Definition 3.2 Opportunity cost

$$c(a_i) = \max \{u(a_1), u(a_2), \ldots, u(a_{i-1}), u(a_{i+1}), \ldots, u(a_n)\}.$$

This is just to say that the opportunity cost of act a_i equals the maximum utility of the other acts.

Figure 3.3 represents a decision problem in which utilities and opportunity costs of four acts have been been identified. The number on the left is the utility; the number in parentheses is the opportunity cost.

Exercise 3.3 Opportunity costs This exercise refers to Figure 3.3. Suppose that a fifth act (call it a_5) becomes available. Assume that a_5 has a utility of 9.

(a) What would the tree look like now?
(b) What would happen to the opportunity costs of the different alternatives?

There is a tight connection between opportunity costs, utilities, and the rational thing to do. As it happens, you are rational – that is, you maximize utility – just in case you take opportunity costs properly into account.

Proposition 3.4 a_i *is a rational choice* $\Leftrightarrow u(a_i) \geqslant c(a_i)$

Proof. We need to prove the claim both ways. The first part goes as follows: assume that a_i is the rational choice. Given our definition of rationality, this means that $u(a_i) \geqslant u(a_j)$ for all $j \neq i$. If so,

$$u(a_i) \geqslant \max \{u(a_1), u(a_2), \ldots, u(a_{i-1}), u(a_{i+1}), \ldots, u(a_n)\}$$

But because of the way we defined opportunity costs in Definition 3.2, this means that $u(a_i) \geqslant c(a_i)$. The second part is the same thing over again, except reversed. □

This proposition establishes formally what we already knew to be the case, namely, that it is irrational to invest in real estate whenever there is a more valuable alternative available, even if investing in real estate would generate a profit. Notice that

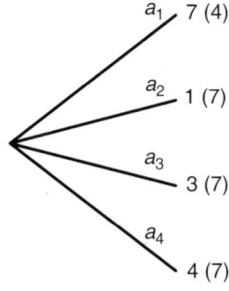

Figure 3.3 Decision tree with utilities and opportunity costs (in parentheses)

the condition holds even if there is more than one optimal element. Whenever this happens, the utility of the optimal alternative will equal its opportunity cost.

The concept of opportunity cost has considerable explanatory power.

Exercise 3.5 Opportunity costs, cont.   Using the language of opportunity cost, explain why highly paid people are less likely than poor people to mow their own lawns, clean their own houses, maintain their own cars, and so on.

In practice, however, people frequently often overlook opportunity costs. In the context of investment decisions, many people are pleased with their performance if their investments increase in value over time, whether or not there is another investment that would have generated a larger profit. Or think about going to the movies. It is rational to go to the movies only if there is not *a single act* available to you that would lead to a utility greater than that of going to the movies. Yet many people may have more valuable uses of their time. Here is another example.

Example 3.6 Ignoring opportunity costs   Imagine that after visiting your parents in Kansas a few times, you earn a voucher that can be exchanged for a free airplane ticket anywhere in the country. You decide to go to Las Vegas. You would not actually have bought a ticket to Vegas, but because it was free you figured you might as well. Now you would like to visit your parents in Kansas, and wish you did not have to pay so much money for the ticket.

In this case, you may be acting irrationally because you did not consider the opportunity cost of using the ticket to go to Vegas. Insofar as you would have preferred to use the voucher to visit your parents in Kansas, you failed to consider what you could have used it for instead. Though the ticket was purchased using a voucher rather than cash, the decision to use it to go to Vegas is associated with a substantial opportunity cost. As this example illustrates, people are particularly likely to ignore the opportunity cost of spending a **windfall**, that is, an unexpectedly large or unforeseen profit. Yet the best way to spend a dollar is not a function of how it ended up in your pocket.

It is easy to think of other scenarios where people might ignore opportunity costs. Think about unpaid work. Even if you can save money by mowing your own lawn, this does not mean that it is rational to do so: if your hourly wage exceeds the hourly charge to have a lawn care company mow your lawn, and you have no particular desire to mow the lawn rather than spending another hour in the office, then the rational choice is to stay in the office and pay somebody to mow your lawn. Or think about investments in public safety. Even if recruiting more police officers might save lives, this does not necessarily mean that it is rational to do so. If there is an alternative investment that would save even more lives – street lights, for example – or in other ways generate more value, it would be irrational to recruit more police officers. In general, even if some business move, political reform, military intervention, or any other initiative can be shown to have hugely beneficial consequences, this does not automatically make it rational: everything hinges on what the opportunity cost is.

Exercise 3.7 Advertising campaigns   Your latest efforts to boost revenue led to an advertising campaign that turned out to be hugely successful: an investment of

$1000 led to a $5000 boost in revenue. Does this mean that the investment in the advertising campaign was rational?

Why do people ignore opportunity costs? The first thing to note is how very difficult it would be to live up to the requirement to take opportunity costs into proper account. The requirement does not say that you have to consciously consider all the different alternatives available to you. But it does say that you must never choose an alternative whose opportunity cost is higher than its utility. This is an extremely demanding condition. Consider what would be required in order to rationally choose whom to marry. You must have complete and transitive preferences over all alternatives and you must make sure that your choice of spouse is not inferior to any other choice. And the set of alternatives in this case might include about half of humankind, though for many of us the budget set would be rather smaller. Hence, we should not be surprised that people sometimes overlook opportunity costs. (Section 3.5 discusses another reason why people may fail to take opportunity costs properly into account.)

Notice that it is irrational to fail to take opportunity costs properly into account, given the account of rationality that we developed in the previous chapter and used in this one. Certainly, in many cases this is right: if you fail to consider the opportunity cost of using your free ticket to go to Vegas, for example, it might be acceptable to call you irrational. But the fact that considering all possible alternatives is so very demanding – when getting married, for instance – means that there can be legitimate disagreement about whether failing to consider opportunity costs under those conditions is irrational or not. And if it can be rational to ignore opportunity costs, the theory that we have studied here is normatively incorrect.

It is important not to exaggerate people's inability to take opportunity costs properly into account. Although the opportunity cost of going to college can be huge, since it includes the amount that can be gained from working instead of studying, people still do go to college. Does this mean they are irrational? Not necessarily. The opportunity cost of *not* going to college can be even greater, since the foregone alternative in this case includes the higher lifetime earnings that a college degree can confer. If so, going to college can be perfectly rational in spite of the sizeable opportunity cost of doing so. (The decision problem here – as in the case of investments in real estate and the stock market – is complicated by the fact that it involves choice over time, which is discussed further in Part IV of this book.)

Problem 3.8 The opportunity cost of an economics education   *What is (or would be) the opportunity cost, for you, of taking a course in behavioral economics? Upon reflection, is it (or would it be) worth it?*

The notion of opportunity cost has other applications. According to psychologist Barry Schwartz, the fact that we face opportunity costs helps explain why many of us are so unhappy in spite of the extraordinary freedom that we enjoy. In this analysis, it is the very fact that we are free, in the sense of having many options available to us, that prevents us from being happy:

> [The] more alternatives there are from which to choose, the greater our experience of the opportunity costs will be. And the greater our experience of the opportunity costs, the less satisfaction we will derive from our chosen alternative... [A] greater variety of choices actually makes us feel worse.

Schwartz calls it "the paradox of choice." Notice, though, that this would be a case where we pay too much, rather than too little, attention to opportunity costs.

3.3 Sunk costs

Suppose that you are the manager of the research and development (R&D) department of a big corporation and that you have to decide whether to spend $1M to complete a project that, you are aware, is going to fail. In one scenario, your corporation has already invested $9M in the project, and you have to decide whether to invest the additional $1M required to complete it. In another scenario, you have not yet invested anything in the project, and you have to decide whether to invest the $1M required to complete it. What would you do? You might be willing to invest in the first scenario but unwilling to do so in the second. Assuming that the two decision problems are otherwise identical, this would be irrational. And it would be irrational because you would be **honoring sunk costs**; you would, as people say, be "throwing good money after bad."

Most decisions are not as simple as the decision trees we saw in Section 3.2. Some decision problems have several stages. Assuming that you want a soft drink, for example, you may first have to decide where to get one. Thus, you may have to choose, first, whether to go to Piggly Wiggly or Publix, and second, whether to get Coke or Pepsi. While the fact that this decision problem has two stages complicates matters somewhat, decision trees allow you to represent problems of this type too, as Figure 3.4 shows.

As always, the theory does not say whether you should choose Coke or Pepsi. However, it does say a few things about how your choices in one part of the tree should relate to your choices in other parts of the tree. Let us assume, for simplicity, that your universe consists of these two alternatives only, and that you are not indifferent between them. If you choose Coke rather than Pepsi at node #2, you also have to choose Coke rather than Pepsi at node #3; if you choose Pepsi rather than Coke at node #2, you also have to choose Pepsi rather than Coke at node #3. As we established in Exercise 2.18(b) on page 18, if you strictly prefer x to y, you must not also prefer y to x. And at #2 you are indeed facing the exact same options as you are at #3. (If you are indifferent between Coke and Pepsi, you can rationally choose either.)

Would anybody fail to act in the same way at nodes #2 and #3? There is a wide class of cases where people do. These are cases in which there are **sunk costs**: costs

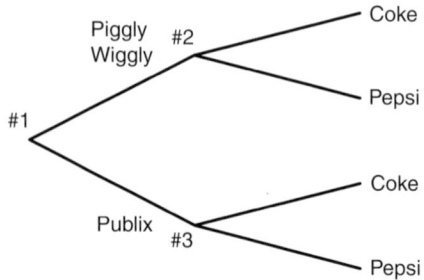

Figure 3.4 Multi-stage drinking problem

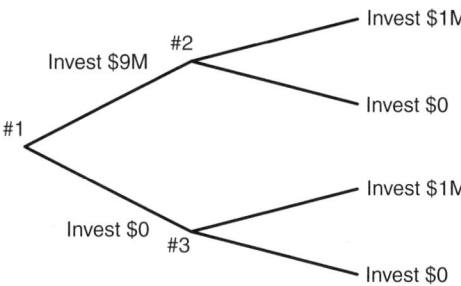

Figure 3.5 Multi-stage investment problem

beyond recovery at the time when the decision is made. Consider the R&D scenario outlined earlier in this section. It can be represented as in Figure 3.5. Faced with these two problems, many people say they would invest at node #2 but not invest at node #3. Yet, at node #2, the $9M is a sunk cost: it cannot be recovered. Whether or not making the further $1M investment is worth it should not depend on whether you find yourself at node #2 or #3. Failing to ignore sunk costs is referred to as **honoring sunk costs**, or as committing the **sunk-cost fallacy**. The sunk-cost fallacy is sometimes called the **Concorde fallacy**, since French and British governments continued to fund the supersonic passenger jet long after it became clear that it would not be commercially viable, supposedly because they had already invested so much money and prestige in the project. As these examples illustrate, the sunk-cost fallacy can be costly.

Example 3.9 The basketball game Imagine that you paid $80 for a ticket for a college basketball game to be played in about an hour's drive away. The ticket cannot be sold. On the day of the game, there is a freak snowstorm that makes driving hazardous. Would you go to the game?

Now, imagine that the ticket instead was given to you for free. Would you be more or less likely to go to the game?

Many people would be more likely to go to the game if they paid actual money for the ticket. Yet the cost of the ticket is a sunk cost at the time when the decision is made. Whether or not you paid for the ticket should not affect whether you go to the game or not.

The sunk-cost fallacy is evident in a wide range of everyday decisions. For one thing, it can make people hold on to failed investments. If you refuse to sell an underperforming asset on the basis that you would lose the difference between what you paid for it and what you would get for it if you sold it now, you are honoring the sunk cost of the original investment; the rational thing to do is to hold on to the asset if you think it is the best investment available to you right now and to sell if it is not. The sunk-cost fallacy can also make people stay in failed relationships. If a friend refuses to ditch her current boyfriend, even though she realizes that he is an utter loser, on the basis that leaving him would mean that she would have wasted some of the best years of her life, she would be honoring the sunk cost of the time and effort that she has already committed to him. As these examples show, honoring sunk costs can be expensive, not just in terms of money, but also in terms of time, effort, and heartache.

Exercise 3.10 Sunk costs Draw decision trees for people who (a) hold on to failed investments and (b) stay in bad relationships, in such a way that it becomes clear that the people in question are committing the sunk-cost fallacy.

Note that the rational decision is determined by what is going on only to the right of the node where you find yourself. What happens in other parts of the tree – in particular, to the left of your node – is completely irrelevant. In this sense, rational choices are completely forward-looking: things that happened in the past matter only insofar as they affect future outcomes.

Exercise 3.11 Sunk costs, cont. Students at an expensive liberal arts college may take courses at a nearby public university at no additional charge. One of their professors tells them that it would make no sense to do so, since they would be losing the money they paid for tuition at the more pricey college. Given that a student has already paid tuition at the liberal arts college, but judges that the course offerings at the public university are better for her, where should she sign up? Explain.

The sunk-cost fallacy can start a vicious circle sometimes referred to as an **escalation situation**. Once a project – whether an R&D effort, a marriage, a financial investment, or whatever – is beginning to go downhill, the sunk-cost fallacy encourages people irrationally to make additional investments in the project. Once the additional investment has been made, unless it turns the project around, people find themselves with an even greater sunk cost, which is even harder to ignore, thereby encouraging even greater investments. The sunk-cost fallacy and escalation behavior are often invoked when explaining why the US spent so many years fighting a losing war in Vietnam. According to this analysis, once soldiers were committed and started dying, it became impossible to withdraw for fear that the dead would have "died in vain"; thus, more soldiers were committed, more soldiers died, and it became even harder to withdraw. Interestingly, the scenario was outlined as early as 1965 by George Ball, then Undersecretary of State. In a memo to President Johnson, Ball wrote:

> The decision you face now is crucial. Once large numbers of US troops are committed to direct combat, they will begin to take heavy casualties in a war they are ill-equipped to fight in a noncooperative if not downright hostile countryside. Once we suffer large casualties, we will have started a well-nigh irreversible process. Our involvement will be so great that we cannot – without national humiliation – stop short of achieving our complete objectives. Of the two possibilities I think humiliation will be more likely than the achievement of our objectives – even after we have paid terrible costs.

Some wars are justified and some wars are not. But the justification can never take the form of simply pointing out how much money and how many lives have already been sacrificed; if the war is justified, it must be for other reasons. One important insight is this: before you embark on a risky project, you may want to ask yourself whether it will be possible for you to call it off in case it starts going downhill. If not, this is a reason not to embark on the project in the first place.

An awareness of our tendency to honor sunk costs can be useful. The loser boyfriend from earlier in this section can appeal to sunk costs when trying to keep his girlfriend. Less obnoxiously, you can use knowledge of the sunk-cost fallacy to market your products. One of the reasons why outlet malls are located so far away from where people live is that executives want shoppers to think of the sunk cost of a long drive to the mall as an investment that will be lost if they do not shop enough. More upliftingly, it turns out that you can make money by teaching people about rational-choice theory.

Example 3.12 How to sell tires   The following story was related by Cory, a former student of behavioral economics:

> I co-manage a local tire/automotive service retailer. Today, one of my good customers came into my store. He had purchased a set of tires from a separate online tire seller and came to get them installed. Before we started working on his car, he asked what other options would have been available to him. I proceeded to tell him about a brand new tire that I stocked that was overall much better than the one he bought – better traction features, better mileage, etc. I politely asked if he would like to buy them and have me send the others back. His response was: "No, that's okay, I've already bought these. I better just stick with them." I told him how easy the return process would be, how much longer the new tire would last, how it would save him money in the long run, etc., but his response remained the same: "Already paid for these; better stick with them." Finally, I told him that he was honoring sunk costs.
>
> So of course he asked what I meant, and I explained the concept at length. He was simply fascinated by this random lecture that he was receiving from somebody he thought to be just a "tire guy." I concluded the conversation by humorously declaring: "If you decide to stick with your original purchase, you are violating the theory of rational decision-making."
>
> He then looked at me with a ponderous stare. "You know what? I learned a lot from you. I think I *will* buy your tires and send the others back. Thanks for helping me!" So he bought the tires from me, had them installed, and I made a nice commission. I thought to myself: "Wow, I have been finished with behavioral economics for only one day, and already it is paying dividends!"

Knowledge of a tendency to honor sunk costs can also help us resist other people's manipulative behavior. If you are the loser's girlfriend, it might help to remind yourself that the wasted years in your past are no reason to stay with him, and if you are the shopper at the outlet mall, you can remind yourself that the long drive out there is no reason to buy stuff you do not want.

Notice that there are cases that may superficially look like the sunk-cost fallacy, but that really are not. In order for you to commit the sunk-cost fallacy in a decision problem like that in Figure 3.5, the options available to you at nodes #2 and #3 need to be identical. If they are not, you could rationally choose any combination of options. For example, your boss might demote you for failing to invest at node #2 but not so at node #3. If that is the case, it may well be rational for you to invest at #2 but not at #3, even if the investment would lead to large losses for the company. Similarly, if calling off a misguided military adventure would have unfortunate consequences – perhaps because the national humiliation would be unbearable, the military would look weak, the administration would look unmanly, and/or the next election would be lost – a president could rationally continue to fight the war. (Notice that we are concerned with rationality here, not morality.)

Either way, it is important not to accuse people of committing the sunk-cost fallacy if their behavior is better captured by standard theory.

Problem 3.13 Revenge   *When wronged, many people feel a strong urge to take revenge. Assuming revenge is costly, would not a revenge simply be a matter of honoring the sunk cost of whatever injury they have already sustained? Or are there conditions under which taking revenge can be rational?*

3.4   Menu dependence and the decoy effect

Spend a moment considering which of the subscription offers in Table 3.1 you would prefer. You will notice that there is something strange about the three options. Why would anybody choose the print subscription, given that you can get an online and a print subscription for the very same price? Given that nobody in their right mind would choose option 2, why was it included? It turns out that there is a good reason for *The Economist* to present potential customers with all three options. When researchers presented MBA students with options 1 and 3 only, 68 percent chose option 1 and 32 percent chose option 3. When the authors presented MBA students with options 1, 2, and 3, 0 percent chose option 2. But only 16 percent chose option 1 whereas 84 percent chose option 3. Thus, it appears that the inclusion of an option that nobody in their right mind would choose can affect people's preferences over the remaining options.

Recall from Section 2.6 that the rational choice depends on your budget set; that is, your menu. When your menu expands, more options become available to you, and one of them may turn out to be more preferred than the one you would have chosen from the smaller menu. However, the theory from the previous chapter does impose constraints on what happens when your menu expands. Suppose you go to a burger restaurant and are told that you can choose between a hamburger and a cheeseburger. Imagine that you prefer a hamburger and say so. Suppose, furthermore, that the server corrects herself and points out that there are snails on the menu as well. In this case, you can legitimately say that you will stick with the hamburger, in the case when hamburgers rank higher than snails in your preference ordering (as in columns (A) and (B) in Figure 3.6). Or you can switch to snails, in the case when snails rank higher than hamburgers (as in column (C) in the figure). It would be odd, however, if you said: "Oh, I see. In that case I'll have the cheeseburger." Why? No rational preference ordering permits you to change your mind in this way. Either you prefer cheeseburgers to hamburgers, in which case you should have ordered the cheeseburger from the start, or you do not, in which case you should not choose it whether or not there are snails on the menu. (This chain of reasoning assumes that

Table 3.1   *The Economist* subscription offers

	Economist.com offers	Price
Option 1	Web subscription	$59
Option 2	Print subscription	$125
Option 3	Print + web subscription	$125

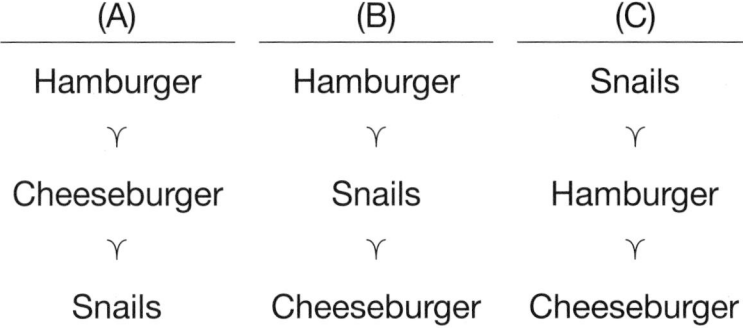

Figure 3.6 Preference orderings over food

we are talking about strict preference; if you are indifferent, you can choose anything you like.)

Formally speaking, the theory implies something we call the **expansion condition**.

Proposition 3.14 Expansion condition   *If x is chosen from the menu {x, y}, assuming that you are not indifferent between x and y, you must not choose y from the menu {x, y, z}.*

Proof. If you choose x when y is available, given that you are not indifferent between the two, you must strictly prefer x to y. If you choose y when x is available, given that you are not indifferent between the two, you must strictly prefer y to x. But we know from Proposition 2.14(ii) on page 18 that the strict preference relation is anti-symmetric; so this is impossible.   □

Plainly put, Proposition 3.14 simply says that the introduction of an inferior product should not change your choice. The choice of y from the expanded menu would signal that you changed your preferences between the first and second decision. The theory, however, does not permit you to change your preferences as a result of an expanding menu or for any other reason. As we know from Section 2.8, the theory assumes that preferences are stable and do not change over time. The plausibility of the expansion condition can also be seen by reflecting on the nature of indifference curves and budget sets. If some option is optimal, given a set of indifference curves and a budget line, this fact cannot be changed by adding another (clearly inferior) option to the budget set. Thus, the introduction of another alternative inside the shaded area of Figure 2.6 on page 23 would not make the alternative marked X suboptimal.

Yet there is evidence that people's preferences do change when the menu expands. We talk about this as a case of **menu dependence**. Suppose that you market a product, which we call the **target**. The problem is that another company markets a similar product, which we call the **competitor**. The consumer can afford each of these; both the target and the competitor are on the budget line. The problem is that the consumer prefers the competitor. Thus, the decision problem facing the consumer looks like Figure 3.7(a). The two products here (the target and the competitor) can be understood as before, as commodity bundles consisting of so many units of apples

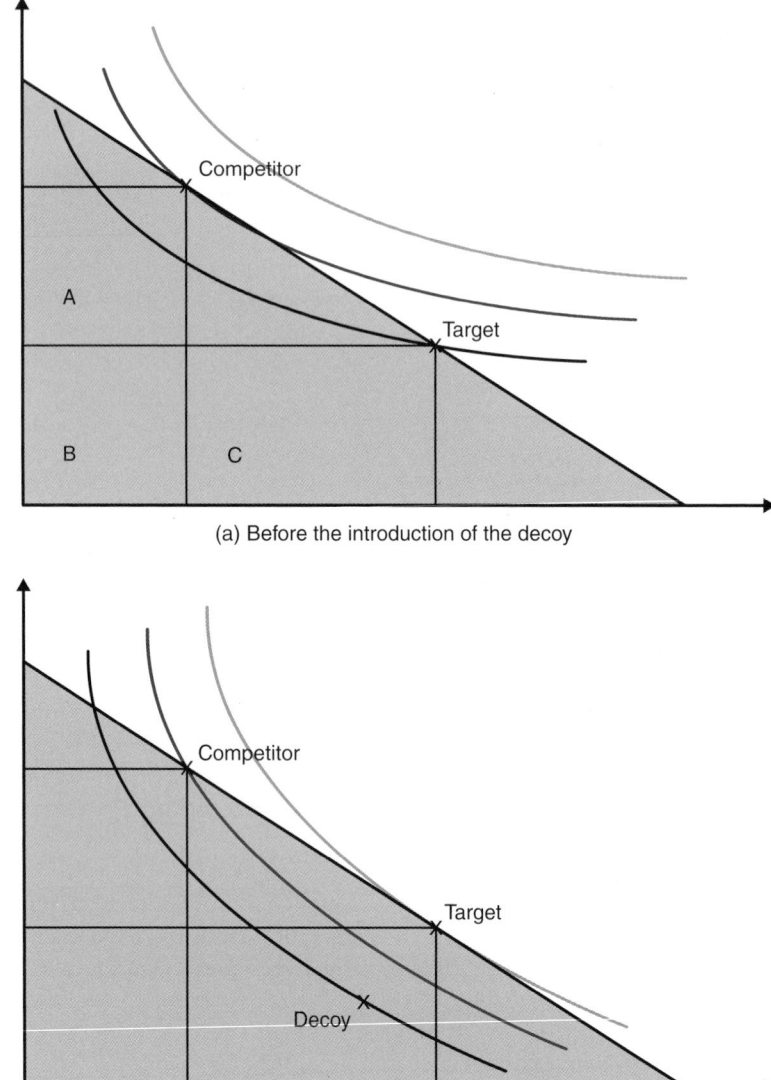

(a) Before the introduction of the decoy

(b) After the introduction of the decoy

Figure 3.7   Decoy effect

and so many units of bananas. They can also be understood as goods that differ along two dimensions: say, as cars that differ along the dimensions of speed and safety. Either way, it should be clear that the consumer in this figure will choose the competitor.

It turns out, however, that you can manipulate the consumer's choices by introducing a product that is in every respect inferior to the target. We say that one product x **dominates** another y just in case x is better than y in every possible respect. In terms of Figure 3.7(a), the target dominates every product in the boxes marked B and C. The competitor dominates every product in boxes A and B. Given a menu and a good x, we say that a product y is **asymmetrically dominated** by x

just in case y is dominated by x but not by any other member of the menu. Suppose, now, that the menu includes a third item, which we call the **decoy**, and which is asymmetrically dominated by the target. This means that the decoy is located in the box marked C in Figure 3.7(a). In spite of the fact that few consumers would bother buying such a good – since it is in every respect worse than the target – its introduction can change people's choices. There is evidence that the introduction of the decoy changes people's indifference curves in the manner illustrated by Figure 3.7(b).

Notice that the indifference curves appear to have rotated clockwise around the competitor, as it were, toward the decoy. As a result, the target is now on a higher indifference curve than the competitor. Thus, in spite of the fact that the rational consumer would not dream of buying the decoy, the introduction of it still succeeds in changing people's indifference curves and therefore their choices. Because the presence of the dominated option appears to increase the attractiveness to the consumer of the dominating alternative, the decoy effect is sometimes referred to as the **attraction effect**. Notice that such shifts violate the expansion condition (Proposition 3.14) and consequently are irrational.

Exercise 3.15 Decoy effect For this question, refer to Figure 3.8.

(a) If you are in charge of marketing the target product, in what area would you want to put the decoy?
(b) Assuming the decoy works as anticipated, does the figure show the indifference curves the way they look *before* or *after* the introduction of the decoy?

Exercise 3.16 Real-estate sales Suppose that you are a real-estate agent showing two properties to potential customers. The one is in good shape but far from the clients' office; the other is only in decent shape but close to the office.

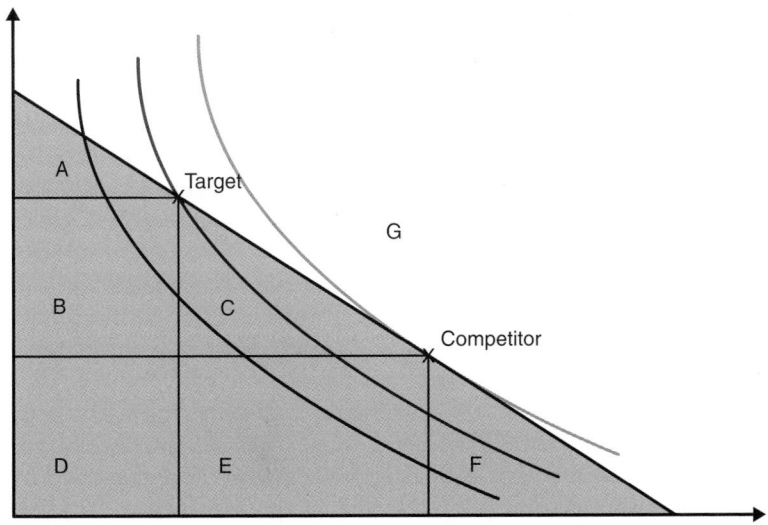

Figure 3.8 Decoy effect exercise

(a) If you want the customers to choose the former, what third property should you show?

(b) If you want the customers to choose the latter, what third property should you show?

The following example is designed to show just how useful the study of behavioral economics can be. Remember that with great power comes great responsibility.

Exercise 3.17 Wingmen and wingwomen   To improve your chances on the dating scene, you have decided to recruit a wingman or wingwoman.

(a) How, in general terms, should you choose your wingman or wingwoman?

(b) Imagine that your attractiveness and intelligence are both rated 9 on a 10-point scale. You have two competitors: one whose attractiveness is 10 and intelligence 8; and another whose attractiveness is 8 and intelligence 10. In what range would you want your wingman or wingwoman's attractiveness and intelligence to fall?

(c) If somebody asks you to be his or her wingman or wingwoman, what does this analysis suggest he or she thinks about your attractiveness and intelligence?

How does this help us explain the subscription offers in Table 3.1? Each option can be represented as a bundle of three different goods: online access, paper subscription, and a low price. Thus, option 1 can be represented as $\langle 1,0,1 \rangle$ because it includes online access, does not include a paper subscription, but has a low price. Similarly, option 2 can be represented as $\langle 0,1,0 \rangle$ and option 3 as $\langle 1,1,0 \rangle$. From this way of representing the options, it is quite clear that option 2 is (weakly) asymmetrically dominated by option 3. If the analysis offered in this section is correct, the introduction of the (inferior) option 2 might still drive customers to option 3, which is what *The Economist* wanted and expected.

How do we best explain the decoy effect? Perhaps consumers look for a *reason* to pick one option over another, or to reject one of the options, in order to feel better about their decision. The introduction of the decoy may give the consumer a reason to reject the competitor and to choose the target, in that the target no longer scores lowest along either one of the two dimensions. This would suggest that the search for reasons for action – or **reason-based choice** – may actually be responsible for making us behave irrationally. This is interesting, because having reasons for actions is otherwise frequently seen as the hallmark of rationality.

Either way, the decoy effect can explain a wide variety of marketing practices, including why the number of options available to customers keeps increasing (see the discussion of the paradox of choice in Section 3.2). And the decoy effect is obviously relevant to anybody who wants to sell things. Given the decoy effect, it might make sense to introduce a product you do not expect anyone to buy. For that reason, you cannot assess a product's contribution to corporate profits by simply looking at the sales of that product.

Notice that there are cases that look like menu dependence but which may be better described as something different. Suppose you enter a restaurant in a part of town you do not know very well and are offered the choice between fish, veal, and nothing at all. You choose the fish. Suppose, next, that the waiter returns to tell you that the menu also includes crack-cocaine. It would be perfectly possible, at this point, to decide you would rather not have anything at all without violating rational-choice theory. Why? When the waiter comes back, he does not just expand your menu, he also tells you something about the establishment – and also that you do not want to eat any of their food. Notice that this is not even a case of choice under certainty. The decoy scenarios are different: in this analysis, it is not the case that you learn something about the target by learning that the decoy is also on the menu.

3.5 Loss aversion and the endowment effect

The theory that we studied in the previous chapter makes preferences independent of your endowment, meaning what you have at the time when you make the decision. Consider your preferences for coffee mugs (Figure 3.9). Obviously, the theory does not tell you how much you should value the mug. However, it does say a few things about how you must order mugs and other things. Assuming you prefer more money to less, you prefer $1 to $0, $2 to $1, and so on. Because of completeness, if you are rational, there must be a dollar amount p (not necessarily in whole dollars and cents) such that you are indifferent between p and the mug. If p is $1, your preference ordering can be represented as Figure 3.10. If you have the mug, and somebody asks you what it would take to give it up, your answer would be "No less than $1," which is to say that your willingness-to-accept (WTA) equals $1. If you do not have a mug, and somebody asks you what you would pay in order to get one, your answer would be "No more than $1," which is to say that your willingness-to-pay (WTP) equals $1 too; that is, your preference between the mug and the dollar bill does not depend on whether or not you already have a mug, and your WTA equals your WTP. (Your preference for a second mug might depend, however, on whether you already have a mug, as Figure 3.11 shows.)

Figure 3.9 The value of a coffee mug. Illustration by Cody Taylor

Figure 3.10 Preference ordering with mug

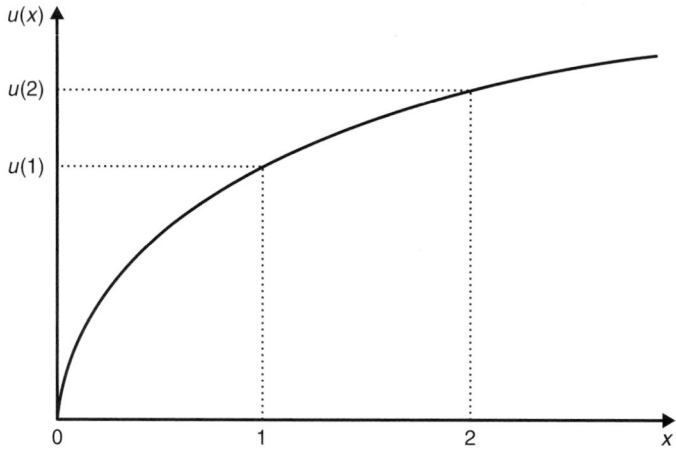

Figure 3.11 Utility over mugs

The independence of your preferences from your endowment is reflected in a fact about utility functions. Suppose your utility function over mugs looks like Figure 3.11. When you move from zero to one mug (rightwards along the x-axis), your utility increases from $u(0) = 0$ to $u(1)$. Similarly, when you move from one to zero mugs (leftwards along the x-axis) your utility decreases from $u(1)$ to zero. Because the increase in utility resulting from receiving the mug equals the decrease in utility resulting from losing it, the utility of the first mug is independent of your endowment, that is, whether or not you have the mug. We can show this numerically. Suppose $u(x) = 3\sqrt{x}$, so that $u(1) = 3$ and $u(0) = 0$. If so, the amount of utility received from acquiring your first mug (3) equals the amount of utility lost when giving it up (3). Again, a second mug would increase your utility by a smaller amount: $u(2) - u(1) = 3\sqrt{2} - 3\sqrt{1} \approx 1.24$.

However, people do not in general behave this way. Frequently, people require a lot more to give up a cup when they already have one than they would be willing to pay when they do not. In one study using Cornell University coffee mugs, the median owner asked for $5.25 when selling a mug, while the median buyer was only willing to pay $2.25 to $2.75 to purchase one. This phenomenon is referred to as the **endowment effect**, because people's preferences appear to depend on their endowment, or what they already possess. Since the manner in which people assess various options might depend on a reference point – in this case, their current endowment – phenomena like these are sometimes referred to as **reference-point phenomena**.

The endowment effect and reference point phenomena are instances of **framing effects**, which occur when people's preferences depend on how the options are *framed*. There are many kinds of framing effects. In 2007, the Associated Press reported that Irishman David Clarke was likely to lose his license after being caught driving 180 km/h (112 mph) in a 100 km/h (62 mph) zone. However, the judge reduced the charge, "saying the speed [in km/h] seemed 'very excessive,' but did not look 'as bad' when converted into miles per hour." The judge's assessment appears to depend on whether Clarke's speeding was described in terms of km/h or mph. Similarly, people traveling to countries with a different currency sometimes fall prey to what is called **money illusion**. Even if you know that one British pound equals about one and a half US dollars, paying two pounds for a drink might strike you as better than paying three dollars.

The endowment effect and other reference-point phenomena are typically explained as the result of **loss aversion**: the apparent fact that people dislike losses more than they like commensurate gains. Loss aversion is reflected in the fact that many people are more upset when they lose something than pleased when they find the same thing. Consider, for example, how upset you would be if you realized that you had lost a $10 bill, as compared to how pleased if you found one. Using the language of framing, we will say that how much you value a $10 bill depends on whether it is framed as a (potential) loss, as in the first case, or as a (potential) gain, as in the second case, and that *losses loom larger than gains*.

Example 3.18 WTA vs. WTP In the presence of loss aversion, your willingness-to-accept (WTA) does not in general equal your willingness-to-pay (WTP). When eliciting your WTA, you are asked to imagine that you have some good and to state what dollar amount you would be willing to accept in order to give the good up, meaning that the good will be evaluated in the loss frame. When eliciting your WTP, you are asked to imagine that you do not have some good and to state what dollar amount you would be willing to pay in order to acquire the good, meaning that the good will be evaluated in the gain frame. Given that losses loom larger than gains, we should expect your WTA to exceed your WTP.

As the example shows, loss aversion has radical implications for the practice of cost–benefit analysis (to which we will return in Section 6.3). It is quite common to assess the value of goods by eliciting people's willingness-to-accept (WTA) or willingness-to-pay (WTP). The elicitation of WTAs and WTPs is particularly common in the case of public goods, like nature preserves, and other goods that are not traded on an open market. As we saw earlier in this section, standard theory entails that WTAs and WTPs should be more or less the same. Loss aversion entails that people value something that they have more than something that they do not have, meaning that we should expect their WTA to exceed their WTP.

Behavioral economists capture loss aversion by means of a **value function** $v(\cdot)$, which represents how an agent evaluates a change. The value function is an essential part of **prospect theory**, which is one of the most prominent theories to emerge from behavioral economics and to which we will return frequently below (e.g., in Sections 7.2 and 7.6). The value function has two critical features. First, unlike the utility function, which ranges over *total* endowments, the value function ranges over *changes* in the endowment. Second, the value function has a kink at the reference point – in this case, the current endowment – in such a way that the curve is steeper to the left of the origin: see Figure 3.12 for an illustration of a typical value function. Notice that in this picture the vertical distance between the origin and $v(-1)$ is much greater than the vertical distance between the origin and $v(+1)$. Mathematically, $|v(-1)| > |v(+1)|$. Again, this captures the fact that losses loom larger than gains, that is, that people dislike losses more than they like the commensurate gains.

A value function like that in Figure 3.12 is consistent with the fact that people frequently reject gambles with an expected value of zero. It is easy to confirm graphically (using a technique we will learn in Section 6.5) that the value of a gamble that gives you a 50 percent chance of winning x and a 50 percent chance of losing x will never exceed the value of ±0. Another implication of loss aversion is that if you gain something and then lose it, you may feel worse off even though you find yourself where you started, which makes little sense from a traditional economic perspective. Suppose your parents promise to buy you car if you graduate with honors, but after you do they reveal that they were lying. Figure 3.13 shows how you might represent this change. By just looking at the picture, it is evident that the gain of a car, $v(+1)$, is smaller than the (absolute value of the) loss of a car, $v(-1)$. Thus, the net effect is negative: you will be worse off (in terms of value) after you find out that your parents tricked you into thinking that you would get a new car, than you would have been if they had not, even though you find yourself with the same number of cars (zero).

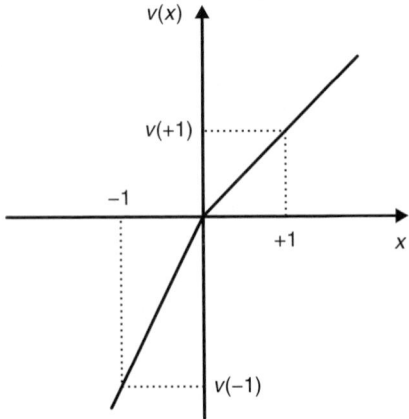

Figure 3.12 Value function

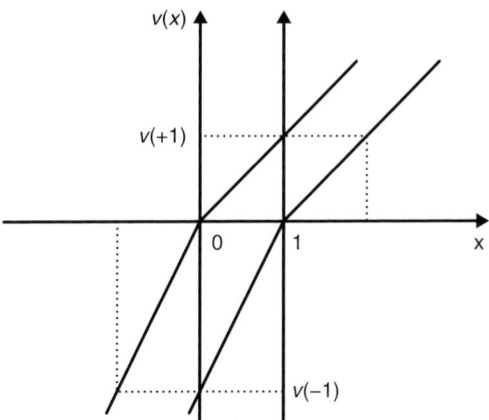

Figure 3.13 Value function and the car problem

It is possible to analyze loss aversion formally, by defining a value function $v(\cdot)$ that is steeper for losses than for gains. For example, we can define a value function along the following lines:

$$v(x) = \begin{cases} x/2 & \text{for gains}(x \ge 0) \\ 2x & \text{for losses}(x < 0) \end{cases}$$

It is easy to confirm that such a specification will generate graphs like Figure 3.12. The next example and exercises illustrate how the value function can be used in practice.

Example 3.19 The stock market Alicia and Benice own stock in the same company. When they bought the stock, it was worth $10. It later rose to $17, but then dropped to $12. Alicia and Benice are loss averse and have the same value function: $v(x) = x/2$ for gains and $v(x) = 2x$ for losses. (a) Alicia uses the purchase price ($10) as her reference point. If you ask her, how much would she say that she lost in terms of value when the price dropped from $17 to $12? (b) Benice uses the peak price ($17) as her reference point. If you ask her, how much would she say that she lost in terms of value when the price dropped from $17 to $12? (c) Who was more disappointed when the price dropped, Alicia or Benice?

(a) Alicia thinks of the drop in value as a change from a gain of seven to a gain of 2. In terms of value, $v(+2) - v(+7) = 1 - 7/2 = -5/2$. (b) Benice thinks of the drop in value as a change from a loss of plus/minus zero to a loss of five. In terms of value, $v(0) - v(-5) = 0 - 10 = -10$. (c) Benice was more disappointed.

The key is to see that Alicia evaluates the change as a *foregone gain*, whereas Benice evaluates the change as an *actual loss*. Given that losses loom larger than gains, Benice suffers more than Alicia does.

Exercise 3.20 The tax cut Suppose Alex and Bob are loss averse, so that their value function is $v(x) = x/2$ for gains and $v(x) = 2x$ for losses. Because of an upcoming election, politician R promises a tax cut which would give each citizen an additional two dollars in his or her pocket every day. Politician D opposes the tax cut. Ultimately D wins the election. Neither Alex nor Bob receives the additional two dollars per day.

(a) Alex thought D would win the election and never thought of the additional two dollars as part of his endowment. He thinks of the two dollars as a foregone gain. What would he say D's election cost him in terms of value?

(b) Bob was sure that R would win the election, and started thinking of the two dollars as part of his endowment. He thinks of the two dollars as an actual loss. What would he say D's election cost him in terms of value?

(c) Who is likely to be more disappointed, Alex or Bob?

Exercise 3.21 The car problem   This exercise refers to Figure 3.13. When you gain a car, incorporate it into your endowment, and then lose it, what is the total change in value that you experience? Assume that you are loss averse and have the value function $v(x) = x/2$ for gains and $v(x) = 2x$ for losses.

Loss aversion can explain a wide range of other phenomena. For example, it can explain why many companies have 30-day-no-questions-asked return policies. Although costly in other ways, such policies may serve to convince a customer who otherwise would not make the purchase to take the product home and try it out. Once taken home, however, the product becomes part of the customer's endowment and loss aversion kicks in, meaning that the customer is unlikely to return the product. Loss aversion serves to explain why credit-card companies permit merchants to offer "cash bonuses" but prevent them from imposing "credit-card surcharges." Clients find it easier to forego a cash bonus than to suffer the loss of a surcharge, so they are more likely to use a credit card in the presence of the former than of the latter. Loss aversion helps explain why politicians argue about whether cancelling tax cuts amounts to raising taxes. Voters find the foregone gain associated with a cancelled tax cut easier to stomach than they do the loss associated with a tax increase. Consequently, politicians favoring higher taxes will talk about "cancelled tax cuts" whereas politicians opposing higher taxes will talk about "tax increases." Loss aversion can also explain why so many negotiations end in stalemate, even in the presence of potential, mutually beneficial agreements. Suppose two partners are negotiating the division of a pie and that both partners think they are owed two-thirds of the pie. Any division that strikes an outside observer as fair (including a 50–50 split) will feel like a loss to both partners, and an agreement might be hard to come by. Loss aversion can also explain why the volume of real-estate sales decreases in an economic downturn. Sellers may find it so hard to sell their house at a loss, relative to the price at which the property was purchased, that they would rather not sell it at all. This kind of behavior even prevents people from upgrading from a smaller to a larger property, which is economically rational to do during a downturn.

In addition, loss aversion helps account for some of the phenomena studied earlier in this book, including the fact that people fail to take opportunity costs properly into account. If people treat out-of-pocket costs as losses and opportunity costs as foregone gains, loss aversion entails that out-of-pocket costs will loom larger than opportunity costs. Loss aversion may also help explain why people are so prone to honoring sunk costs. Since a sunk cost is often experienced as a loss, loss aversion entails that such costs will loom large, which in turn might drive people to honor sunk costs.

Loss aversion has other, and perhaps even more radical, implications for microeconomics. Because standard theory presupposes that preferences are independent of endowments, it implies that indifference curves are independent of endowments. Thus, if your indifference curves look like those in Figure 3.14(a), they do so independently of whether you happen to possess bundle x or y. This indifference curve is **reversible**, in the sense that it describes your preference over (actually, indifference between) x and y independently of your endowment.

By contrast, loss aversion entails that your indifference curves will not be independent of your current endowment. Suppose, for instance, that your value function is $v(x) = x$ for gains and $v(x) = 2x$ for losses, and that this is true for both apples and bananas. If you begin with bundle $y = \langle 3,1 \rangle$ and lose an apple, you will require two additional bananas to make up for that loss. Hence, the indifference curve going through y will also go through $\langle 2,3 \rangle$. If you start out with bundle y and lose a banana,

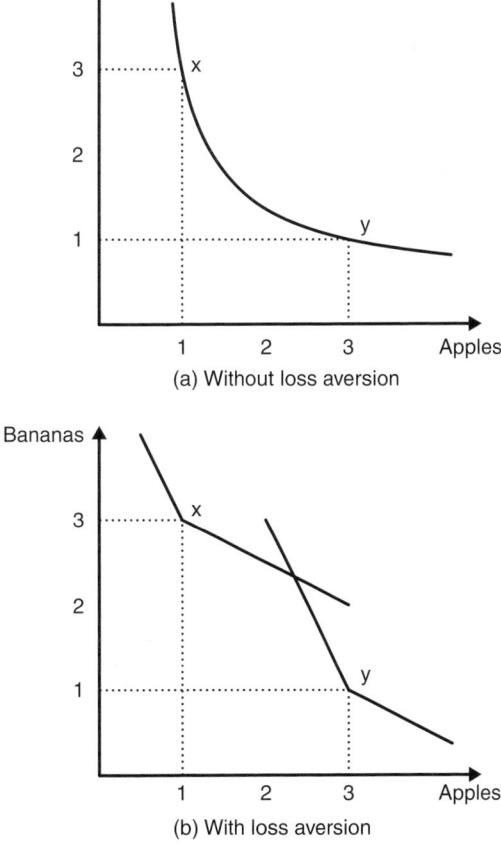

Figure 3.14 Indifference curves and loss aversion

you will require two additional apples to make up for that loss. Hence, the very same indifference curve will also go through $\langle 5,0 \rangle$. The result is similar if you begin with bundle $x = \langle 1,3 \rangle$. If you are loss averse, then, your indifference curves will look like those in Figure 3.14(b). Notice that there are two indifference curves here – really, two sets of indifference curves – one for initial endowment x and one for initial endowment y.

Exercise 3.22 Value functions Suppose that you are loss averse, and that your value function is $v(x) = x$ for gains and $v(x) = 3x$ for losses.

(a) Represent the value function graphically, in the manner of Figure 3.12.
(b) Represent your indifference curves graphically, in the manner of Figure 3.14(b), assuming that your initial endowment is $\langle 3,4 \rangle$.

A related feature of having kinks in your indifference curves – as in Figure 3.14(b) – is that if you begin with x and are offered to trade it for y, you will reject the offer. At the same time, if you begin with y and are offered to trade it for x, you will reject this offer too. This phenomenon is sometimes referred to as **status quo bias**, because you exhibit a tendency to prefer the existing state of affairs under any circumstances. In the study of Cornell coffee mugs, a median number of 2 out of 22 mugs changed hands when participants were allowed to trade mugs for money; in the absence of status quo bias, one would expect the number of trades to equal about 11.

Exercise 3.23 Health care Broadly speaking, in Europe, health care is provided by the government and paid for by taxes. That is, individuals are taxed by the government, which then uses the tax money to provide health care services for the citizens. In the US, again broadly speaking, health care is largely purchased privately. That is, individuals pay lower taxes, and (if they so choose) use their money to purchase health care services.

(a) Use the notion of status quo bias to provide a detailed explanation of the following paradox: most Americans prefer their system to a European-style one, whereas most Europeans prefer their system to an American-style one.
(b) Illustrate your answer with a graph showing the indifference curves of a typical American and a typical European.
(c) Imagine that the US were to adopt a European-style health-care system. How should we expect Americans to feel about their new health-care system then, and how easy would it be for the opposition party to switch back?

Status quo bias can explain why many people oppose human genetic enhancement. Many of us would be unwilling to give up our natural, pristine "unenhanced" state in exchange for an increase in intelligence quotient (IQ); yet, if we were the beneficiaries of genetic enhancement, it is hard to imagine that we would willingly accept a decrease in IQ in exchange for the natural, pristine "unenhanced" state. Also, status quo bias explains why many people oppose free trade when they do not have it but are in favor of it when they do. Many people who hesitate to support free-trade agreements with other countries (with which they do not already trade freely) would protest loudly if somebody proposed eliminating free-trade agreements already in existence, for example, with adjoining states. In all these cases, people are unmoved by the prospect of gaining a benefit that they do not already have, but deeply averse to losing some benefit that they already have.

So far, we have assumed that the reference point is determined by a person's current endowment. This is not always the case. A person's reference point can be determined by her aspirations and expectations, among other things. The fact that reference points can be fixed by aspirations and expectations explains how people who get a five percent raise can feel cheated if they expected a ten percent raise, but be absolutely elated if they did not expect a raise at all.

Exercise 3.24 Bonuses   Draw a graph that illustrates how a person who gets a five percent raise can be elated if she did not expect a raise at all, but feel cheated if she expected a ten percent raise.

Exercise 3.25 Exam scores   Assume that Alysha and Billy have the following value function over exam scores: $v(x) = x/2$ for gains and $v(x) = 2x$ for losses. Both of them use the expected exam score as their reference point.

(a) Alysha expects to score 75 out of 100 on her upcoming midterm exam. She does better than expected. What is her gain, in terms of value, if her final score is 93?
(b) Billy also expects to score 75 out of 100 on his upcoming midterm exam. He does worse than expected. What is his loss, in terms of value, if his final score is 67?
(c) Insofar as you use your expectation as a reference point, what does value theory seem to say about maximizing value in your life: should you perform well or poorly in exams? Should you set high or low expectations for yourself?

The most spectacular example of the outsize role that expectations can play is baseball player Barry Bonds:

> When Pittsburgh Pirate outfielder Barry Bonds's salary was raised from $850,000 in 1990 to $2.3 million in 1991, instead of the $3.25 million he had requested, Bonds sulked, "There is nothing Barry Bonds can do to satisfy Pittsburgh. I'm so sad all the time."

A person's reference point can also be determined by other people's achievements or endowments. Such **social comparisons** help explain the fact that whether a person is happy with his or her salary will depend in part on the salaries of neighbors, friends, and relatives. In this respect, income is similar to speed. Is 70 mph (110 km/h) fast or slow? If everybody else on the highway is driving 50 mph, 70 mph feels fast. But if everybody else is driving 80 mph, 70 mph feels slow. Thus, your sense for how fast you are traveling depends not just on your absolute speed, but on your relative speed. Similarly, your sense for how much money you earn depends not just on your absolute income, but on your relative income.

Exercise 3.26 Salary comparisons   Insofar as you use other people's salaries as a reference point, what does value theory seem to say about maximizing value in your life?

Example 3.27 Salary comparisons, cont.   At one university library, there is a single book that is so popular that it is chained to the checkout counter. It is the book that lists the salaries of all university employees. Presumably, no one would use the book to look up one's own salary: that information is more easily accessible on one's monthly pay stub. In all likelihood, the book is so popular because people like to look up their colleagues' salaries.

As the last example illustrates, it is hard to deny that people engage in social comparisons. Social comparisons can also explain why bronze-medal winners can be more satisfied with their performance than silver-medal winners. Assuming that a bronze-medal winner compares himself or herself with the athletes who did not win a medal, the bronze medal represents achievement. But assuming that the silver-medal winner compares his or her performance with the gold-medal winner's, the silver medal represents defeat.

Loss aversion must not be confused with diminishing marginal utility. If people would be willing to pay less for a mug that they do not own than they would accept in return for the mug that they do own, this may reflect diminishing marginal utility for mugs. Going back to Figure 3.11, notice that the utility derived from the second mug (that is, the marginal utility of the second mug) is much lower than the utility derived from the first mug. It is important not to attribute loss aversion to agents whose behavior is better explained in terms of diminishing marginal utility.

3.6 Anchoring and adjustment

Imagine that you subject people to the following two experiments. If your research participants protest that they do not know the answers to the questions, tell them to offer their best guesses.

Example 3.28 Africa and the UN   Spin a wheel of fortune to come up with a number between 0 and 100, and invite your participants to answer the following two questions: (a) Is the percentage of African nations in the United Nations (UN) greater than or less than the number? (b) What is the actual percentage of African nations in the UN?

You probably would not expect the answer to (b) to reflect the random number generated by the wheel of fortune. Yet evidence suggests that you would find a correlation between the two. In one study, when the starting point was 10, the median answer to (b) was 25; when the starting point was 65, the median answer was 45.

Example 3.29 Multiplication   Give people 5 seconds to come up with an answer to either one of the following multiplication problems:

(a) Compute: $1*2*3*4*5*6*7*8$
(b) Compute: $8*7*6*5*4*3*2*1$

Given that (a) and (b) are mathematically equivalent, you might expect your research participants to come up with more or less the same answer independently of which question they were asked. Yet, when a group of high school students were asked the first question, the median answer was 512; when they were asked the second question, the median answer was 2250. (The correct answer is 40, 320.)

These phenomena are frequently explained by reference to **anchoring and adjustment**, which is a cognitive process that can be used when forming judgments.

As the name suggests, anchoring and adjustment is a two-stage process: first, you pick an initial estimate called an **anchor**, and second, you adjust the initial estimate up or down (as you see fit) in order to come up with a final answer. When deciding what a used car with a $15k price tag is worth, for example, you might start by asking yourself whether it is worth $15k and then adjust your estimate as required. If you think $15k is too much, you adjust your estimate of its worth downward; if you think $15k is too little, you adjust it upward.

According to one prominent account of human judgment and decision-making – the **heuristics-and-biases program** – we make judgments not by actually computing probabilities and utilities but by following rules of thumb or **heuristics**. Thus, a heuristic is a rule of thumb that can be used when forming judgments. Heuristics are thought to be functional, in the sense that they reduce the time and effort required to solve everyday problems and produce approximately correct answers under a wide range of conditions. But they are not assumed to be perfect: under certain circumstances, they are thought to fail in predictable fashion. Because the consistent application of a heuristic can lead to answers that are systematically and predictably wrong, we say that it can lead to **bias**. Thus, an account according to which we follow heuristics can help explain both why we oftentimes are able to make quick and perfectly appropriate judgments, and why we sometimes go wrong.

Anchoring and adjustment is one of the heuristics identified by the heuristics-and-biases program. Like all heuristics, anchoring and adjustment is thought to be functional but at the same time lead to bias under certain conditions. Evidence suggests that the adjustment is often insufficient. This means that the final judgment will to some extent be a function of the anchor, which may be perfectly arbitrary. If the anchor is very different from the true answer, anchoring and insufficient adjustment can generate highly inaccurate answers.

Consider Example 3.28. People's answer to the question about the percentage of African nations in the UN can be explained by saying that they take the random number as an anchor and adjust the answer up or down as they see fit. If the random number is 65, they begin by 65, then (assuming this number strikes them as too high) adjust downward. If, instead, the random number is 10, then (assuming this strikes them as too low) they adjust upward. Insofar as the adjustment is insufficient, we should expect the final estimate to be higher if the random number is 65 than if it is 10.

Consider Example 3.29. Under time pressure, students presumably perform a few steps of the multiplication problem (as time allows) and adjust upward to compensate for the missing steps. Insofar as the adjustment is insufficient, you would expect the answers to be too low. Moreover, because people who answer (a) will get a lower number after a few steps than people who answer (b), you would expect the former to offer a lower estimate than the latter. As you can tell, this is exactly what happened.

Anchoring and adjustment might affect a wide range of judgments. Consider the following famous story.

Exercise 3.30 Invention of chess   According to legend, the inventor of chess was asked by the emperor what he (the inventor) wanted in return for his invention. The inventor responded: "One grain of rice for the first square on the chess-board, two grains for the second square, four grains for the third square, and so on."

The emperor was happy to oblige. There are 64 squares on the chess board, so on the 64th day, the inventor could demand $2^{64-1} \approx 10^{19} = 10,000,000,000,000,000,000$ grains of rice, a figure much greater than what the emperor had expected and could afford. Use the idea of anchoring and adjustment to explain how the emperor could underestimate the number so dramatically.

So far we have talked about anchoring and adjustment as something that affects belief, but there is evidence that it also affects preferences. In one study, experimenters showed MBA students various products, and asked them, first, whether they would be willing to buy the product for a price equal to the last two digits of their social security number, and second, to state their WTP. When people in the lowest quintile (the lowest 20 percent of the distribution with respect to social security numbers) were willing to pay $8.64 on the mean for a cordless trackball, people in the highest quintile were willing to pay $26.18. When people in the lowest quintile were willing to pay $11.73 for a bottle of fine wine, people in the highest quintile were willing to pay $37.55. Thus, people in the highest quintile were sometimes willing to pay more than three times as much as people in the lowest quintile. These results are easily explained by anchoring and (insufficient) adjustment, if we assume that the study participants used the last two digits of their social security number as an anchor.

From the discussion in the beginning of Section 3.5, it should be clear why this behavior pattern is irrational. The behavior pattern can be said to violate **procedure invariance**: the proposition that a stated preference should not differ depending on the method used to elicit it.

Anchoring and adjustment can explain a whole range of phenomena. It can explain, for instance, why it is so common to lure customers by lines such as these: "Used to be $50! Now only $24.99!" or "A $500 value for only $399" or "Suggested retail price: $14.99. Now, only $9.99." Sellers might hope that potential customers will form a judgment about the dollar value of the product by using the first amount as an anchor. The seller might realize that the customer would not be willing to pay $24.99 for the product if asked a direct question; however, the seller may be hoping that the customer will use the $50 figure as an anchor and insufficiently adjust downward, and therefore end up with a final WTP exceeding $24.99. That is, the seller hopes that people will use the greater number as an anchor. Anchoring and adjustment might also explain why realtors often publish an asking price that is higher than what they expect to receive for the property: by publishing a higher number, they might hope to influence what potential buyers would be willing to pay.

It is important not to exaggerate people's susceptibility to anchoring-and-adjustment-related bias. It may be that people respond to suggested retail prices (and the like) because they take a high suggested retail price to signal high quality. If so, their behavior may not be due to anchoring-and-adjustment at all. They would not even be making a choice under certainty. That said, this line of argument cannot explain how roulette wheels and social security numbers can affect behavior, on the assumption that no one would take such numbers as a mark of quality.

Either way, the heuristics-and-biases program has been enormously influential, and we will continue to discuss it below (for example in Sections 5.2 and 5.6). Because it carries so much explanatory power, we will return to anchoring and adjustment repeatedly (see, for example, Exercise 4.29 on page 70).

3.7 Discussion

This chapter has reviewed a number of different phenomena that appear to pose a problem for the theory that we learned in Chapter 2. Most of these phenomena are presented as challenges to the descriptive adequacy of rational-choice theory. Thus, behavioral economists think of the manner in which people ignore opportunity costs but honor sunk costs, exhibit menu dependence, overweight losses relative to gains, and permit arbitrary anchors to unduly affect their behavior as inconsistent with the view that people actually behave in accordance with rational-choice theory. Though far from universal, the deviations appear to be substantial, systematic, and predictable. Examples have illustrated that these phenomena can be costly indeed, not just in terms of time, effort, and money, but also in terms of human lives. Some of the phenomena that we have studied can also be construed as challenges to the normative adequacy of the theory. When it comes to opportunity costs, for example, we noted how extraordinarily demanding the theory can be. It has been argued that this makes the theory unsuitable as a normative theory.

Obviously, this chapter does not pretend to have presented a complete list of phenomena that are at odds with standard theory of choice under certainty. For example, the decoy effect is not the only form of menu dependence. Another effect that has received a great deal of attention especially in marketing literature is the **compromise effect**: people's tendency to choose an alternative that represents a compromise or middle option in the menu. Some sellers try to drive business from a cheap to an expensive product by introducing a super-expensive product; while the super-expensive product might not sell, it might make the expensive product stand out as an attractive compromise between the cheap and the super-expensive one. These phenomena are sometimes referred to as **context effects**, because people's decisions appear to be responsive to the context of the decisions.

We have also reviewed some basic building blocks of theories that behavioral economists have proposed to account for phenomena that cannot be captured within standard economics. Thus, we have studied the value function of prospect theory, which is one of the most prominent theories to emerge from behavioral economics. We have also come across the notion of a heuristic, which is essential to the enormously influential heuristics-and-biases program. We will return to prospect theory and the heuristics-and-biases program repeatedly below. Studying these theories will give you a better idea of what behavioral economists do, beyond finding fault with standard theory.

In the process, we have come across a variety of ways in which knowledge of behavioral economics permits you to influence the behavior of others. By appealing to sunk costs, introducing asymmetrically dominated alternatives, altering the frame in which options are presented, or introducing arbitrary anchors you can affect other people's evaluation of various options. Since standard economic models frequently treat the options available to consumers as ordered n-tuples of price and product characteristics, it leaves out many variables of interest to marketers, medical doctors, public health officials, and the like. By bringing things such as framing and reference points into the picture, behavioral economics offers a wider range of levers that can be used to influence people's behavior (for good or for evil). But knowledge of behavioral economics can also help you resist other people's efforts to manipulate your behavior. By being aware of the manner in which sunk costs, inferior alternatives, framing, and heuristics affect your behavior, you may be less likely to fall for other people's tricks.

We will return to these themes in later chapters, after we have studied the standard theory of judgment under risk and uncertainty.

Additional exercises

Exercise 3.31 AEA The following question was famously asked of 200 professional economists at the 2005 meeting of the American Economic Association (AEA). By looking up the answer in the answer key, you can compare your performance with theirs:

> You won a free ticket to see an Eric Clapton concert (which has no resale value). Bob Dylan is performing on the same night and is your next-best alternative activity. Tickets to see Dylan cost $40. On any given day, you would be willing to pay up to $50 to see Dylan. Assume there are no other costs of seeing either performer. Based on this information, what is the opportunity cost of seeing Eric Clapton? (a) $0, (b) $10, (c) $40, or (d) $50.

Exercise 3.32 Mr Humphryes The following quote is from a 2009 news story titled "Tension builds around courthouses' reopening." The controversy concerns whether to reopen a satellite courthouse in a building that the county owns or one in a building that the county leases. What fallacy does Mr Humphryes commit?

> The county owns the Centerpoint Building and leases Gardendale and Forestdale buildings. [Commissioner Bobby] Humphryes believes it would make economic sense to open one of the buildings [the] county leases. "I think it's senseless to shut down a building we have leases on when we let the others remain idle, we don't have leases on and don't owe money on," Humphryes said.

Exercise 3.33 Pear Corporation The Pear computer company is introducing a new line of tablet computers. The Macro has huge storage capacity but is not very affordable. The Micro has limited storage capacity but is very affordable.

(a) Market research suggests that a typical consumer tends to be indifferent between the Micro and the Macro. Draw a graph with storage capacity on the x-axis and affordability on the y-axis. Use a solid line to represent a typical consumer's indifference curves going through the Micro and the Macro.
(b) Pear wants to steer customers toward the more expensive tablet computer. They decide to use a decoy, which they will call the Dud, to accomplish this goal. Use an "X" to mark the location of the Dud in the graph.
(c) Use dashed lines to show what the typical consumer's indifference curves would look like if the introduction of the Dud had the intended effect.

Exercise 3.34 Match each of the vignettes below with one of the following phenomena: *anchoring and adjustment, compromise effect, failure to consider opportunity costs, loss aversion,* and *sunk-cost fallacy*. If in doubt, pick the best fit.

(a) Adam has just arrived at the movie theater when he realizes that he has lost the $10 ticket he bought just before dinner. The theater staff informs him that there are more tickets available. "I'm not buying another ticket," he tells them. "This movie may be worth ten bucks but there's no way I'm going to pay 20 for it." He is angry with himself all night.

Additional exercises cont'd

(b) Bruce is buying a new car, which he intends to keep for a long time. The car dealership has two new cars for sale. There is no difference except for the color: one is red and one is metallic blue. The red one used to be $15,995 and the metallic blue one $16,495; both are on sale for $14,995. Bruce has no particular preference for blue, and fears that the metallic finish will make him look unmanly. Still, thinking about what these cars used to cost, it seems to him that it would be worth paying more for the blue one, which makes it seem like a better deal. He tells the car salesman that he will take the blue one, though he secretly wonders how his friends will react.

(c) The owners of the local organic grocery store decide that they want to encourage their customers to use fewer plastic bags. They decide that the customers would be upset if the store started charging money for the bags – after all, people expect their plastic bags to be free. Instead, they gradually raise the prices of their goods by an average of 25 cents per customer, and give people who bring their own bags a 25-cent discount. Current customers have no problem with this arrangement.

(d) A philosophy department is hiring a new professor. There are two candidates. Dr A does aesthetics. Dr E does ethics. Everybody agrees that Dr E is the most accomplished philosopher. However, Prof. P maintains that Dr A should be hired anyway, because the Department used to have a spectacularly talented professor in aesthetics.

(e) Erica is a highly paid neurosurgeon with no shortage of work. Every second Friday afternoon she leaves work early to go home and mow the lawn. She takes no pleasure in mowing the lawn, but she cannot bring herself to pay the lawn guy $75 to do it for her.

(f) Frank is looking at strollers for his first child. He is undecided between the basic SE model and the slightly more upscale CE model. Suddenly, he realizes that there exists a third option, the extra-special XS model. He settles on the CE model.

Problem 3.35   *Drawing on your own experience, make up stories like those in Exercise 3.34 to illustrate the various ideas that you have read about in this chapter.*

Further reading

The idea that choices can lead to unhappiness is explored in Schwartz (2004, pp. 122–3). The classic analysis of sunk costs is Arkes and Blumer (1985), but see also Hastie and Dawes (2010, pp. 34–42); escalation behavior is analyzed in Staw and Ross (1989), the source of the George Ball quote (p. 216). Decoy effects are discussed in Huber et al. (1982) and Ariely (2008); the latter is the source of the example involving subscription offers (pp. 1–6). The classic text on reason-based choice is Shafir et al. (1993). A great review of loss aversion, the endowment effect, and status quo bias is Kahneman et al. (1991); the fate of the speeding Irishman was reported by the Associated Press (2007) and Barry Bonds was quoted in Myers (1992, p. 57). The classic discussion of anchoring and adjustment is Tversky and Kahneman (1974), which is also the source of the examples and data cited early in the section; the follow-up experiments are described in Ariely et al. (2003). The study of professional economists is discussed in Frank (2005) and Mr Humphryes is cited by FOX6 WBRC (2009).

Judgment under Risk and Uncertainty

Chapter 4

Probability Judgment

Introduction

Though the theory of choice explored in Part I is helpful for a range of purposes, most real-life decision are not choices under certainty. When you decide whether to start a company, buy stocks, propose to the love of your life, or have a medical procedure, you will not typically know at the time of making the decision what the outcome of each available act would be. In order to capture what people do, and what they should do, in such situations, we need another theory. Part II explores theories of judgment: how people form and change beliefs. In Part III, we will return to the topic of decision-making.

In this chapter, we explore the theory of probability. There is wide – but far from complete – agreement that this is the correct normative theory of probabilistic judgment, that is, that it correctly describes how we should make probabilistic judgments. Consequently, the theory of probability is widely used in statistics, engineering, finance, public health, and elsewhere. Moreover, the theory can be used as a descriptive theory about how people make judgments, and it can be used as part of a theory about how they make decisions.

Like the theory of rational choice under certainty, probability theory is axiomatic. Thus, we begin by learning a set of axioms – which will be called "rules" – and which you will have to take for granted. Most of the time, this is not hard: once you understand them, the rules may strike you as intuitively plausible. We will also adopt a series of definitions. Having done that, though, everything else can be derived. Thus, we will spend a great deal of time below proving increasingly interesting and powerful principles on the basis of axioms and definitions.

4.2 Fundamentals of probability theory

Here are two classic examples of probability judgment.

Example 4.1 Mrs Jones's children   You are visiting your new neighbor, Mrs Jones. Mrs Jones tells you that she has two children, who are playing in their room. Assume that each time somebody has a child, the probability of having a girl is the same as the probability of having a boy (and that whether the mother had a boy or a girl the first time around does not affect the probabilities involved the second time around). Now, Mrs Jones tells you that at least one of the children is a girl. What is the probability that the other child is a girl too?

Example 4.2 The Linda problem   Linda is 31 years old, single, outspoken and very bright. She majored in philosophy. As a student, she was deeply concerned with issues of discrimination and social justice and also participated in anti-nuclear demonstrations.

(a) What is the probability that Linda is a bank teller?
(b) What is the probability that Linda is a bank teller and a feminist?

Answers to these questions will be given once we have developed the apparatus required to address them rigorously. For now, I will just note that one reason why this theory is interesting is that people's intuitive probability judgments – and therefore many of their decisions – tend to fail in predictable ways.

Before we start, we need to develop a conceptual apparatus that will permit us to speak more clearly about the subject matter. For example, we want to talk about the different things that can conceivably happen. When you flip a coin, for instance, you can get heads or you can get tails; when you roll a six-sided die, you can get any number between one and six.

Definition 4.3 Definition of "outcome space"   *The **outcome space** is the set of all possible individual outcomes.*

We represent outcome spaces following standard conventions, using curly brackets and commas. To denote the outcome space associated with flipping a coin, we write: {Heads, Tails} or {H, T}. To denote the outcome space associated with rolling a six-sided die, we write: {1, 2, 3, 4, 5, 6}.

Oftentimes, we want to talk about what actually happened or about what may happen. If so, we are talking about actual outcomes, as in "the coin came up tails" and "I might roll snake eyes (two ones)."

Definition 4.4 Definition of "outcome"   *An **outcome** is a subset of the outcome space.*

We write outcomes following the same conventions. Thus, some of the outcomes associated with one roll of a six-sided die include: {1} for one, {6} for six, {1, 2, 3} for a number less than or equal to three, and {2, 4, 6} for an even number. There is one exception: when the outcome only has one member, we may omit the curly brackets and write 6 instead of {6}. Notice that in all these cases, the outcomes are subsets of the outcome space.

Definition 4.5 Definition of "probability"   *The **probability function** is a function $Pr(\cdot)$ that assigns a real number to each outcome. The **probability** of an outcome A is the number $Pr(A)$ assigned to A by the probability function $Pr(\cdot)$.*

Hence, the probability of rolling an even number when rolling a six-sided die is denoted $Pr(\{2, 4, 6\})$. The probability of rolling a six is denoted $Pr(\{6\})$, or relying on the convention introduced above, $Pr(6)$. The probability of getting heads when flipping a coin is denoted $Pr(\{H\})$ or $Pr(H)$. The probability of an outcome, of course, represents (in some sense) the chance of that outcome happening. Sometimes people talk about odds instead of probabilities. Odds and probabilities are obviously related, but they are not identical. Refer to the text box on page 69 for more about odds.

The next propositions describe the properties of this probability function. They will be referred to as the **rules** or **axioms** of probability.

Axiom 4.6 The range of probabilities   *The probability of any outcome A is a number between 0 and 1 inclusive, that is, $0 \leqslant Pr(A) \leqslant 1$.*

Thus, probabilities have to be numbers no smaller than zero and no greater than one. Equivalently, probabilities can be no lower than 0 percent and no greater than 100 percent. You might not know the probability that your internet startup company will survive its first year. But you do know this: the probability is no lower than 0 percent and no greater than 100 percent.

In general, it can be difficult to compute probabilities. People such as engineers and public health officials spend a lot of time trying to determine the probabilities of events such as nuclear disasters and global pandemics. There is one case in which computing probabilities is easy, however, and that is in the case when individual outcomes are equally probable, or **equiprobable**.

Axiom 4.7 The EQUIPROBABILITY rule   *If there are n equally probable individual outcomes* $\{A_1, A_2, \ldots, A_n\}$*, then the probability of any one individual outcome* A_i *is 1/n, that is,* $Pr(A_i) = 1/n$.

Suppose we are asked to compute the probability of getting a four when rolling a fair die. Because all outcomes are equally likely (that is what it means for the die to be fair) and because there are six outcomes, the probability of getting a four is 1/6. So $Pr(4) = 1/6$. Similarly, the probability of getting heads when flipping a fair coin is 1/2. So $Pr(H) = 1/2$.

Exercise 4.8   Suppose that you are drawing one card each from two thoroughly shuffled but otherwise normal decks of cards. What is the probability that you draw the same card from the two decks?

You could answer this question by analyzing all $52^2 = 2704$ different outcomes associated with drawing two cards from two decks. The easiest way to think about it, though, is to ask what it would take for the second card to match the first.

As it happens, we have already developed enough of an apparatus to address Example 4.1. First, we need to identify the outcome space associated with having two children. Writing G for "girl" and B for "boy," and BG for "the oldest child is a boy and the youngest child is a girl," the outcome space is {GG, GB, BG, BB}. Once you learn that at least one of the children is a girl, you know for a fact that it is not the case that both children are boys. That is, you know that BB does not obtain. This means that the outcome space has been reduced to {GG, GB, BG}. In only one of three cases (GG) is the other child a girl also. Because these three outcomes are equally likely, you can apply the EQUIPROBABILITY rule to find that the probability that the other child is a girl equals $Pr(GG) = 1/3$.

Exercise 4.9 Mrs Jones's children   Instead of telling you that at least one of the children is a girl, Mrs Jones tells you that her oldest child is a girl. Now, what is the probability that the other child is also a girl?

Exercise 4.10 Mr Peters's children   Your other neighbor, Mr Peters, has three children. Having just moved to the neighborhood, you do not know whether the children are boys or girls. Let us assume that every time Mr Peters had a child, he was equally likely to have a boy and a girl (and that there are no other possibilities).

(a) What is the relevant outcome space?
(b) Imagine that you learn that at least one of the children is a girl. What is the new outcome space?
(c) Given that you know that at least one of the children is a girl, what is the probability that Mr Peters has three girls?
(d) Imagine that you learn that at least two of the children are girls. What is the new outcome space?
(e) Given that you know that at least two of the children are girls, what is the probability that Mr Peters has three girls?

Exercise 4.11 Three-card swindle   Your friend Bill is showing you his new deck of cards. The deck consists of only three cards. The first card is white on both sides. The second card is red on both sides. The third card is white on one side and red on the other. Now Bill shuffles the deck well, occasionally turning individual cards over in the process. Perhaps he puts them all in a hat and shakes the hat for a long time. Then he puts the stacked deck on the table in such a way that you can see the visible face of the top card only.

(a) What is the outcome space? Write "W/R" to denote the outcome where the visible side of the top card is white and the other side is red, and so on.
(b) After shuffling, the visible side of the top card is white. What is the new outcome space?
(c) Given that the visible side of the top card is white, what is the probability that the other side of the top card is red?

This last exercise is called the "three-card swindle," because it can be used to fool people into giving up their money. If you bet ten dollars that the other side is white, you will find that many people are willing to accept the bet. This is so because they (mistakenly) believe that the probability is 50 percent. You might lose. Yet, because you have got the probabilities on your side, on average you will make money. It is not clear that this game deserves the name "swindle" since it involves no deception. Still, because this might be illegal where you live, you did not hear it from me.

Exercise 4.12 Four-card swindle   Your other friend Bull has another deck of cards. This deck has four cards: one card is white on both sides; one card is black on both sides; one card is red on both sides; and one card is white on one side and red on the other. Imagine that you shuffle the deck well, including turning individual cards upside down every so often.

(a) What is the outcome space? Write "W/R" to denote the outcome where the visible side of the top card is white and the other side is red, and so on.
(b) Suppose that after shuffling, the visible side of the top card is black. What is the new outcome space?
(c) Given that the visible side of the top card is black, what is the probability that the other side of the card is black as well?
(d) Suppose that after shuffling, the visible side of the top card is red. What is the new outcome space?

(e) Given that the visible side of the top card is red, what is the probability that the other side of the card is white?

We end this section with one more exercise.

Exercise 4.13 The Monty Hall Problem You are on a game show. The host gives you the choice of three doors, all of which are closed. Behind one door there is a car; behind the others are goats. Here is what will happen. First, you will point to a door. Next, the host, who knows what is behind each door and who is doing his best to make sure you do not get the car, will open one of the other two doors (which will have a goat). Finally, you can choose to open either one of the remaining two closed doors; that is, you can keep pointing to the same door, or you can switch. If you do not switch, what is the probability of finding the car?

4.3 Unconditional probability

The theory should also allow us to compute unknown probabilities on the basis of known probabilities. In this section we study four rules that do this.

Axiom 4.14 The or rule *If two outcomes A and B are mutually exclusive (see below), then the probability of A OR B equals the probability of A plus the probability of B, that is, $Pr(A \lor B) = Pr(A) + Pr(B)$.*

Suppose that you want to know the probability of rolling a one or a two when you roll a fair six-sided die. The or rule tells you that the answer is $Pr(1 \lor 2) = Pr(1) + Pr(2) = 1/6 + 1/6 = 1/3$. Or suppose that you want to know the probability of flipping heads or tails when flipping a fair coin. The same rule tells you that $Pr(H \lor T) = Pr(H) + Pr(T) = 1/2 + 1/2 = 1$.

Notice that the rule requires that the two outcomes be **mutually exclusive**. What does this mean? Two outcomes A and B are mutually exclusive just in case at most one of them can happen. In the previous two examples, this condition holds. When flipping a coin, H and T are mutually exclusive since at most one of them can occur every time you flip a coin. No coin can land heads and tails at the same time. Similarly, when you roll one die, one and two are mutually exclusive, since at most one of them can occur. Notice that the latter two outcomes are mutually exclusive even though neither one may occur.

Exercise 4.15 Mutual exclusivity Which pairs of outcomes are mutually exclusive? More than one answer may be correct.

(a) It is your birthday; you have a test.
(b) It rains; night falls.
(c) You get Bs in all of your classes; you get a 4.0 GPA.
(d) Your new computer is a Mac; your new computer is a PC.
(e) You are a remarkable student; you get a good job after graduation.

Exercise 4.16 What is the probability of drawing an ace when drawing one card from a regular (well-shuffled) deck of cards? If you intend to apply the or rule, do not forget to check that the relevant outcomes are mutually exclusive.

The importance of checking whether two outcomes are mutually exclusive is best emphasized by giving an example. What is the probability of rolling a fair die and getting number that is either strictly less than six or strictly greater than one? It is quite obvious that you could not fail to roll a number strictly less than six or strictly greater than one, so the probability must be 100 percent. If you tried to take the probability that you roll a number strictly less than six *plus* the probability that you roll a number strictly greater than one, you would end up with a number greater than one, which would be a violation of Axiom 4.6. So there is good reason for the OR rule to require that outcomes be mutually exclusive.

The answer to the question in the previous paragraph follows from the following straightforward rule:

Axiom 4.17 The EVERYTHING rule   *The probability of the entire outcome space is equal to one.*

So, $Pr(\{1,2,3,4,5,6\}) = 1$ by the EVERYTHING rule. We could also have computed this number by using the OR rule, because $Pr(\{1,2,3,4,5,6\}) = Pr(1 \text{ OR } 2 \text{ OR } 3 \text{ OR } 4 \text{ OR } 5 \text{ OR } 6) = Pr(1) + Pr(2) + Pr(3) + Pr(4) + Pr(5) + Pr(6) = 1/6 * 6 = 1$. The OR rule (Axiom 4.14) applies because the six individual outcomes are mutually exclusive; the EQUIPROBABILITY rule (Axiom 4.7) applies because all outcomes are equally probable. What the EVERYTHING rule tells us that we did not already know is that the probability of the entire outcome space equals one whether or not the outcomes are equiprobable. The next rule is easy too.

Axiom 4.18 The NOT rule   *The probability that some outcome A will not occur is equal to one minus the probability that it does. That is, $Pr(\neg A) = 1 - Pr(A)$.*

For example, suppose that you want to know the probability of rolling anything but a six when rolling a six-sided die. By the NOT rule, the probability that we roll anything but a six can be computed as $Pr(\neg 6) = 1 - Pr(6) = 1 - 1/6 = 5/6$. Given that the outcomes are mutually exclusive, we could have computed this using the OR rule too. (How?) In general, it is good to check that you get the same number when solving the same problem in different ways. If you do not, there is something wrong with your calculations.

Axiom 4.19 The AND rule   *If two outcomes A and B are independent (see below), then the probability of A AND B equals the probability of A multiplied by the probability of B, that is, $Pr(A \& B) = Pr(A) * Pr(B)$.*

Suppose you flip a fair coin twice. What is the probability of getting two heads? Writing H_1 for heads on the first coin, and so on, by the AND rule, $Pr(H_1 \& H_2) = Pr(H_1) * Pr(H_2) = 1/2 * 1/2 = 1/4$. You could also solve this problem by looking at the outcome space $\{H_1H_2, H_1T_2, T_1H_2, T_1T_2\}$ and using the EQUIPROBABILITY rule. Similarly, it is easy to compute the probability of getting two sixes when rolling a fair die twice: $Pr(6_1 \& 6_2) = Pr(6_1) * Pr(6_2) = 1/6 * 1/6 = 1/36$.

Exercise 4.20   Are you more likely to get two sixes when rolling one fair die twice or when simultaneously rolling two fair dice?

Notice that the AND rule requires that the two outcomes be **independent**. What does this mean? Two outcomes A and B are independent just in case the fact that one occurs does not affect the probability that the other one does. This condition is satisfied when talking about a coin flipped twice. H_1 and H_2 are independent since the coin has no memory: whether or not the coin lands heads or tails the first time you flip it will not affect the probability of getting heads (or tails) the second time.

Exercise 4.21 Independence What pairs of outcomes are independent? More than one answer may be correct.

(a) You sleep late; you are late for class.
(b) You are a remarkable student; you get a good job after graduation.
(c) You write proper thank-you notes; you get invited back.
(d) The first time you flip a silver dollar you get heads; the second time you flip a silver dollar you get tails.
(e) General Electric stock goes up; General Motors stock goes up.

Exercise 4.22 Luck in love According to a well-known saying: "Lucky in cards, unlucky in love." Is this to say that luck in cards and luck in love are independent or not independent?

The importance of checking whether two outcomes are independent is best emphasized by giving an example. What is the probability of simultaneously getting a two and a three when you roll a fair die once? The answer is not $1/6 * 1/6 = 1/36$, of course, but zero. The outcomes are not independent, so you cannot use the AND rule. This example also tells you is that when two outcomes are mutually exclusive they are not independent.

Exercise 4.23 When rolling two fair dice, what is the probability that the number of dots add up to 11? If you intend to use the OR rule, make sure the relevant outcomes are mutually exclusive. If you intend to use the AND rule, make sure the relevant outcomes are independent.

Exercise 4.24 Suppose you draw two cards from a well-shuffled deck of cards *with replacement*, meaning that you put the first card back into the deck (and shuffle the deck once more) before drawing the second card.

(a) What is the probability that you draw the ace of spaces twice?
(b) What is the probability that you draw two aces? (Here, you can use your answer to Exercise 4.16.)

We are now in a position to address Example 4.2. Obviously, the theory of probability by itself will not tell you the probability that Linda is a bank teller. But it can tell you something else. Let F mean that Linda is a feminist and B that Linda is a bank teller. Then the probability that she is both a feminist and a bank teller is $\Pr(B\&F) = \Pr(B) * \Pr(F)$. (In order to apply the AND rule here, I am assuming that the outcomes are independent; the general result, however, holds even if they are not.) Because $\Pr(F) \leqslant 1$ by Axiom 4.6, we know that $\Pr(B) * \Pr(F) \leqslant \Pr(B)$. For, if you multiply a positive number x with a fraction (between zero and one) you will end up with something less than x. So whatever the relevant probabilities involved are, it must be the case that $\Pr(B\&F) \leqslant \Pr(B)$; that is, the probability that Linda is a bank teller and a feminist has to be smaller than the probability that she is a bank teller. Many people will tell you that Linda is more likely to be a bank teller and a feminist than she is to be a bank teller. This mistake is referred to as the **conjunction fallacy**, about which you will hear more in Section 5.3.

We end this section with one more exercise.

Exercise 4.25 For the following questions, assume that you are rolling two fair dice:

(a) What is the probability of getting *two* sixes?
(b) What is the probability of getting *no* sixes?
(c) What is the probability of getting *exactly one* six?
(d) What is the probability of getting *at least one* six?

To compute the answer to (c), note that there are two ways to roll exactly one six. When answering (d), note that there are at least two ways to compute the answer. You can recognize that *rolling at least one six* is the same as *rolling two sixes or rolling exactly one six* and add up the answers to (a) and (c). Or you can recognize that *rolling at least one six* is the same as *not rolling no sixes* and compute the answer using the NOT rule.

Exercise 4.26 In computing the answer to Exercise 4.25(d), you may have been tempted to add the probability of rolling a six on the one die (1/6) to the probability of rolling a six on the other die (1/6) to get the answer $2/6 = 1/3$. That, however, would be a mistake. Why?

If the answers to Exercise 4.25 are not completely obvious already, refer to Figure 4.1. Here, the numbers to the left represent what might happen when you roll the first die and the numbers on top represent what might happen when you roll the second die. Thus, the table has $6 * 6 = 36$ cells representing all the possible outcomes of rolling two dice. The dark gray area represents the possibility that both dice are sixes; because there is only one way to roll two sixes, this area contains but one cell and the answer to (a) is 1/36. The white area represents the possibility that both dice are non-sixes; because there are $5 * 5$ ways to roll two non-sixes, this area contains 25 cells and the answer to (b) is 25/36. The light gray areas represent the possibility that one die is a six and the other one is a non-six; because there are $5 + 5$ ways to attain this outcome, these areas contain ten cells and the answer to (c) is 10/36. You

	1	2	3	4	5	6
1						
2						
3		25/36				5/36
4						
5						
6		5/36				1/36

Figure 4.1 The two dice

can compute the answer to (d) by counting the $5+5+1=11$ cells in the two light gray and the one dark gray areas and get an answer of 11/36. But a smarter way is to realize that the gray areas cover everything that is not white, which allows you to get the answer by computing $1 - 25/36 = 11/36$. Why this is smarter will be clear in Section 5.3.

Odds

Sometimes probabilities are expressed in terms of **odds** rather than probabilities. Imagine that you have an urn containing 2 black and 3 white balls, so that the probability of drawing a black ball is 2/5. One way to get this figure is to divide the number of favorable outcomes (outcomes in which the event of interest obtains) by the total number of outcomes. By contrast, you get the odds of drawing a black ball by dividing the number of favorable outcomes by the number of unfavorable outcomes, so that the odds of drawing a black ball are 2 to 3 or 2:3. Under the same assumptions, the odds of drawing a white ball are 3:2. If there is an equal number of black and white balls in the urn, the odds are 1-to-1 or 1:1. Such odds are also said to be **even**. When people talk about a 50–50 chance, they are obviously talking about even odds, since $50/50 = 1$. How do odds relate to probabilities? If you have the probability p and want the odds o, you apply the following formula:

$$o = \frac{p}{1-p}$$

When p equals 2/5, it is easy to confirm that o equals 2/5 divided by 3/5 which is 2/3 or 2:3. If the probability is 1/2, the odds are 1/2 divided by 1/2 which is 1 or 1:1. If you have the odds o and want the probability p, you apply the inverse formula:

$$p = \frac{o}{o+1}$$

When o equals 2:3, you can quickly confirm that p equals 2/3 divided by 5/3 which is 2/5. If the odds are even, the probability is 1 divided by 1+1, which is 1/2. The use of odds instead of probabilities can come across as old-fashioned. But there are areas – for example, some games of chance and some areas of statistics – where odds are consistently used. It is good to know how to interpret them.

Conditional probability

In Exercise 4.24, you computed the probability of drawing two aces when drawing two cards with replacement. Suppose, instead, that you draw two aces *without replacement*, meaning that you put the first card aside after looking at it. What is the probability of drawing two aces without replacement? You know you cannot use Axiom 4.19, since the two outcomes we are interested in (drawing an ace the first time and drawing an ace the second time) are not independent. You can, however, approach the problem in the following way. First, you can ask what is the probability that the first card is an ace. Because there are 52 cards in the deck, and 4 of those are aces, you know that this probability is 4/52. Second, you can ask what is the probability is that the second card is an ace, *given that the first card was an ace*. Because there are 51 cards left in the deck, and only 3 of them are aces, this probability is 3/51. Now you can multiply these numbers and get:

$$\frac{4}{52} * \frac{3}{51} = \frac{12}{2652} = \frac{1}{221}.$$

This procedure can be used to calculate the probability of winning certain types of lotteries. According to the Consumer Federation of America, about one in five Americans believe that "the most practical way for them to accumulate several hundred thousand dollars is to win the lottery." The poor, least educated, and oldest are particularly likely to think of the lottery as a smart way to get rich. So it might be useful to ask just how likely or unlikely it is to win common lotteries.

Exercise 4.27 Lotto 6/49 Many states and countries operate lotteries in which the customer picks n of m numbers, in any order, where n is considerably smaller than m. In one version of this lottery, which I will call Lotto 6/49, players circle 6 numbers out of 49 using a ticket like that in Figure 4.2. The order in which numbers are circled does not matter. You win the grand prize if all 6 are correct. What is the probability that you win the Lotto 6/49 any one time you play? Notice that this is similar to picking six consecutive aces out of a deck with 49 cards, if 6 of those cards are aces.

		LOTTO 6/49				
1	2	3	4	5	6	7
8	9	10	11	12	13	14
15	16	17	18	19	20	21
22	23	24	25	26	27	28
29	30	31	32	33	34	35
36	37	38	39	40	41	42
43	44	45	46	47	48	49

Figure 4.2 Lotto 6/49 ticket

The fact that the probability of winning the lottery is low does not imply that it is necessarily irrational to buy these tickets. (We will return to this topic in Part III.) Nevertheless, it may be fun to ask some questions about these lotteries.

Problem 4.28 Lotto 6/49, cont. *What does probability of winning the Lotto 6/49 tell you about the wisdom of buying Lotto tickets? What does it tell you about people who buy these tickets?*

Exercise 4.29 Lotto 6/49, cont. Use the idea of anchoring and adjustment from Section 3.6 to explain why people believe that they have a good chance of winning these lotteries.

The probability that something happens given that some other thing happens is called a **conditional probability**. We write the probability that A given C, or the probability of A conditional on C, as follows: $\Pr(A|C)$. Conditional probabilities are useful for a variety of purposes. It may be easier to compute conditional probabilities than unconditional probabilities. Knowing the conditional probabilities is oftentimes quite enough to solve the problem at hand.

Notice right away that $\Pr(A|C)$ is not the same thing as $\Pr(C|A)$. Though these two probabilities may be identical, they need not be. Suppose, for example, that S means that Joe is a smoker, while H means that Joe is human. If so, $\Pr(S|H)$ is the probability that Joe is a smoker given that Joe is human, which is a number somewhere between zero and one. Meanwhile, $\Pr(H|S)$ is the probability that Joe is human given that Joe is a smoker, which is one (or at least close to one). Joe may not be a human being for quite as long if he is a smoker, but that is another matter.

Exercise 4.30   Suppose that H means "The patient has a headache" and T means "The patient has a brain tumor." (a) How to you interpret the two conditional probabilities $\Pr(H|T)$ and $\Pr(T|H)$? (b) Are the two numbers more or less the same?

It should be clear that the two conditional probabilities in general are different, and that it is important for both doctors and patients to keep them apart. (We will return to this topic in sections 5.4 and 5.6.)

Suppose that you draw one card from a well-shuffled deck, and that you are interested in the probability of drawing the ace of spades given that you draw an ace. Given that you just drew an ace, there are four possibilities: the ace of spades, ace of clubs, ace of hearts, or ace of diamonds. Because only one of the four is the ace of spades, and because all four outcomes are equally likely, this probability is $1/4$. You can get the same answer by dividing the probability that you draw the ace of spades by the probability that you draw an ace: $1/52$ divided by $4/52$, which is $1/4$. This is no coincidence, as the formal definition of conditional probability will show.

Definition 4.31 Conditional probability   *If A and B are two outcomes, $\Pr(A \mid B) = \Pr(A \ \& \ B)/\Pr(B)$.*

As another example of conditional probability, recall the problem with the two aces. Let A denote "the second card is an ace" and let B denote "the first card is an ace." We know that the probability of drawing two aces without replacement is $1/221$. This is $\Pr(A\&B)$. We also know that the probability that the first card is an ace is $1/13$. This is $\Pr(B)$. So by definition:

$$\Pr(A|B) = \frac{\Pr(A\&B)}{\Pr(B)} = \frac{1/221}{1/13} = \frac{3}{51}.$$

But we knew this: $3/51$ is the probability that the second card is an ace given that the first card was: $\Pr(A\&B)$. So the formula works. Because you cannot divide numbers by zero, things get tricky when some probabilities are zero; here, I will ignore these complications.

One implication of the definition is particularly useful:

Proposition 4.32 The general AND rule $Pr(A \& B) = Pr(A \mid B)^* Pr(B)$.

Proof. Starting off with Definition 4.31, multiply each side of the equation by $Pr(B)$. □

According to this proposition, the probability of drawing two aces equals the probability of drawing an ace the first time multiplied by the probability of drawing an ace the second time given that you drew an ace the first time. But again, we knew this. In fact, we implicitly relied on this rule when computing the answers to the first exercises in this chapter. Notice that this rule allows us to compute the probability of A AND B without requiring that the outcomes be independent. This is why it is called the general AND rule.

Exercise 4.33 The general AND rule   Use the general AND rule to compute the probability that you will draw the ace of spades twice when drawing two cards from a deck *without* replacement.

The general AND rule permits us to establish the following result.

Proposition 4.34 $Pr(A \mid B)^* Pr(B) = Pr(B \mid A)^* Pr(A)$.

Proof. By Proposition 4.32, $Pr(A\&B) = Pr(A \mid B) * Pr(B)$ but also $Pr(B\&A) = Pr(B \mid A) * Pr(A)$. Because by logic $Pr(A\&B) = Pr(B\&A)$, it must be the case that $Pr(A \mid B) * Pr(B) = Pr(B \mid A) * Pr(A)$. □

Suppose that you draw one card from a well-shuffled deck, and that A means that you draw an ace and that D means that you draw a diamond. If so, it follows that $Pr(A \mid D) * Pr(D) = Pr(D \mid A) * Pr(A)$. You can check that this is true by plugging in the numbers: $1/13 * 13/52 = 1/4 * 4/52$.

This notion of conditional probability allows us to sharpen our definition of independence. We said that two outcomes A and B are independent if the probability of A does not depend on whether B occurred. Another way of saying this is to say that $Pr(A \mid B) = Pr(A)$. In fact, there are several ways of saying the same thing.

Proposition 4.35 Independence conditions   *The following three claims are equivalent:*

(i) $Pr(A \mid B) = Pr(A)$
(ii) $Pr(B \mid A) = Pr(B)$
(iii) $Pr(A\&B) = Pr(A) * Pr(B)$

Proof. See Exercise 4.36. □

Exercise 4.36 Independence conditions   Prove that the three parts of Proposition 4.35 are equivalent. The most convenient way of doing so is to prove (a) that (i) implies (ii), (b) that (ii) implies (iii), and (c) that (iii) implies (i).

Notice that part (iii) is familiar: it is the principle that we know as the AND rule (Axiom 4.19). Thus, the original AND rule follows logically from the general AND rule and the assumption that the two outcomes in question are independent. This is pretty neat.

4.5 Total probability and Bayes's rule

Conditional probabilities can also be used to compute unconditional probabilities. Suppose that you are running a frisbee factory and that you want to know the probability that one of your frisbees is defective. You have two machines producing frisbees: a new one (B) producing 800 frisbees per day and an old one (¬B) producing 200 frisbees per day. Thus, the probability that a randomly selected frisbee from your factory was produced by machine B is $\Pr(B) = 800/(800 + 200) = 0.8$; the probability that it was produced by machine ¬B is $\Pr(\neg B) = 1 - \Pr(B) = 0.2$. Among the frisbees produced by the new machine, one percent are defective (D); among those produced by the old one, two percent are. The probability that a randomly selected frisbee produced by machine B is defective is $\Pr(D \mid B) = 0.01$; the probability that a randomly selected frisbee produced by machine ¬B is defective is $\Pr(D \mid \neg B) = 0.02$. It may be useful to draw a tree illustrating the four possibilities (see Figure 4.3).

What is the probability that a randomly selected frisbee from your factory is defective? There are two ways in which a defective frisbee can be produced: by machine B and by machine ¬B. So the probability that a frisbee is defective $\Pr(D)$ equals the following probability: that the frisbee is produced by machine B and turns out to be defective or that the frisbee is produced by machine ¬B and turns out to be defective, that is, $\Pr([D\&B] \vee [D\&\neg B])$. These outcomes are obviously mutually exclusive, so the probability equals $\Pr(D\&B) + \Pr(D\&\neg B)$. Applying the general AND rule twice, this equals $\Pr(D \mid B) * \Pr(B) + \Pr(D \mid \neg B) * \Pr(\neg B)$. But we have all these numbers, so:

$$\Pr(D) = \Pr(D \mid B) * \Pr(B) + \Pr(D \mid \neg B) * \Pr(\neg B) = 0.01 * 0.8 + 0.02 * 0.2 = 0.012.$$

The probability that a randomly selected frisbee produced by your factory is defective is 1.2 percent. These calculations illustrate **the rule of total probability**.

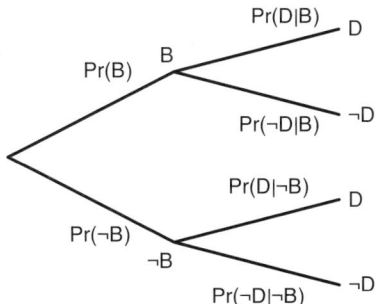

Figure 4.3 The frisbee factory

Proposition 4.37 The rule of total probability

$$\Pr(D) = \Pr(D \mid B) * \Pr(B) + \Pr(D \mid \neg B) * \Pr(\neg B).$$

Proof. By logic, D is the same as $[D\&B] \vee [D\&\neg B]$. So $\Pr(D) = \Pr([D\&B] \vee [D\&\neg B])$. Because the two outcomes are mutually exclusive, this equals $\Pr(D\&B) + \Pr(D\&\neg B)$ by the OR rule (Axiom 4.14). Applying the general AND rule (Proposition 4.32) twice, we get $\Pr(D) = \Pr(D \mid B) * \Pr(B) + \Pr(D \mid \neg B) * \Pr(\neg B)$. □

Exercise 4.38 Cancer Use the rule of total probability to solve the following problem. You are a physician meeting with a patient who has just been diagnosed with cancer. You know there are two mutually exclusive types of cancer that the patient could have: type A and type B. The probability that he or she has A is 1/3 and the probability that he or she has B is 2/3. Type A is deadly: four patients out of five diagnosed with type A cancer die (D) within one year. Type B is less dangerous: only one patient out of five diagnosed with type B cancer dies (D) within one year.

(a) Draw a tree representing the four possible outcomes.
(b) Compute the probability that your patient dies within a year.

There is another type of question that you may ask as well. Suppose you pick up one of the frisbees produced in your factory and find that it is defective. What is the probability that the defective frisbee was produced by the new machine? Here you are asking for the probability that a frisbee was B conditional on D, that is, $\Pr(B \mid D)$.

We know that there are two ways in which a defective frisbee can be produced. Either it comes from the new machine, which is to say that D&B, or it comes from the old machine, which is to say that D&¬B. We also know the probabilities that these states will obtain for any given frisbee (not necessarily defective): $\Pr(D\&B) = \Pr(D \mid B) * \Pr(B) = 0.01 * 0.8 = 0.008$ and $\Pr(D\&\neg B) = \Pr(D \mid \neg B) * \Pr(\neg B) = 0.02 * 0.2 = 0.004$. We want the probability that a frisbee comes from the new machine given that it is defective, that is, $\Pr(B \mid D)$. By looking at the figures, you can tell that the first probability is twice as large as the second one. What this means is that in two cases out of three, a defective frisbee comes from the new machine. Formally, $\Pr(D \mid B) = 0.008/0.012 = 2/3$. This may be surprising, in light of the fact that the new machine has a lower rate of defective frisbees than the old one. But it is explained by the fact that the new machine also produces far more frisbees than the old one.

The calculations you have just performed are an illustration of **Bayes's rule**, or **Bayes's theorem**, which looks more complicated than it is.

Proposition 4.39 Bayes's rule

$$\Pr(B \mid D) = \frac{\Pr(D \mid B) * \Pr(B)}{\Pr(D)}$$

$$= \frac{\Pr(D \mid B) * \Pr(B)}{\Pr(D \mid B) * \Pr(B) + \Pr(D \mid \neg B) * \Pr(\neg B)}.$$

Proof. The rule has two forms. The first form can be obtained from Proposition 4.34 by dividing both sides of the equation by $\Pr(D)$. The second form can be obtained from the first by applying the rule of total probability (Proposition 4.37) to the denominator. □

Exercise 4.40 Cancer, cont. Suppose that your patient from Exercise 4.38 dies in less than one year, before you learn whether he or she has type A or type B cancer. Given that the patient died in less than a year, what is the probability that she had type A cancer?

Bayes's rule is an extraordinarily powerful principle. To show how useful it can be, consider the following problem. If it is not immediately obvious how to attack this problem, it is almost always useful to draw a tree identifying the probabilities.

Exercise 4.41 The dating game You are considering asking L out for a date, but you are a little worried that L may already have started dating somebody else. The probability that L is dating somebody else, you would say, is 1/4. If L is dating somebody else, he/she is unlikely to accept your offer to go on a date: in fact, you think the probability is only 1/6. If L is not dating somebody else, though, you think the probability is much better: about 2/3.

(a) What is the probability that L is dating somebody else but will accept your offer to go on a date anyway?
(b) What is the probability that L is *not* dating somebody else and will accept your offer to go on a date?
(c) What is the probability that L will accept your offer to go on a date?
(d) Suppose L accepts your offer to go on a date. What's the probability that L is dating somebody else, given that L agreed to go on a date?

There are more exercises on Bayes's rule in sections 4.6 and 5.3. See also Exercise 5.24 on page 94.

4.6 Bayesian updating

Bayes's rule is often interpreted as describing how we should update our beliefs in light of new evidence. We update beliefs in light of new evidence all the time. In everyday life, we update our belief that a particular presidential candidate will win the election in light of evidence about how well he or she is doing. The evidence here may include poll results, our judgments about his or her performance in presidential debates, and so on. In science, we update our assessment about the plausibility of a hypothesis or theory in light of evidence, which may come from experiments, field studies, or other sources. Consider, for example, how a person's innocent belief that the Earth is flat might be updated in light of the fact that there are horizons, the fact that the Earth casts a circular shadow onto the Moon during a lunar eclipse, and the fact that one can travel around the world. Philosophers of science talk about the **confirmation** of scientific theories, so the theory of how this is done is called **confirmation theory**. Bayes's rule plays a critical role in confirmation theory.

To see how this works, think of the problem of belief updating as follows: what is at stake is whether a given hypothesis is true or false. If the hypothesis is true,

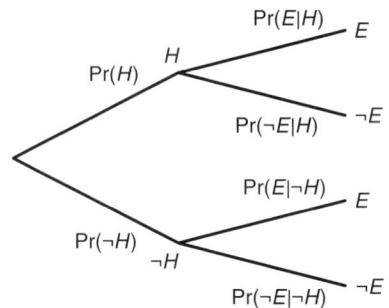

Figure 4.4 Bayesian updating

there is some probability that the evidence obtains. If the hypothesis is false, there is some other probability that the evidence obtains. The question is how you should change your belief – that is, the probability that you assign to the possibility that the hypothesis is true – in light of the fact that the evidence obtains. Figure 4.4 helps to bring out the structure of the problem.

Let H stand for the **hypothesis** and E for the **evidence**. The probability of H, $\Pr(H)$, is called the **prior probability**: it is the probability that H is true before you learn whether E is true. The probability of H given E, $\Pr(H \mid E)$, is called the **posterior probability**: it is the probability that H obtains given that the evidence E is true. The question is what the posterior probability should be. This question is answered by a simple application of Bayes's rule. Substituting H for B and E for D in Proposition 4.39, we can write Bayes's rule as follows:

$$\Pr(H \mid E) = \frac{\Pr(E \mid H) * \Pr(H)}{\Pr(E \mid H) * \Pr(H) + \Pr(E \mid \neg H) * \Pr(\neg H)}.$$

The result tells you how to update your belief in the hypothesis H in light of the evidence E. Specifically, Bayes's rule tells you that the probability you assign to H being true should go from $\Pr(H)$ to $\Pr(H \mid E)$. If you change your beliefs in accordance with Bayes's rule, we say that you engage in **Bayesian updating**.

Suppose that John and Wes are arguing about whether a coin brought to class by a student has two heads or whether it is fair. Imagine that there are no other possibilities. For whatever reason, the student will not let them inspect the coin, but she will allow them to observe the outcome of coin flips. Let H be the hypothesis that the coin has two heads, so that $\neg H$ means that the coin is fair. Let us consider John first. He thinks the coin is unlikely to have two heads: his prior probability, $\Pr(H)$, is only 0.01. Now suppose the student flips the coin, and that it comes up heads. Let E mean "The coin comes up heads." The problem is this: What probability should John assign to H given that E is true?

Given Bayes's rule, computing John's posterior probability $\Pr(H \mid E)$ is straightforward. We are given $\Pr(H) = 0.01$, and therefore know that $\Pr(\neg H) = 1 - \Pr(H) = 0.99$. From the description of the problem, we also know the conditional probabilities: $\Pr(E \mid H) = 1$ and $\Pr(E \mid \neg H) = 0.5$. All that remains is to plug the numbers into the theorem, as follows:

$$Pr(H \mid E) = \frac{Pr(E \mid H) * Pr(H)}{Pr(E \mid H) * Pr(H) + Pr(E \mid \neg H) * Pr(\neg H)}$$

$$= \frac{1 * 0.01}{1 * 0.01 + 0.5 * 0.99} \approx 0.02.$$

The fact that John's posterior probability $Pr(H \mid E)$ differs from his prior probability $Pr(H)$ means that he updated his belief in light of the evidence. The observation of heads increased his probability that the coin has two heads, as it should. Notice how the posterior probability reflects both the prior probability and the evidence E.

Now, if John gets access to ever more evidence about the coin, there is no reason why he should not update his belief again. Suppose that the student flips the coin a second time and gets heads again. We can figure out what John's probability should be after observing this second flip by simply treating his old posterior probability as the new prior probability and applying Bayes's rule once more:

$$Pr(H \mid E) = \frac{1 * 0.02}{1 * 0.02 + 0.5 * 0.98} \approx 0.04.$$

Notice that his posterior probability increases even more after he learns that the coin came up heads the second time.

Exercise 4.42 Bayesian updating Suppose Wes, before the student starts flipping the coin, assigns a probability of 50 percent to the hypothesis that it has two heads. (a) What is his posterior probability after the first trial? (b) After the second?

Figure 4.5 illustrates how John's and Wes's posterior probabilities develop as the evidence comes in. Notice that over time both increase the probability assigned to the hypothesis. Notice, also, that their respective probabilities get closer and closer. As a result, over time (after some 15–20 trials) they are in virtual agreement that the probability of the coin having two heads is almost 100 percent. We will return to questions of rational updating in the next chapter. Until then, one last exercise.

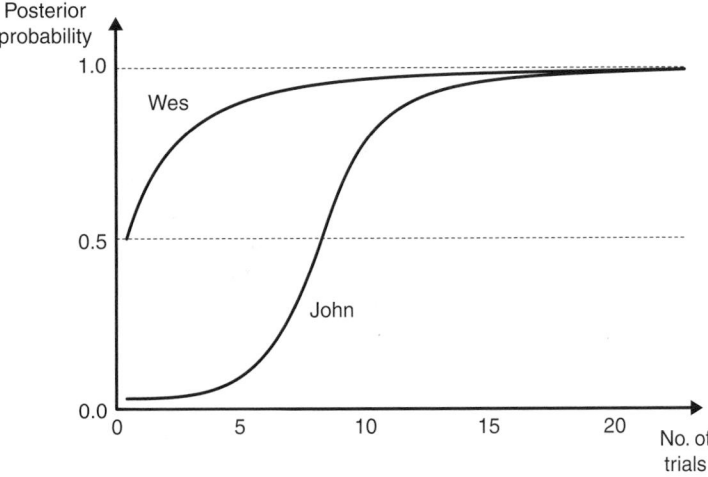

Figure 4.5 John's and Wes's probabilities after repeated trials

Exercise 4.43 Bayesian updating, cont. Suppose that, on the third trial, instead of flipping heads, the student flips tails. What would John's and Wes's posterior probability be? To solve this problem, let E mean "The coin comes up tails."

4.7 Discussion

In this chapter we have explored the theory of probability. This theory is critical to a wide range of applications, among other things as the foundations of statistical inference. It is relevant here because it can be interpreted as a theory of judgment, that is, as a theory of how to revise beliefs in light of evidence. The section of Bayesian updating (Section 4.6) shows how the argument goes. As long as you are committed to the axioms and rules of the probability calculus, we established that you will (as a matter of mathematical necessity) update your probabilities consistently with Bayes's rule. Notice how neat this is. While the theory says nothing about what your prior probabilities are or should be, it does tell you exactly what your posterior probability will or should be after observing the evidence.

How plausible is this theory? Again, we must separate the descriptive question from the normative question. Do people in fact update their beliefs in accordance with Bayes's rule? Should they? The axioms might seem weak and uncontroversial, both from a descriptive and from a normative standpoint. Yet the resulting theory is anything but weak. As in the case of the theory of choice under certainty, we have built a remarkably powerful theory on the basis of a fairly modest number of seemingly weak axioms. It is important to keep in mind that the theory is not as demanding as some people allege. It is not intended to describe the actual cognitive processes you go through when updating your beliefs: the theory does not say that you must apply Bayes's theorem in your head. But it does specify exactly how your posterior probability relates to your prior, given various conditional and unconditional probabilities.

In the next chapter, we will see how the theory fares when confronted with evidence.

Additional exercises

Exercise 4.44 SAT test   When you take the SAT test, you may think that the correct answers to the various questions would be completely random. In fact, they are not. The authors of the test want the answers to *seem* random, and therefore they make sure that not all correct answers are, say, (d). Consider the following three outcomes. A: The correct answer to question 12 is (d). B: The correct answer to question 13 is (d). C: The correct answer to question 14 is (d). Are outcomes A, B, and C mutually exclusive, independent, both, or neither?

Exercise 4.45 Mr Langford   Multiple lawsuits allege that area gambling establishments, on multiple occasions, doctored equipment so as to give Birmingham mayor Larry Langford tens of thousands of dollars in winnings. Langford, already in prison for scores of corruption-related charges, has not denied winning the money; he does deny that the machines were doctored.

We do not know exactly what the probability of winning the jackpot on a machine that has *not* been doctored might be, but we can make some intelligent guesses.

Additional exercises cont'd

Suppose that Langford on three occasions bet $1 and won $25,000. For each jackpot, in order to break even, a gambling establishment needs 24,999 people who bet $1 and do not win. So we might infer that the probability of winning when betting a dollar is somewhere in the neighborhood of 1/25,000. If the establishment wants to make a profit, which it does, the probability would have to be even lower, but let us ignore this fact.

What is the probability that Langford would win the jackpot three times in a row when playing three times on undoctored machines?

Note that the probability that Langford would win three times in a row given that the machines were not doctored is different from the conditional probability that the machines were not doctored given that Langford won three times in a row.

Exercise 4.46 Gov. Schwarzenegger   After vetoing a bill from the California State Assembly in 2009, California Governor Arnold Schwarzenegger published a letter (see Figure 4.6). People immediately noticed that the first letter on each line together spelled out a vulgarity. When confronted with this fact, a spokesperson said: "It was just a weird coincidence."

(a) Assuming that a letter has eight lines, and that each of the 26 letters in the alphabet is equally likely to appear at the beginning of each line, what is the probability that this exact message would appear by chance?

(b) It is true that the Governor writes many letters each year, which means that the probability of any one letter spelling out this vulgarity is higher than your answer to (a) would suggest. Suppose that the Governor writes 100 eight-line letters each year. What is the probability that at least one of them will spell out the vulgarity?

```
To the Members of the California State Assembly:

I am returning Assembly Bill 1176 without my s . . .

For some time now I have lamented the fact tha . . .
unnecessary bills come to me for consideration . . .
care are major issues my Administration has br . . .
kicks the can down the alley.

Yet another legislative year has come and gone . . .
overwhelmingly deserve. In light of this, and . . .
unnecessary to sign this measure at this time.

Sincerely,

Arnold Schwarzenegger
```

Figure 4.6   Governor Schwarzenegger's letter

Exercise 4.47 Max's bad day   Max is about to take a multiple-choice test. The test has ten questions, and each has two possible answers: "true" and "false." Max does not

Additional exercises cont'd

have the faintest idea of what the right answer to any of the questions might be. He decides to pick answers randomly.

(a) What is the probability that Max will get all ten questions right?
(b) What is the probability that Max will get the first question right and the other questions wrong?
(c) What is the probability that Max will get the second question right and the other questions wrong?
(d) What is the probability that Max will get the third question right and the other questions wrong?
(e) What is the probability that Max will get exactly nine questions right?
(f) Max really needs to get an A on this test. In order to get an A, he needs to get nine or more questions right. What is the probability that Max will get an A?

Exercise 4.48 Pregnancy tests   You are marketing a new line of pregnancy tests. The test is simple. You flip a fair coin. If the coin comes up heads, you report that the customer is pregnant. If the coin comes up tails, you report that the customer is not pregnant.

(a) Your first customer is a man. What is the probability that the test accurately predicts his pregnancy status?
(b) Your second customer is a woman. What is the probability that the test accurately predicts her pregnancy status?
(c) After you have administered the test ten times, what is the probability that you have not correctly predicted the pregnancy status of any of your customers?
(d) After you have administered the test ten times, what is the probability that you correctly predicted the pregnancy status of *at least one* of your customers?

Notice how high is the probability of getting at least one customer right. This suggests the following scheme for getting rich. Issue ten, or a hundred, or whatever, newsletters offering advice about how to pick stocks. No matter how unlikely each newsletter is to give good advice, if you issue enough of them at least one is very likely to give good advice. Then sell your services based on your wonderful track record, pointing to the successful newsletter as evidence. You would not be the first. We will return to this kind of problem in Section 5.3.

Problem 4.49 Pregnancy tests, cont.   *The pregnancy test of Exercise 4.48 is needlessly complicated. Here is another test that is even simpler: just report that the customer is not pregnant. Roughly, what is the probability that you would get the pregnancy status of a randomly selected college student right when using the simplified test?*

Further reading

There are numerous introductions to probability theory. Earman and Salmon (1992) deals with probability theory in the context of the theory of confirmation and is the source of the stories about frisbees and coins (pp. 70–4); it also contains a discussion about the meaning of probability (pp. 74–89). The Consumer Federation of America (2006) discusses people's views about the most practicable way to get rich. The fate of Birmingham mayor Larry Langford is discussed in Tomberlin (2009) and that of California governor Arnold Schwarzenegger in McKinley (2009).

Chapter 5

Judgment under Risk and Uncertainty

Introduction

The previous chapter showed how a powerful theory of probabilistic judgment can be built on the foundation of a limited number of relatively uncontroversial axioms. Though the axioms might seem weak, the resulting theory is anything but. In fact, the theory is open to criticism, especially on descriptive grounds. In this section, we consider whether the theory can serve as a descriptively adequate theory, that is, whether it captures how people actually make probabilistic judgments, and we explore a series of phenomena that suggest that it does not. The discrepancy suggests that a descriptively adequate theory of judgment must differ from the theory that we just learned. We will also continue our study of the building blocks of behavioral theory. In particular, we will continue the discussion of the heuristics-and-biases program in Chapter 3, by reviewing more heuristics and discussing the biases that these heuristics can lead to. Thus, this chapter gives a better idea of how behavioral economists respond to discrepancies between observed behavior and standard theory.

5.2 The gambler's fallacy

The notion of independence that we encountered in Section 4.3 is absolutely critical in economics and finance. If you are managing investments, for example, you are supposed to diversify. It would be unwise to put all of your eggs in one basket, investing all your money in a single asset such as Google stock. But in order to diversify, it is not enough to invest in two or more assets: if you invest in stocks that will rise and fall together, you do not actually have a diversified portfolio. What you should do is to invest your money in assets that are sufficiently independent. In real-world investment management, a great deal of effort goes into exploring whether assets can be assumed to be independent or not.

The notion of independence is also very important in fields like engineering. If you are in the process of designing a new nuclear power plant, you should include multiple safety systems that can prevent nuclear meltdown. But having five safety systems instead of one gives you additional safety only when a breakdown in one system is sufficiently independent from a breakdown in the other. If, for example, all safety systems are held together with one bolt, or plugged into the same outlet, a breakdown in the one system is not independent from a breakdown in the other, and your plant will not be as safe as it could be. In the nuclear power plant design, and elsewhere, a great deal of effort goes into making sure that different systems (if they are all critical to the operation of the machine) are sufficiently independent from each other.

In principle, there are two ways in which you might make a mistake about independence: you may think that two outcomes are independent when in fact they are not, or you may think that two outcomes are not independent when in fact they are. People make both kinds of mistake. We will consider them in order.

Thinking that two outcomes are independent when in fact they are not happens, for instance, when people invest in stocks and bonds on the assumption that they are completely independent. In fact they are not. One of the important take-home lessons of the recent economic crisis is that a vast range of assets – US stocks, Norwegian real estate, etc. – are probabilistically dependent because of the highly international nature of modern finance and the complicated ways in which mortgages and the like are packaged and sold. Thinking that two outcomes are independent when in fact they are not also happens when people build nuclear power plant safety systems that have parts in common or that depend on the sobriety of one manager or the reliability of one source of electric power.

Thinking that two outcomes are dependent when in fact they are not occurs, for example, when people think that they can predict the outcomes of roulette wheels. People cannot: these things are set up in such a way as to make the outcomes completely independent. And they are set up that way because it is a good way for the casino to make sure customers are unable to predict the outcomes. Nevertheless, many people believe that they can predict the outcome of a roulette game. For evidence, the internet offers a great deal of advice about how to beat the casino when playing roulette: "monitor the roulette table," "develop a system," "try the system on a free table before operating it for financial gain," and so on. Do an internet search for "roulette tips," and you will find a long list of webpages encouraging you to think of various outcomes as probabilistically dependent, when they are not.

One specific case of thinking that two outcomes are dependent when in fact they are not is the **gambler's fallacy**: thinking that a departure from the average behavior of some system will be corrected in the short term. People who think they are "due for" a hurricane or a car accident or the like because they have not experienced one for a few years are committing the gambler's fallacy. Here, I am assuming that hurricanes and car accidents are uncorrelated from year to year. It is possible that thinking you are due for a car accident makes you more likely to have one; if so, a number of accident-free years might in fact make it more likely for you to have an accident.

The following exercises illustrate how easy it is to go wrong.

Exercise 5.1 Gambler's fallacy   Carefully note the difference between the following two questions:

(a) You intend to flip a fair coin eight times. What is the probability that you end up with eight heads?
(b) You have just flipped a fair coin seven times and ended up with seven heads. What is the probability that when you flip the coin one last time you will get another heads, meaning that you would have flipped eight heads in a row?

The gambler's fallacy is sometimes explained in terms of **representativeness**. We came across heuristics in Section 3.6 on anchoring and adjustment. According to the heuristics-and-biases program, people form judgments by following heuristics, or rules of thumb, which by and large are functional but which sometimes lead us astray. The representativeness heuristic is such a heuristic. When you employ the representativeness heuristic, you estimate the probability that some outcome was the result of a given process by reference to the degree to which the outcome is representative of that process. If the outcome is highly representative of the process, the probability that the former was a result of the latter is estimated to be high; if the outcome is highly unrepresentative of the process, the probability is estimated to be low.

The representativeness heuristic can explain the gambler's fallacy if we assume that a sequence like HHHHHHHH seems less representative of the process of flipping a fair coin eight times than a sequence like HHHHHHHT, which seems less representative than a sequence like HTTTHHTH. If you use the representativeness heuristic, you will conclude that the first sequence is less likely than the second, and that the second is less likely than the third. In reality, of course, the three are equally likely *ex ante*. The representativeness heuristic might be perfectly functional in a wide variety of contexts. If it is used, for example, to infer that kind acts are more likely to be performed by kind people, and that mean acts more likely to be performed by mean people, the representativeness heuristic can protect us from adverse events. But because it can generate predictable and systematic patterns of mistakes, it can lead to bias, just as anchoring and adjustment can. For another example, consider the following case:

Exercise 5.2 Let us assume that whenever one gets pregnant, there is a 1/100 chance of having twins, and that being pregnant with twins once will not affect the probability of being pregnant with twins later.

(a) You are not yet pregnant, but intend to get pregnant twice. What is the probability that you will be pregnant with twins twice?
(b) You have just had a set of twins, and intend to get pregnant one more time. What is the probability that you will end up pregnant with twins again, that is, that you will have been pregnant with twins twice?

Again, having two sets of twins might strike a person as extraordinarily unrepresentative of the process that generates children. Thus, people relying on the representativeness heuristic will think of the probability of having a second set of twins conditional on having one set already as considerably smaller than the probability of having a set of twins the first time around. But by assumption, of course, these probabilities are equal.

Exercise 5.3 Mr Langford, cont. Suppose that Langford from Exercise 4.45 on page 78 has just won two jackpots in a row and is about to play a third time. What is the probability that he will win a third time, so as to make it three jackpots in a row?

One way to explain the ubiquity of the gambler's fallacy is to say that people believe in the **law of small numbers**. That is, people exaggerate the degree to which small samples resemble the population from which they are drawn. In the case of the coins, the "population" consists of half heads and half tails. A believer in the law of small numbers would exaggerate the degree to which a small sample (such as a sequence of eight coin flips) will resemble the population and consist of half heads and half tails.

It is important to note, however, that there are games of chance in which outcomes are correlated. In Black Jack, for example, cards are drawn from a deck without being replaced, which means that the probability of drawing a given card will vary from draw to draw. In principle, then, you can beat the house by counting cards, which is why that practice is not permitted in casinos.

5.3 Conjunction and disjunction fallacies

We have already (in Section 4.3) come across the conjunction fallacy. "A AND B" is a conjunction; you commit the conjunction fallacy when you overestimate the probability of a conjunction. The conjunction fallacy is particularly important in the context of **planning**. Complex projects are puzzles with many pieces, and typically each piece needs to be in place for the project to be successful. Even if the probability that any one piece will fall into place is high, the probability that all pieces of the puzzle will fall into place may be low. Planners who commit the conjunction fallacy will overestimate the probability of the conjunction – the proposition that the first piece is in place AND the second piece is in place AND the third piece is in place, and so on – meaning that they will overestimate the probability that the project will succeed.

Example 5.4 Boeing aircraft   A Boeing 747–400 has around 6 million parts. Suppose that each part is very reliable and only fails with probability 0.000,001. Assuming that failures are independent events, what is the probability that all parts work?

The probability that any one part works is 0.999,999, so the probability that all parts work is $(0.999,999)^{6,000,000} \approx 0.0025 = 0.25$ percent.

Given these numbers, the probability that all parts in a 747 work is only about a quarter of a percent! If this figure was lower than you expected, you may have committed the conjunction fallacy. Still, airplane crashes remain rare because planes are built with a great deal of redundancy, so that any one failure does not necessarily lead to a crash. That said, not all machines can be built in this way: some helicopters famously depend on a single rotor-retaining nut in such a way that if the nut fails, the whole machine will come crashing down. The term "Jesus nut" is sometimes used to denote a part whose failure would lead to a breakdown of the whole system. Presumably, the name is due to the only thing that can save you if the nut fails, though this assumes that a Jesus intervention is sufficiently independent of a nut failure.

There is a related fallacy called the **disjunction fallacy**. "A OR B" is a disjunction; you commit the disjunction fallacy when you underestimate the probability of a disjunction. To illustrate, let us build upon Exercise 4.25 on page 68, in which you computed the probability of rolling at least one six when rolling two dice.

Example 5.5   Compute the probability of getting at least one six when rolling (a) one die, (b) two dice, (c) three dice, (d) ten dice.

(a)   The probability of rolling at least one six when rolling one die equals one minus the probability of rolling a non-six, which equals $1 - 5/6 \approx 16.6$ percent.
(b)   The probability of rolling at least one six when rolling two dice equals one minus the probability of rolling no sixes in two trials, which equals $1 - (5/6)^2 \approx 30.6$ percent.

(c) The probability of rolling at least one six when rolling three dice equals one minus the probability of rolling no sixes in three trials, which equals $1 - (5/6)^3 \approx$ 42.1 percent.

(d) Finally, the probability of rolling at least one six when rolling ten dice equals one minus the probability of rolling no sixes in ten trials, which equals $1 - (5/6)^{10} \approx$ 83.8 percent.

Notice how quickly the probability of rolling at least one six rises as the number of trials increases. The probability will never reach 100 percent, but it will approach it asymptotically. If the resulting numbers here are greater than you expected, you may have committed the disjunction fallacy. For the probability of rolling at least one six in multiple trials equals the probability of rolling a six in the first trial, OR rolling a six in the second trial, OR . . . And given the definition above, if you underestimate the probability of the disjunction, you are committing the disjunction fallacy.

Exercise 5.6 Hiking You plan to go on a hike in spite of the fact that a tornado watch is in effect. The national weather service tells you that for every hour in your area, there is a 30 percent chance that a tornado will strike. That is, there is a 30 percent chance that a tornado will strike your area between 10 am and 11 am, a 30 percent chance that a tornado will strike your area between 11 am and noon, and so on.

(a) What is the probability of a tornado striking your area at least once during a two-hour hike?

(b) What is the probability of a tornado striking your area at least once during a three-hour hike?

(c) What is the probability of a tornado striking your area at least once during a ten-hour hike?

Exercise 5.7 Flooding Imagine that you live in an area where floods occur on average every ten years. The probability of a flood in your area is constant from year to year. You are considering whether to live in your house for a few more years and save up some money, or whether to move before you lose everything you own in the next flood.

(a) What is the probability that there will no floods in your area over the course of the next two years?

(b) What is the probability that there will be exactly one flood in your area over the course of the next two years?

(c) What is the probability that there will be at least one flood over the course of the next two years?

(d) What is the probability that there will be at least one flood over the course of the next ten years?

Exercise 5.8 Terrorism Compute the probability that at least one major terrorist attack occurs over the course of the next ten years, given that there are approximately 365 days a year, if the probability of an attack on any given day is 0.000,1.

That last exercise illustrates an infamous statement by the Irish Republican Army (IRA), which for decades fought a guerilla war for the independence of Northern Ireland from Great Britain. In the aftermath of an unsuccessful attempt to kill British Prime Minister Margaret Thatcher in 1984 by planting a bomb in her hotel, the IRA released a statement that ended with the words: "You have to be lucky all the time. We only have to be lucky once."

The disjunction fallacy is particularly important in the context of **risk assessment**. When assessing the risk that some complex system will fail, it is often the case that the system as a whole – whether a car or an organism – critically depends on multiple elements in such a way that the failure of any one of these elements would lead to a breakdown of the system. Even if the probability that any one element will fail is low, the probability that at least one element will fail may be high. Assessors who commit the disjunction fallacy will underestimate the probability of the disjunction – the proposition that the first element fails OR the second element fails OR the third element fails, and so on – meaning that they will underestimate the probability of a system breakdown.

There is an obvious symmetry between the two fallacies discussed in this section. According to a principle referred to as **de Morgan's law**, $A\&B$ is logically equivalent to $\neg[\neg A \vee \neg B]$. So if you overestimate the probability $\Pr(A\&B)$, this is the same as saying that you overestimate $\Pr(\neg[\neg A \vee \neg B])$. But by the NOT rule, that is the same as saying that you overestimate $1 - \Pr(\neg A \vee \neg B)$, which is to say that you underestimate $\Pr(\neg A \vee \neg B)$. In the context of the Linda example, overestimating the probability that she is a feminist bank teller is (according to de Morgan's law) the same as underestimating the probability that she is a non-feminist or a non-bank teller. In sum, if you adhere to de Morgan's law, then you commit the conjunction fallacy if and only if you commit the disjunction fallacy.

Both the conjunction and disjunction fallacies can be explained in terms of anchoring and adjustment (see Section 3.6). People overestimate the probability of conjunctions – and therefore commit the conjunction fallacy – if they use the probability of any one conjunct as an anchor and adjust downwards insufficiently. They underestimate the probability of disjunctions – and therefore commit the disjunction fallacy – if they use the probability of any one disjunct as an anchor and adjust upwards insufficiently. Here are more exercises:

Exercise 5.9 What is the probability of drawing at least one ace when drawing cards from an ordinary deck, with replacement, when you draw: (a) 1 card, (b) 2 cards, (c) 10 cards, and (d) 52 cards?

Exercise 5.10 The birthday problem Suppose that there are 30 students in your behavioral economics class. What is the probability that no two students have the same birthday? To make things easier, assume that every student was born the same non-leap year and that births are randomly distributed over the year.

Exercise 5.11 The preface paradox In the preface to your new book, you write that you are convinced that every sentence in your book is true. Yet you recognize that for each sentence there is a 1 percent chance that the sentence is false. (a) If your book has 100 sentences, what is the probability that at least one sentence is false? (b) What if your book has 1000 sentences?

Finally, an exercise about aviation safety.

Exercise 5.12 Private jet shopping Suppose you are fortunate (or delusional) enough to be shopping for a private jet. You have to decide whether to get a jet with one or two engines. Use p to denote the probability that an engine fails during any one flight. A "catastrophic engine failure" is an engine failure that makes the plane unable to fly.

(a) One of the jets you are looking to buy has only one engine. What is the probability of a catastrophic engine failure during any one flight with this plane?

(b) Another jet you are looking to buy has two engines, but is unable to fly with only one functioning engine. Assume that engine failures are independent events. What is the probability of a catastrophic engine failure during any one flight with this plane?

(c) Which jet strikes you as safer?

(d) What if the twin-engine jet can fly with only one functioning engine?

The answer to Exercise 5.12(b) is far from obvious. To help you out, consider constructing a table as in Figure 4.1 on page 68.

5.4 Base-rate neglect

One source of imperfect reasoning about probabilities results from the confusion between conditional probabilities $\Pr(A \mid B)$ and $\Pr(B \mid A)$. It might seem obvious that these two are distinct. As we know from Section 4.4, the probability that a randomly selected human being is a smoker is obviously different from the probability that a randomly selected smoker is a human being. However, there are contexts in which it is easy to mix these two up. In this section, we will consider some of these contexts.

Example 5.13 Mammograms Doctors often encourage women over a certain age to participate in routine mammogram screening for breast cancer. Suppose that from past statistics about some population, the following is known. At any one time, 1 percent of women have breast cancer. The test administered is correct in 90 percent of the cases. That is, if the woman does have cancer, there is a 90 percent probability that the test will be positive and a 10 percent probability that it will be negative. If the woman does not have cancer, there is a 10 percent probability that the test will be positive and a 90 percent probability that it will be negative. Suppose a woman has a positive test during a routine mammogram screening. Without knowing any other symptoms, what is the probability that she has breast cancer?

When confronted with this question, most people will answer close to 90 percent. After all, that is the accuracy of the test. Luckily, we do not need to rely on vague intuitions; we can compute the exact probability. In order to see how, consider Figure 5.1, in which C denotes the patient having cancer and P denotes the

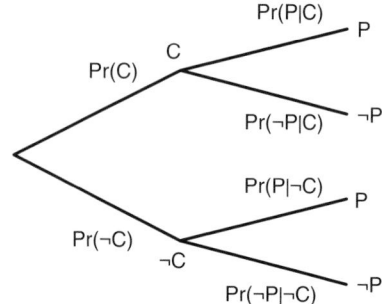

Figure 5.1 Breast cancer screening

patient testing positive. Plugging the numbers into Bayes's rule (Proposition 4.39), we get:

$$\Pr(C \mid P) = \frac{\Pr(P \mid C) * \Pr(C)}{\Pr(P \mid C) * \Pr(C) + \Pr(P \mid \neg C) * \Pr(\neg C)}$$

$$= \frac{0.9 * 0.01}{0.9 * 0.01 + 0.1 * 0.99} \approx 0.08.$$

Notice that the probability that somebody who has been identified as having cancer in fact has cancer is not equal to – in fact, not even remotely similar to – the accuracy of the test (which in this case is 90 percent). The probability that the woman has cancer is only about 8 percent – much lower than people think. This is paradoxical because we know that the test is reasonably good: it gives the correct outcome in 90 percent of cases. What we are forgetting is that relatively few people actually have cancer. Out of 1000 people, only about ten can be expected to have cancer. Of those, nine will test positive. Of the 990 women who do not have cancer, only 10 percent will test positive, but that is still 99 people. So only nine of the 108 people who test positive actually have cancer, and that is about 8 percent. Notice that this case is similar to the frisbee case: although the new machine has a lower failure rate than the old one, the average frisbee produced in the factory is more likely than not to come from the new machine, simply because it produces so many more frisbees.

The fraction of all the individuals in the population who have cancer (or some other characteristic of interest) is called the **base rate**. In the cancer case, the base rate is only one percent. One way to diagnose the mistake that people make is to say that they fail to take the base rate properly into account. Thus, the mistake is sometimes referred to as **base-rate neglect** or the **base-rate fallacy**. The judgment that we make in these situations should reflect three different factors: first, the base rate; second, the evidence; third, the conditional probabilities that we would see the evidence when the hypothesis is true and when it is false. We commit the base-rate fallacy when we fail to take the first of these three factors properly into account.

Incidentally, this example makes it clear why younger women are not routinely tested for breast cancer. In younger women, the base rate would be even lower; so the ratio of true positives to all positives would be even lower. Notice that in the previous example, when a woman from the relevant population gets a positive result the probability that she has cancer only increases from 1 percent to about eight percent, which is not a very large increase. If the base rate were even lower, the increase would be even smaller, and the conditional probability $\Pr(C\,|\,P)$ would not be very different from the base rate $\Pr(C)$. When this is the case, the test does not give the doctor any additional information that is relevant when producing a diagnosis, and so the test is said to be **non-diagnostic**. If the base rate were very high, the test would still not be diagnostic. In order for a test to be diagnostic, it helps if the base rate is somewhere in the middle.

Exercise 5.14 Mammograms, cont. Men can get breast cancer too, although this is very unusual. Using the language of "base rates" and "diagnosticity," explain why men are not routinely tested for breast cancer.

Testimony can be non-diagnostic, as the following classic example illustrates.

Exercise 5.15 Testimony A cab company was involved in a hit-and-run accident at night. Two cab companies, the Green and the Blue, operate in the city. You are given the following data: 85 percent of the cabs in the city are Green, 15 percent are Blue. A witness identified the cab involved in the accident as Blue. The court tested the reliability of the witness under the same circumstances that existed on the night of the accident and concluded that the witness correctly identified each one of the two colors 80 percent of the time and failed 20 percent of the time. What is the probability that the cab involved in the accident was Blue rather than Green?

Exercise 5.16 Iron Bowl At an Auburn–Alabama game, 80 percent of attendees wore Alabama gear and 20 percent wore Auburn gear. During the game, one of the attendees apparently robbed a beer stand outside the stadium. A witness (who was neither an Alabama nor an Auburn fan) later told police that the robber wore Auburn gear. The witness, however, was the beer stand's best customer, and it was estimated that he would only be able to identify the correct gear about 75 percent of the time. What is the probability that the robber wore Auburn gear, given that the witness said that he did?

Here is a slightly different kind of problem.

Exercise 5.17 Down syndrome The probability of having a baby with Down syndrome increases with the age of the mother. Suppose that the following is true. For women 34 and younger, about one baby in 1000 is affected by Down syndrome. For women 35 and older, about one baby in 100 is affected. Women 34 years and younger have about 90 percent of all babies. What is the probability that a baby with Down syndrome has a mother who is 34 years or younger?

Base-rate neglect can explain the **planning fallacy**: the tendency to believe that one's own project will be finished on time, even while knowing that the vast majority of similar projects have run late. Many projects – senior theses, doctoral dissertations, dams, bridges, tunnels, railroads, highways, and wars – frequently take longer, and cost more, than planned. Here is one famous example:

Many people consider the Sydney Opera House to be the champion of all planning disasters. According to original estimates in 1957, the opera house would be completed early in 1963 for $7 million. A scaled-down version of the opera house finally opened in 1973 at a cost of $102 million.

From the point of view of the theory we explored in the previous chapter, the ubiquity of overruns is surprising. If people updated their beliefs in Bayesian fashion, they would take previous overruns into account and gradually come up with a better estimate of future projects. We can, however, understand the optimistic estimates as a result of base-rate neglect. It is possible to think of the fraction of past projects that were associated with overruns as the base rate, and assume that people tend to ignore the base rate in their assessments.

The last problems in this section all relate to the war on terror.

Exercise 5.18 Jean Charles de Menezes In the aftermath of the July 21, 2005, terrorist attacks in London, British police received the authority to shoot terrorism suspects on sight. On July 22, plainclothes police officers shot and killed a terrorism suspect in the London underground. Use Bayes's rule to compute the probability that a randomly selected Londoner, identified by the police as a terrorist, in fact is a terrorist. Assume that London is a city of 10 million people, and that ten of them (at any given time) are terrorists. Assume also that police officers are extraordinarily competent, so that their assessments about whether a given person is a terrorist or not are correct 99.9 percent of the time.

The suspect, Jean Charles de Menezes, 27, was shot seven times in the head and once in the shoulder. He was later determined to be innocent. Notice, again, that the probability that somebody who has been identified as a terrorist is in fact a terrorist is not equal to – in fact, not even remotely similar to – the accuracy of the test. Notice, also, the time line: in this case, it is as though the police went out of their way to prove as soon as possible that they cannot be entrusted with the authority to execute people on sight.

Exercise 5.19 Behavior detection The following passage is from *USA Today*:

> Doug Kinsey stands near the security line at Dulles International Airport, watching the passing crowd in silence. Suddenly, his eyes lock on a passenger in jeans and a baseball cap.
>
> The man in his 20s looks around the terminal as though he's searching for something. He chews his fingernails and holds his boarding pass against his mouth, seemingly worried.
>
> Kinsey, a Transportation Security Administration [TSA] screener, huddles with his supervisor, Waverly Cousins, and the two agree: The man could be a problem. Kinsey moves in to talk to him.
>
> The episode this month is one of dozens of encounters airline passengers are having each day – often unwittingly – with a fast-growing but controversial security technique called behavior detection. The practice, pioneered by Israeli airport security, involves picking apparently suspicious people out of crowds and asking them questions about travel plans or work. All the while, their faces, body language and speech are being studied.
>
> The TSA has trained nearly 2,000 employees to use the tactic, which is raising alarms among civil libertarians and minorities who fear illegal arrests and ethnic profiling. It's also worrying researchers, including some in the Homeland Security Department, who say it's unproven and potentially ineffectual.

The government is unlikely to reveal data on the efficacy of this program, but we can make some reasonable assumptions. Every month, roughly 60 million people fly on US carriers. Let us imagine that 6 of them are terrorists. Let us also imagine that the TSA personnel are highly competent and will correctly identify a person as a terrorist or non-terrorist in 98/100 of cases. Questions:

(a) What is the probability that a passenger selected at random is a terrorist and is correctly identified as such by TSA personnel?
(b) What is the probability that a passenger selected at random is *not* a terrorist but is nevertheless (incorrectly) identified as a terrorist by TSA personnel?
(c) What is the probability that a passenger in fact is a terrorist conditional on having been identified as such by TSA personnel?
(d) Is this test diagnostic?

Notice that in the story above, the man was apparently a false positive, meaning that the story inadvertently ended up illustrating the lack of diagnosticity of the test.

Exercise 5.20 Diagnosticity Let us take it for granted that the behavior-detection test (from Exercise 5.19) is not diagnostic. The test may still be diagnostic in another setting, say, at a checkpoint at the US embassy in Kabul, Afghanistan. Explain how this is possible.

On a related note: since 2004, the US Department of Homeland Security's US-VISIT Program collects digital fingerprints and photographs from international travelers at US visa-issuing posts and ports of entry. Before long, the database might contain hundreds of millions of fingerprints. If a terrorist's fingerprint – recovered from a crime scene, perhaps – is found to match one in the database, what do you think the probability is that the match is the actual terrorist? If you find yourself caught up in this kind of dragnet, the only thing standing between you and the electric chair might be a jury's understanding of Bayes's rule. Good luck explaining it to them.

5.5 Confirmation bias

One striking feature of Bayesian updating in Section 4.6 is that John and Wes come to agree on the nature of the coin so quickly. As you will recall, after only about 15 flips of the coin, both assigned a probability of almost 100 percent to the possibility that the coin had two heads. People sometimes refer to this phenomenon as **washing out of the priors**. That is, after so many flips, John and Wes will assign roughly the same probability to the hypothesis, independently of what their priors used to be. This represents a hopeful picture of human nature: when rational people are exposed to the same evidence, over time they come to agree regardless of their starting point. (As is often the case, things get tricky when probabilities are zero; I continue to ignore such complications.)

In real life, unfortunately, people do not in general come to agree over time. Sometimes that is because they are exposed to very different evidence: conservatives tend to read conservative newspapers and blogs that present information selected because it supports conservative viewpoints; liberals tend to read liberal newspapers and blogs that present information selected because it supports liberal viewpoints. Yet sometimes people have access to the very same evidence presented in the very same way (as Wes and John do) but nevertheless fail to agree over time. Why is this?

Part of the story is a phenomenon psychologists call **confirmation bias**: a tendency to interpret evidence as supporting prior beliefs to a greater extent than warranted. In one classic study, participants who favored or opposed the death penalty read an article containing ambiguous information about the advantages and disadvantages of the death penalty. Rather than coming to agree as a result of being exposed to the same information, both groups of people interpreted the information as supporting their beliefs. That is, after reading the article, those who were previously opposed to the death penalty were even more strongly opposed and those who favored it were even more in favor. In the presence of confirmation bias, then, the picture of how people's beliefs change as they are exposed to the evidence may look less like Figure 4.5 on page 77 and more like Figure 5.2.

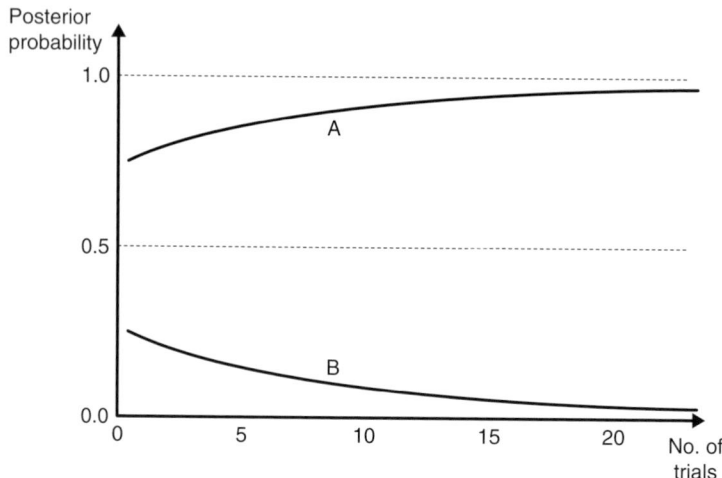

Figure 5.2 Confirmation bias

Exercise 5.21 Confirmation bias Imagine that John is suffering from confirmation bias. Which of the curves labeled A, B, and C in Figure 5.3 best represents the manner in which his probabilities change over time as the evidence comes in?

Example 5.22 The jealous lover From literature or life, you may be familiar with the character of the jealous lover, who refuses to accept any evidence that his or her affections are reciprocated and who everywhere finds evidence fueling suspicions. As Marcel Proust, author of *In Search of Lost Time*, wrote: "It is astonishing how jealousy, which spends its time inventing so many petty but false suppositions, lacks imagination when it comes to discovering the truth." In more prosaic terms, the jealous lover exhibits confirmation bias.

Confirmation bias can explain a whole range of phenomena. It can explain why racist and sexist stereotypes persist over time. A sexist may dismiss or downplay evidence suggesting that girls are good at math and men are able to care for

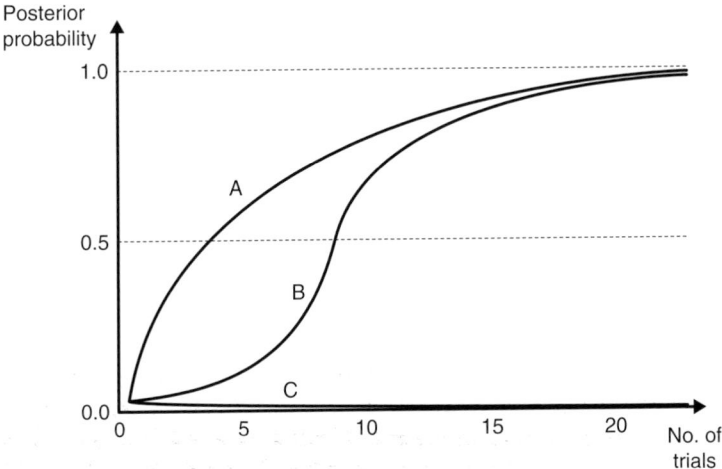

Figure 5.3 John's confirmation bias

children but be very quick to pick up on any evidence that they are not (as in Figure 5.4). A racist may not notice all the people of other races who work hard, feed their families, pay their taxes, and do good deeds, but pay a lot of attention to those who do not. Confirmation bias can also explain why people gamble. Many gamblers believe that they can predict the outcome of the next game, in spite of overwhelming evidence that they cannot (they may, for example, have lost plenty of money in the past by mispredicting the outcomes). This could happen if the gambler notices all the cases when he did predict the outcome (and if the outcome is truly random, there will be such cases by chance alone) and fails to notice all the cases when he does not. The same line of thinking can explain why so many people think that they can beat the stock market, in spite of evidence that (in the absence of inside information) you might as well pick stocks randomly. Finally, confirmation bias can explain how certain conspiracy theories survive in spite of overwhelming contradictory evidence. The conspiracy theorist puts a lot of

Figure 5.4 "How it Works" by Randall Munroe. From http://xkcd.com/385/

weight on morsels of evidence supporting the theory, and dismisses all the evidence undermining it.

Psychological research suggests that confirmation bias is due to a number of different factors. First, people sometimes fail to notice evidence that goes against their beliefs, whereas they quickly pick up on evidence that supports them. Second, when the evidence is vague or ambiguous, and therefore admits of multiple interpretations, people tend to interpret it in such a way that it supports their beliefs. Third, people tend to apply a much higher standard of proof to evidence contradicting their beliefs than to evidence supporting them.

Problem 5.23 Preventing confirmation bias *In matters of politics, philosophy, religion, and so on, do you expose yourself to the ideas of people "on the other side" as you do to the ideas of people "on your side"? Are you paying as much attention to what they say? Are you applying the same standards of evidence? If you can honestly answer yes to all these questions, you belong to a small but admirable fraction of the population. If not, you might give it a try; it is an interesting exercise.*

5.6 Availability

When physicians examine children with headaches, one of the things they look for is brain tumors. The base rate is very low. Children with brain tumors are virtually certain to have headaches, but there are of course many other causes of headaches. As it happens, a simple examination successfully identifies the children with tumors in very many of the cases. That is, of all the children who have been properly examined and judged not to have a tumor, very few actually do.

Exercise 5.24 CT scans In some populations, brain tumors in children are rare: the base rate is only about $1/10,000$. A child with a tumor is very likely to have occasional headaches: 99 out of 100 do. But there are many other reasons a child can have a headache: of those who do not have a tumor 1 in 10 have occasional headaches.

(a) Given that a child has occasional headaches, what is the probability that he or she has a brain tumor?

(b) Let us suppose that a physician, when using a simple test, can detect the presence or absence of a tumor in 99.99 percent of children with headaches. Given that the patient is judged to be healthy after this test is performed, what is the probability that he or she has a tumor anyway?

As these exercises indicate, it is in fact very unlikely that the patient has a brain tumor provided that he or she has been properly examined. CT scans can determine almost conclusively whether the patient has a tumor, but they are prohibitively expensive. Knowing that patients who have been examined by a physician are unlikely to have a tumor, it is widely agreed that CT scans under these conditions are unjustified. However, once a physician happens to have a patient who turns out to have a tumor in spite of the fact that the examination failed to find one, the physician's behavior often changes dramatically. From then on, she wants to order far more CT scans than she previously did. Let us assume that the physician's experience with the last child did not change her values. Assuming that a drastic change in behavior must be due to a change in values or a change in beliefs, it follows that her beliefs must have changed. On the basis of what we know, did the physician update her beliefs rationally?

The story is, of course, far more complicated than it appears here. It is worth noticing, though, that the actual figures are widely known among medical doctors. This knowledge reflects the accumulated experience of far more cases than any one physician will see during her career. As a result, it seems unlikely that rational updating on the basis of one single case should have such a radical impact on a physician's behavior. So what is going on? Behavioral economists explain this kind of behavior in terms of **availability**: the ease with which information can be brought to mind when making a judgment. When the physician faces her next patient, though she at some level of consciousness still knows the figures that suggest a CT scan is uncalled for, chances are that the last case (in which she failed to find the tumor) will come to mind. It is particularly salient, in part because it happened recently, but also because it is highly emotionally loaded.

The **availability heuristic** is another prominent heuristic from the heuristics-and-biases program. When we rely on this heuristic, we assess the probability of some event occurring by the ease with which the event comes to mind. That is, the availability heuristic says that we can treat X as more likely than Y if X comes to mind more easily than Y. As pointed out in Section 3.6, heuristics are often perfectly functional. Suppose, for instance, that you happen to come across an alligator while walking to work. The chances are that images of alligators attacking other animals (including humans) will come to mind more easily than images of alligators acting cute and cuddly. If so, the availability heuristic tells you to assume the alligator is likely to be dangerous, which is obviously a helpful assumption under the circumstances. However, the availability heuristic (being a simple rule of thumb) can sometimes lead you astray, as in the case of the children with headaches. Thus, like anchoring and adjustment, availability can lead to bias.

Exercise 5.25 Contacts Your optometrist tells you that your new contacts are so good that you can wear them night and day for up to 30 days straight. She warns you that there is some chance that you will develop serious problems, but says that she has seen many clients and that the probability is low. After a week, you develop problems and see an ophthalmologist. The ophthalmologist tells you that he is the doctor who removes people's eyes when they have been injured as a result of improper contact use. He tells you that the probability of developing serious problems is high.

Use the concept of availability bias to explain how the optometrist and the ophthalmologist can report such different views about the likelihood of developing serious problems as a result of wearing contacts.

The availability heuristic can explain a variety of phenomena, including why people think violent crime is more common than other kinds of crime. Violent crime comes to mind so easily in part because images of violence can be particularly vivid, but also because it is covered so extensively in the press: "Area Man Not Shot Today" would make for a terrible headline. Availability can also explain why fears of airplane crashes, nuclear meltdowns, and terrorist attacks tend to increase dramatically shortly after such events occur, for the obvious reason that they come to mind particularly easily then. Availability can also explain a variety of marketing practices.

Advertising campaigns for grooming products, cigarettes, alcohol, and all sorts of other products depict users of the product as being particularly attractive and popular. If that is what comes to mind when potential buyers reflect on the consequences of using the products, availability might make attractiveness and popularity seem particularly likely outcomes.

Availability bias also helps explain the base-rate fallacy. Consider the cancer case. Even if you know that there are false positives, so that a positive test does not necessarily mean that you have the disease, the chances are cases of true positives (people who were correctly diagnosed with cancer) are more likely to come to mind than cases of false positives (people who were incorrectly diagnosed with cancer). Insofar as you follow the availability heuristic, you will think of true positives as more likely than false positives. Because the actual probability of having the disease given a positive test is the ratio of true positives to all positives, an overestimation of the probability of a true positive will lead to an inflated probability of having the disease.

5.7 Discussion

This chapter has explored phenomena that appear inconsistent with the theory of probabilistic judgment that we learned about in Chapter 4. While the theory of probability was never designed to capture the precise cognitive processes people use when forming judgments, there appears to be a wide range of circumstances under which people's intuitive probability judgments differ substantially, systematically, and predictably from the demands of the theory. As the examples have shown, differences can be costly. The phenomena are typically construed as undercutting the adequacy of probability theory as a descriptive theory. Yet some of these phenomena can also be invoked when challenging the correctness of probability theory as a normative standard. The fact that living up to the theory is so demanding – surely, part of the explanation for why people fail to live up to it in practice – is sometimes thought to undercut its normative correctness.

The chapter does not purport to offer a complete list of phenomena that are inconsistent with standard theory. For example, we could have discussed **hindsight bias**: the tendency to exaggerate the probability that an event would occur by people who know that it did occur. When your car breaks down on the highway after you postpone its regular service, you might tell yourself that you should have known that it would break down, in spite of the fact that you could know no such thing. We could also have discussed **overconfidence**: the fact that the probability that people (including experts) assign to the probability that their judgments are correct tends to exceed the frequency with which those judgments in fact are correct. In a prominent study, subjects who indicated that they were 100 percent certain that their answers were right were on the average correct 70–80 percent of the time.

We have also discussed some of the theoretical tools used by behavioral economists to capture the manner in which people actually make judgments. Thus, we explored further aspects of the heuristics-and-biases program, which is one prominent effort to develop a descriptively adequate theory of probabilistic judgment. Because heuristics are largely functional, it would be a mistake to try to eliminate reliance on them altogether. But heuristics can lead us astray, and an awareness of the conditions under which this may happen might reduce the likelihood that they do. As the marketing applications make particularly clear, knowledge of behavioral economics in general, and heuristics and biases in particular, permits us to influence other people's judgment, for good or for evil. But knowledge of behavioral economics also permits us to anticipate and to resist other people's efforts to influence our judgment.

The next part of the book will explore how the theory of probability can be incorporated into a theory of rational decision, and explores its strengths and weaknesses.

Additional exercises

Exercise 5.26 Probability matching   Imagine that your friend Anne has a coin that has a 2/3 probability of coming up heads (H) and a 1/3 probability of coming up tails (T). She intends to flip it three times and give you a dollar for every time you correctly predicted how the coin would come up. Would you be more likely to win if you predicted that the coin will come up HHH or HHT?

If your prediction was HHT (or HTH or THH) you might have engaged in **probability matching**: choosing frequencies so as to match the probabilities of the relevant events. Probability matching might result from the use of the representativeness heuristic, since an outcome like HHT (or HTH or THH) might seem so much more representative for the random process than HHH or TTT. As the exercise shows, probability matching is a suboptimal strategy leading to bias.

Exercise 5.27 IVF   In vitro fertilization (IVF) is a procedure by which egg cells are fertilized by sperm outside the womb. Let us assume that any time the procedure is performed the probability of success (meaning a live birth) is approximately 20 percent. Let us also assume, though this is unlikely to be true, that the probabilities of success at separate trials are independent. Imagine, first, that a woman has the procedure done twice.

(a) What is the probability that she will have *exactly* two live births?
(b) What is the probability that she will have *no* live births?
(c) What is the probability that she will have *at least* one live birth?

Imagine, next, that another woman has the procedure done five times.

(d) What is the probability that she will have at least one live birth?

Exercise 5.28 Mandatory drug testing   In July 2011, the state of Florida started testing all welfare recipients for the use of illegal drugs. Statistics suggest that some 8 percent of adult Floridians use illegal drugs; let us assume that this is true for welfare recipients as well. Imagine that the drug test is 90 percent accurate, meaning that it gives the correct response in nine cases out of ten.

(a) What is the probability that a randomly selected Floridian welfare recipient uses illegal drugs and has a positive test?
(b) What is the probability that a randomly selected Floridian welfare recipient does not use illegal drugs but nevertheless has a positive test?
(c) What is the probability that a randomly selected Floridian welfare recipient has a positive test?
(d) Given that a randomly selected Floridian welfare recipient has a positive test, what is the probability the he or she uses illegal drugs?
(e) If a Florida voter favors the law because he thinks the answer to (d) is in the neighborhood of 90 percent, what fallacy might he be committing?

Additional exercises cont'd

Exercise 5.29 CIA   Intelligence services are deeply interested in how people think, both when they think correctly and incorrectly. The following exercise is borrowed from the book *Psychology of Intelligence Analysis*, published by the US Central Intelligence Agency (CIA).

> During the Vietnam War, a fighter plane made a non-fatal strafing attack on a US aerial reconnaissance mission at twilight. Both Cambodian and Vietnamese jets operate in the area. You know the following facts: (a) Specific case information: The US pilot identified the fighter as Cambodian. The pilot's aircraft recognition capabilities were tested under appropriate visibility and flight conditions. When presented with a sample of fighters (half with Vietnamese markings and half with Cambodian) the pilot made correct identifications 80 per cent of the time and erred 20 per cent of the time. (b) Base rate data: 85 per cent of the jet fighters in that area are Vietnamese; 15 per cent are Cambodian.
>
> Question: What is the probability that the fighter was Cambodian rather than Vietnamese?

Exercise 5.30 Juan Williams   In October 2010, National Public Radio (NPR) fired commentator Juan Williams after he made the following remark on Fox News: "When I get on a plane . . . if I see people who are in Muslim garb and I think, you know, they're identifying themselves first and foremost as Muslims, I get worried. I get nervous." Here, I will not comment on the wisdom of firing somebody for expressing such a sentiment or of expressing it in the first place. But we can discuss the *rationality* of the sentiment.

(a) In the United States, there are roughly 300 million people, of whom about 2 million are Muslims. Let us assume that at any one time there are ten terrorists able and willing to strike an airliner, and that as many as nine out of ten terrorists are Muslims. Under these assumptions, what is the probability that a randomly selected Muslim is a terrorist able and willing to strike an airliner?

(b) Use the notion of availability bias to explain how Juan Williams might overestimate the probability that a randomly selected Muslim is a terrorist able and willing to strike an airliner.

Exercise 5.31   Match each of the vignettes below with one of the following phenomena: *availability bias, base-rate neglect, confirmation bias, conjunction fallacy, disjunction fallacy, hindsight bias,* and *overconfidence.* If in doubt, pick the best fit.

(a) Al has always been convinced that people of Roma (gypsy) descent are prone to thievery. In fact, several of his co-workers have a Roma background. But he knows his co-workers are not thieves, and he does not think twice about it. One day during happy hour, however, an old acquaintance shares a story about two people "who looked like gypsies" stealing goods from a grocery store. "I knew it!" Al says to himself.

(b) Beth's car is falling apart. Her friends, who know these things, tell her that the car has a 10 percent probability of breaking down every mile. Beth really wants to go see a friend who lives about ten miles away, though. She ponders the significance of driving a car that has a 10 percent probability of breaking down each mile, but figures that the probability of the car breaking down during the trip cannot be much higher than, say, 15 percent. She is shocked when her car breaks down half way there.

Additional exercises cont'd

(c) Cecile is so terrified of violent crime that she rarely leaves her house, even though she lives in a safe neighborhood. She is out of shape, suffers from hypertension, and would be much happier if she went for a walk every so often. However, as soon as she considers going for a walk, images of what might happen to innocent people quietly strolling down the sidewalk come to mind, and she is sure something horrible is going to happen to her too. As a result, she goes back to watching reruns of *Law and Order*.

(d) David, who has never left the country, somehow manages to get tested for malaria. The test comes back positive. David has never been so depressed. Convinced that he is mortally sick, he starts to draft his will.

(e) Because she has trouble getting up in the morning, Elizabeth often drives too fast on her way to school. After getting a speeding ticket on Monday last week, she religiously followed the law all week. Only this week is she starting to drive faster again.

(f) Fizzy does not think the US will want to start another front in the war on terror, so she believes that is quite unlikely that the US will bomb Iranian nuclear facilities. She does, however, think that it is quite likely that the US will withdraw all troops from Afghanistan. When asked what she thinks about the possibility that the US will bomb Iranian nuclear facilities and withdraw all troops from Afghanistan, she thinks that it is more likely than the possibility that the US will bomb Iranian nuclear facilities.

(g) Georgina has trouble imagining an existence without Apple computers and iPads. Thus, she thinks it was inevitable that a man like Steve Jobs would appear and design such things.

(h) Harry lost all his luggage the last time he checked it. He is never going to check his luggage again, even if it means having unpleasant arguments with flight attendants.

Problem 5.32 *Drawing on your own experience, make up stories like those in Exercise 5.31 to illustrate the various ideas that you have read about in this chapter.*

Further reading

A comprehensive introduction to heuristics and biases in judgment is Hastie and Dawes (2010). The gambler's fallacy and related mistakes are discussed in Tversky and Kahneman (1971). The conjunction and disjunction fallacies are explored in Tversky and Kahneman (1983) and in Tversky and Shafir (1992). Base-rate neglect is examined in Bar-Hillel (1980); the planning fallacy and the Sydney Opera House are discussed in Buehler et al. (1994, p. 366). The *USA Today* story is Frank (2007). An extensive review of confirmation bias is Nickerson (1998); the quote from *In Search of Lost Time* is Proust (2002 [1925], p. 402) and the study of confirmation bias in the context of the death penalty is Lord et al. (1979). Availability is discussed alongside anchoring and adjustment and representativeness in Tversky and Kahneman (1974). The classic article on hindsight bias is Fischhoff (1975); overconfidence, especially when it comes to economic judgment, is discussed in Angner (2006). The CIA's intelligence analysis example comes from Heuer (1999, pp. 157–8) and the Juan Williams affair is described in Farhi (2010).

Part III

Choice under Risk and Uncertainty

Chapter 6
Rational Choice under Risk and Uncertainty

Introduction

In Part II, we left the theory of decision aside for a moment in order to talk about judgment. Now it is time to return to questions of decision, and specifically, rational decision. In this chapter we explore the theory of rational choice under risk and uncertainty. According to the traditional perspective, you face a **choice under uncertainty** when the probabilities of the relevant outcomes are completely unknown or not even meaningful; you face a **choice under risk** when the probabilities of the relevant outcomes are both meaningful and known. At the end of the day, we want a theory that gives us principled answers to the question of what choice to make in any given decision problem. It will take a moment to develop this theory. We begin by discussing uncertainty and then proceed to expected value, before getting to expected utility. Ultimately, expected-utility theory combines the concept of utility from Chapter 2 with the concept of probability from Chapter 4 into an elegant and powerful theory of choice under risk.

6.2 Uncertainty

Imagine that you are about to leave your house and have to decide whether to take an umbrella or to leave it at home (Figure 6.1). You are concerned that it might rain. If you do not take the umbrella and it does not rain, you will spend the day dry and happy; if you do not take the umbrella and it does rain, however, you will be wet and miserable. If you take the umbrella, you will be dry no matter, but carrying the cumbersome umbrella will infringe on your happiness. Your decision problem can be represented as in Table 6.1(a).

In a table like this, the left-most column represents your menu, that is, the options available to you. Other than that, there is one column for each thing that can happen. These things are referred to as **states of the world** or simply **states**, listed in the top row. Together, they constitute the outcome space. In this case, obviously, there are only two states: either it rains, or it does not. Nothing prevents expressing your preferences over the four outcomes by using our old friend the utility function from Section 2.7. Utility payoffs can be represented as in Table 6.1(b). Under the circumstances, what is the rational thing to do? Let us assume that you treat this as a choice under uncertainty. There are a number of different criteria that could be applied.

According to the **maximin criterion**, you should choose the alternative that has the greatest minimum utility payoff. If you take the umbrella, the minimum payoff is three; if you leave the umbrella at home, the minimum payoff is zero. Consequently, maximin reasoning would favor taking the umbrella. According to the **maximax criterion**, you should choose the alternative that has the greatest maximum utility payoff. If you take the umbrella, the maximum payoff is three; if you leave the umbrella at home, the maximum payoff is five. Thus, maximax reasoning would

Figure 6.1 Ready for rain? Illustration by Cody Taylor

Table 6.1 Umbrella problem

	Rain	No rain
Take umbrella	Dry, not happy	Dry, not happy
Leave umbrella	Wet, miserable	Dry, happy

(a) Payoffs

	Rain	No rain
Take umbrella	3	3
Leave umbrella	0	5

(b) Utility payoffs

	Rain	No rain
Take umbrella	0	2
Leave umbrella	3	0

(c) Risk payoffs

favor leaving the umbrella at home. The maximin reasoner is as cautious as the maximax reasoner is reckless. The former looks at nothing but the *worst* possible outcome associated with each act, and the latter looks at nothing but the *best* possible outcome associated with each act.

There are other criteria as well. According to the **minimax-risk criterion**, you should choose the alternative that is associated with the lowest maximum **risk** or **regret**. If you take the umbrella and it rains, or if you leave the umbrella at home and it does not rain, you have zero regrets. If you take the umbrella and it does not rain, your regret equals the best payoff you could have had if you had acted differently (five) minus your actual payoff (three), that is, two. By the same token, if you leave the umbrella at home and it does rain, your regret equals three. These "risk payoffs" can be captured in table form, as shown in Table 6.1(c). Since bringing the umbrella is associated with the lowest maximum regret (two, as opposed to three), minimax-risk reasoning favors taking the umbrella. The term **regret aversion** is sometimes used when discussing people's tendency to behave in such a way as to minimize anticipated regret. Regret aversion may be driven by loss aversion (see Section 3.5), since regret is due to the loss of a payoff that could have resulted from the state that obtains, had the agent acted differently. (We return to the topic of regret in Section 7.4.)

Exercise 6.1 Rational choice under uncertainty This exercise refers to the utility matrix of Table 6.2. What course of action would be favored by (a) the maximin criterion, (b) the maximax criterion, and (c) the minimax-risk criterion? As part of your answer to (c), make sure to produce the risk-payoff matrix.

Table 6.2 Decision under uncertainty

	S_1	S_2
A	1	10
B	2	9
C	3	6

Problem 6.2 The dating game under uncertainty *Imagine that you are considering whether or not to ask somebody out on a date. (a) Given your utility function, what course of action would be favored by (i) the maximin criterion, (ii) the maximax criterion, and (iii) the minimax-risk criterion? (b) In the words of Alfred, Lord Tennyson, "'Tis better to have loved and lost / Than never to have loved at all." What decision criterion do these lines advocate?*

Of all criteria for choice under uncertainty, the maximin criterion is the most prominent. It is, among other things, an important part of the philosopher John Rawls's theory of justice. In Rawls's theory, the principles of justice are the terms of cooperation that rational people would agree to follow in their interactions with each other *if* they found themselves behind a "veil of ignorance," meaning that they were deprived of all morally relevant information about themselves, the society in which they live, and their place in that society. Suppose, for example, that you have to choose whether to live either in a society with masters and slaves or in a more egalitarian society, without knowing whether (in the former) you would be master or slave. According to Rawls, the rational procedure is to rank societies in accordance with the worst possible outcome (for you) in each society – that is, to apply the maximin criterion – and to choose the egalitarian option. Rawls took this to constitute a reason to think that an egalitarian society is more just than a society of masters and slaves.

Critics have objected to the use of maximin reasoning in this and other scenarios. One objection is that maximin reasoning fails to consider relevant utility information, since for each act, it ignores all payoffs except the worst. Consider the two decision problems in Table 6.3. Maximin reasoning would favor A in either scenario. Yet it does not seem completely irrational to favor A over B and B* over A, since B* but not B upholds the prospect of ten billion utiles.

Table 6.3 More decisions under uncertainty

	S_1	S_2		S_1	S_2
A	1	1	A	1	1
B	0	10	B*	0	10^{10}
	(a)			(b)	

Another objection is that maximin reasoning fails to take into account the chances that the various states of the world will obtain. In a famous critique of Rawls's argument, Nobel prize-winning economist John C. Harsanyi offered the following example:

Example 6.3 Harsanyi's challenge Suppose you live in New York City and are offered two jobs at the same time. One is a tedious and badly paid job in New York City itself, while the other is a very interesting and well-paid job in Chicago. But the catch is that, if you wanted the Chicago job, you would have to take a plane from New York to Chicago (for example, because this job would have to be taken up the very next day). Therefore there would be a very small but positive probability that you might be killed in a plane accident.

Assuming that dying in a plane crash is worse than anything that could happen on the streets of New York, as Harsanyi points out, maximin reasoning would favor the tedious NYC job, *no matter* how much you prefer the Chicago job and *no matter* how unlikely you think a plane accident might be. This does not sound quite right.

Perhaps there are scenarios in which the probabilities of the relevant outcomes are completely unknown or not even meaningful, and perhaps in those scenarios maximin reasoning – or one of the other criteria discussed earlier in this section – is appropriate. Yet the upshot is that, whenever possible, it is perfectly reasonable to pay attention to all possible payoffs as well as to the probabilities that the various states might obtain. When facing the umbrella problem in Table 6.1, for example, it seems right to take into account all four cells in the payoff matrix as well as the probability of rain.

6.3 Expected value

From now on I will assume that it is both meaningful and possible to assign probabilities to outcomes; that is, we will be leaving the realm of choice under uncertainty and entering the kingdom of choice under risk. In this section, we explore one particularly straightforward approach – expected value – that takes the entire payoff matrix as well as probabilities into account.

The **expected value** of a gamble is what you can expect to win *on the average, in the long run*, when you play the gamble. Suppose I make you the following offer: I will flip a fair coin, and I will give you $10 if the coin comes up heads (H), and nothing if the coin comes up tails (T). This is a reasonably good deal: with 50 percent probability you will become $10 richer. This gamble can easily be represented in tree and table form, as shown in Figure 6.2. It is clear that on the average, in the long run,

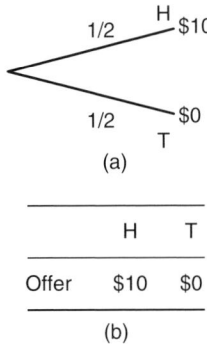

H
1/2 — $10

1/2 — $0
T
(a)

	H	T
Offer	$10	$0

(b)

Figure 6.2 Simple gamble

you would get $5 when playing this gamble; in other words, the expected value of the gamble is $5. That is the same as the figure you get if you multiply the probability of winning (1/2) by the dollar amount you stand to win ($10).

Exercise 6.4 Lotto 6/49   Represent the gamble accepted by someone who plays Lotto 6/49 (from Exercise 4.27 on page 70) as in Figure 6.2(a) and (b). Assume that the grand prize is a million dollars.

Example 6.5 Lotto 6/49, cont.   What is the expected value of a Lotto 6/49 ticket, if the grand prize is a million dollars?

We know from Exercise 4.27 on page 70 that the ticket is a winner one time out of 13,983,816. The means that the ticket holder will receive, on the average in the long run, $1/13,983,816 * \$1,000,000$. You get the same answer if you multiply the probability of winning by the amount won, that is, $0.000,000,07 * \$1,000,000 = \$0.07$. That is 7 cents.

Problem 6.6   *What would you pay to play this gamble? If you are willing to pay to play this game, what do you hope to achieve?*

Sometimes two or more acts are available to you, in which case you have a choice to make. Imagine, for instance, that you can choose between the gamble in Figure 6.2 and $4 for sure. If so, we can represent your decision problem in tree form as shown in Figure 6.3(a). We can also think of the outcome of rejecting the gamble as $4 no matter whether the coin comes up heads or tails. Thus, we can think of the gamble as identical to that in Figure 6.3(b). The latter decision tree makes it obvious how to represent this gamble in table form (see Figure 6.3(c)). The numbers in the row marked "Reject" represent the fact that if you reject the gamble, you keep the four dollars whether or not it turns out to be a winner.

Exercise 6.7 Expected value   For the following questions, refer to Figure 6.3(c). (a) What is the expected value of accepting this gamble? (b) What is the expected value of rejecting it?

You may be wondering if all gambles can be represented in table form: they can. Consider, for instance, what would happen if you win the right to play the gamble

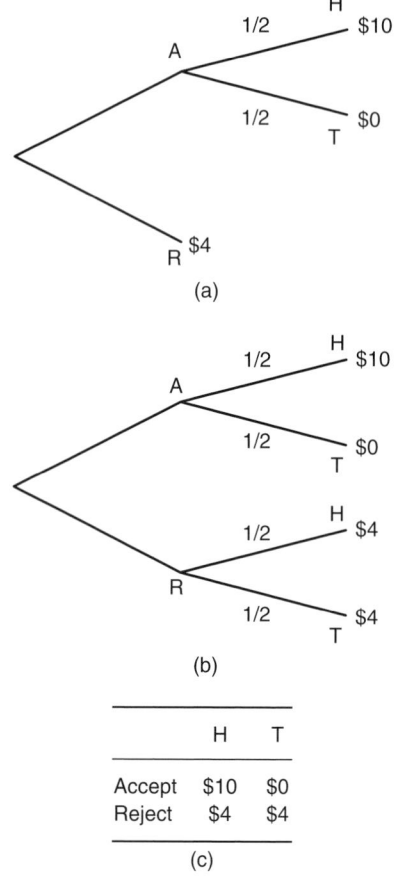

Figure 6.3 Choice between gambles

from Figure 6.2 if you flip a coin and it comes up heads. If so, the complex gamble you are playing would look like Figure 6.4(a). The key to analyzing more complex, multi-stage gambles like this is to use one of the AND rules to construct a simpler one. In this case, the gamble gives you a 1/4 probability of winning $10 and a 3/4 probability of winning nothing. Hence, the gamble can also be represented as in Figure 6.4(b). This makes it obvious how to represent the complex gamble in table form, as in Figure 6.4(c). There can be more than two acts or more than two states. So, in general, we end up with a matrix like Table 6.4. By now, it is obvious how to define expected value.

Definition 6.8 Expected value *Given a decision problem as in Table 6.4, the expected value* $EV(A_i)$ *of an act A_i is given by:*

$$EV(A_i) = \Pr(S_1) * C_{i1} + \Pr(S_2) * C_{i2} + \ldots + \Pr(S_n) * C_{in}$$

$$= \sum_{j=1}^{n} \Pr(S_j) C_{ij}.$$

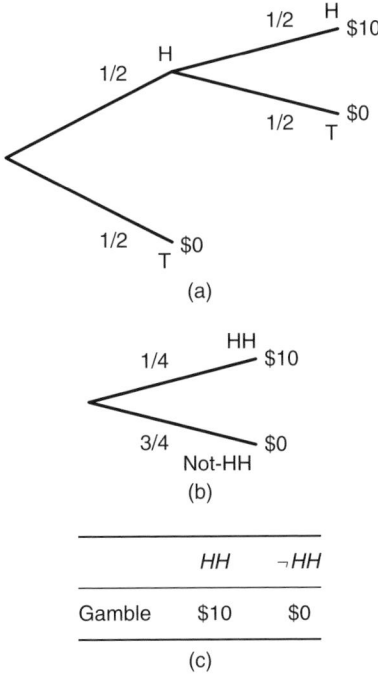

Figure 6.4 Multi-stage gamble

If this equation looks complicated, notice that actual computations are easy. For each state – that is, each column in the table – you multiply the probability of that state occurring with what you would get if it did; then you add all your numbers up. If you want to compare two or more acts, just complete the procedure for each act and compare your numbers. As you can tell, this formula gives some weight to each cell in the payoff matrix and to the probabilities that the various states of the world will obtain.

The table form is often convenient when computing expected values, since it makes it obvious how to apply the formula in Definition 6.8. The fact that more complex gambles can also be represented in table form means that the formula applies even in the case of more complex gambles. Hence, at least as long as outcomes can be described in terms of dollars, lives lost, or the like, the concept is well defined. To illustrate how useful this kind of knowledge can be, let us examine decision problem that you might encounter in casinos and other real-world environments.

Table 6.4 The general decision problem

	S_1	S_2	$\cdots$	S_n
A_1	C_{11}	C_{12}	$\cdots$	C_{1n}
$\vdots$	$\vdots$	$\vdots$		$\vdots$
A_m	C_{m1}	C_{m2}	$\cdots$	C_{mn}

Exercise 6.9 Roulette A roulette wheel has slots numbered $0, 00, 1, 2, 3, \ldots, 36$ (see Figure 6.5). The players make their bets, the croupier spins the wheel, and depending on the outcome, payouts may or may not be made. Players can make a variety of bets. Table 6.5 lists the bets that can be made as well as the associated payoffs for a player who wins after placing a one-dollar bet. Fill in the table.

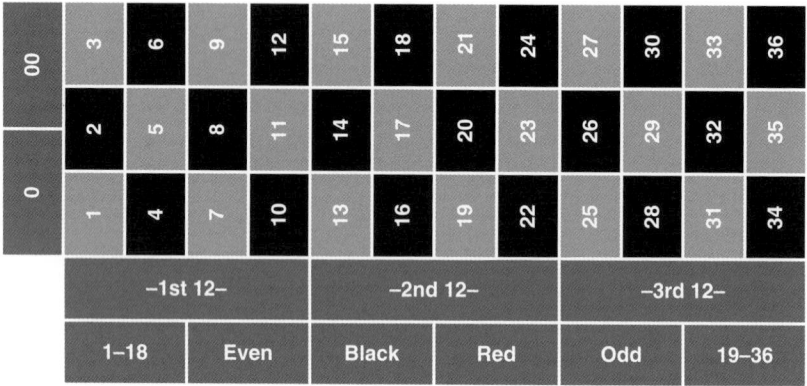

Figure 6.5 Roulette table

Table 6.5 Roulette bets

Bet	Description	Payout	Pr(win)	Expected Value
Straight Up	One number	$36		
Split	Two numbers	$18		
Street	Three numbers	$12		
Corner	Four numbers	$9		
First Five	0, 00, 1, 2, 3	$7		
Sixline	Six numbers	$6		
First 12	1–12	$3		
Second 12	13–24	$3		
Third 12	25–36	$3		
Red		$2		
Black		$2		
Even		$2		
Odd		$2		
Low	1–18	$2		
High	19–36	$2		

Exercise 6.10 Parking You are considering whether to park legally or illegally and decide to be rational about it. Use negative numbers to represent costs in your expected-value calculations.

(a) Suppose that a parking ticket costs $30 and that the probability of getting a ticket if you park illegally is $1/5$. What is the expected value of parking illegally?
(b) Assuming that you use expected-value calculations as a guide in life, would it be worth paying $5 in order to park legally?

It is perfectly possible to compute expected values when there is more than one state with a non-zero payoff.

Example 6.11   You are offered the following gamble: if a (fair) coin comes up heads, you receive $10; if the coin comes up tails, you pay $10. What is the expected value of this gamble?

The expected value of this gamble is $1/2 * 10 + 1/2 * (-10) = 0$.

Exercise 6.12   Suppose somebody intends to roll a fair die and pay you $1 if she rolls a one, $2 if she rolls a two, and so on. What is the expected value of this gamble?

Exercise 6.13 *Deal or No Deal*   You are on the show *Deal or No Deal*, where you are facing so many boxes, each of which contains some (unknown) amount of money (see Figure 6.6). At this stage, you are facing three boxes. One of them contains $900,000, one contains $300,000, and one contains $60, but you do not know which is which. Here are the rules: if you choose to open the boxes, you can open them in any order you like, but you can keep the amount contained in the *last* box only.

(a)   What is the expected value of opening the three boxes?
(b)   The host gives you the choice between a sure $400,000 and the right to open the three boxes. Assuming you want to maximize expected value, which should you choose?
(c)   You decline the $400,000 and open a box. Unfortunately, it contains the $900,000. What is the expected value of opening the remaining two boxes?

Figure 6.6   *Deal or No Deal*

(d) The host gives you the choice between a sure $155,000 and the right to open the remaining two boxes. Assuming you want to maximize expected value, which should you choose?

Expected-value calculations form the core of **cost–benefit analysis**, which is used to determine whether all sorts of projects are worth undertaking. Corporations engage in cost–benefit analysis to determine whether to invest in a new plant, start a new marketing campaign, and so on. Governments might engage in cost–benefit analysis to determine whether to build bridges, railways, and airports; whether to incentivize foreign corporations to relocate there; whether to overhaul the tax system; and many other things. The basic idea is simply to compare expected benefits with expected costs: if the benefits exceed or equal the cost, the assumption is that it is worth proceeding, otherwise not.

So far, we have used our knowledge of probabilities to compute expected values. It is also possible to use Definition 6.8 to compute probabilities, provided that we know enough about the expected values. So, for example, we can ask the following question.

Example 6.14 Parking, cont. If a parking ticket costs $30, and it costs $5 to park legally, what does the probability of getting a ticket need to be for the expected value of parking legally to equal the expected value of parking illegally?

We solve this problem by setting up an equation. Assume, first of all, that the probability of getting a parking ticket when you park illegally is p. Assume, further, that the expected value of parking illegally equals the expected value of parking legally: $p * (-30) = -5$. Solving for p, we get that $p = -5/-30 = 1/6$. This means that if the probability of getting a ticket is $1/6$, the expected values are identical. If p is greater than $1/6$, the expected value of parking legally is greater than the expected value of parking illegally; if p is lower than $1/6$, the expected value of parking legally is smaller than the expected value of parking illegally.

Exercise 6.15 Parking, cont. Assume that the cost of parking legally is still $5.

(a) If the parking ticket costs $100, what does the probability need to be for the expected value of parking legally to equal the expected value of parking illegally?
(b) What if the ticket costs $10?

Problem 6.16 Parking, cont. *Given what you pay for parking and given what parking fines are in your area, what does the probability of getting a ticket need to be for the expected value of parking legally to equal the expected value of parking illegally?*

There is a whole field called **law and economics** that addresses questions such as this, exploring the conditions under which it makes sense for people to break the law, and how to design the law so as to generate the optimal level of crime.

Exercise 6.17 Lotto 6/49, cont. Suppose a Lotto 6/49 ticket costs $1 and that the winner will receive $1,000,000. What does the probability of winning need to be for this lottery to be **actuarially fair**, that is, for its price to equal its expected value?

Exercise 6.18 Warranties A tablet computer costs $325; the optional one-year warranty, which will replace the tablet computer at no cost if it breaks, costs $79. What does the probability p of the tablet computer breaking need to be for the expected value of purchasing the optional warranty to equal the expected value of not purchasing it?

As this example suggests, the price of warranties is often inflated relative to the probability that the product will break (for the average person, anyway).

Unfortunately, when used as a guide in life, expected-value calculations have drawbacks. Obviously, we can only compute expected values when consequences can be described in terms of dollars, lives lost, or similar. The definition of expected value makes no sense if the consequences C_{ij} are not expressed in numbers. Moreover, under many conditions expected-value considerations give apparently perverse advice, and therefore cannot serve as a general guide to decision-making in real life. Consider, for example, what to do if you have 30 minutes in a casino before the mafia comes after you to reclaim your debts. Assuming that you will be in deep trouble unless you come up with, say, $10,000 before they show up, gambling can be a very reasonable thing to do, even if the expected values are low. Consider, finally, the following famous example.

Example 6.19 St Petersburg paradox A gamble is resolved by tossing an unbiased coin as many times as necessary to obtain heads. If it takes only one toss, the payoff is $2; if it takes two tosses, it is $4; if it takes three, it is $8; and so forth (see Table 6.6). What is the expected value of the gamble?

Notice that the probability of getting heads on the first flip (H) is $1/2$; the probability of getting tails on the first flip and heads on the second (TH) is $1/4$; the probability of getting tails on the first two flips and heads on the third (TTH) is $1/8$; and so on. Thus, the expected value of the gamble is:

$$\frac{1}{2} * \$2 + \frac{1}{4} * \$4 + \frac{1}{8} * \$8 + \ldots =$$
$$\$1 + \$1 + \$1 + \ldots = \$\infty.$$

In sum, the expected value of the gamble is *infinite*. This means that if you try to maximize expected value, you should be willing to pay any (finite) price for this gamble. That does not seem right, which is why the result is called the **St Petersburg paradox**. And it would not seem right even if you could trust that you would receive the promised payoffs no matter what happens.

Table 6.6 St Petersburg gamble

	H	TH	TTH	...
St Petersburg gamble	$2	$4	$8	...

6.4 Expected utility

Our calculations in Section 4.4 suggested that games like Lotto 6/49 are simply not worth playing (see Exercise 4.27 on page 70). But the story does not end there. For one thing, as our deliberations in this chapter have illustrated, the size of the prize matters (see, for instance, Example 6.5). Equally importantly, a dollar is not as valuable as every other dollar. You may care more about a dollar bill if it is the first in your pocket than if it is the tenth. Or, if the mafia is coming after you to settle a $10,000 debt, the first 9999 dollar bills may be completely useless to you, since you will be dead either way, whereas the 10,000th can save your life.

To capture this kind of phenomenon, and to resolve the St Petersburg paradox, we simply reintroduce the concept of utility from Section 2.7. The utility of money is often represented in a graph, with money (or wealth, or income) on the x-axis and utility on the y-axis. In Figure 6.7, for example, the dashed line represents the expected value of money if $u(x) = x$; the solid line represents the utility of money if the mafia is coming after you; and the dotted line represents the case when a dollar becomes worth less and less and you get more of them, that is, when the marginal utility of money is diminishing. When the curve bends downwards when you move to the right, as the dotted line does, it is said to be **concave**.

For most goods, it is probably true that the marginal utility is diminishing. When buying a newspaper from a box, you put a few coins in the slot, open a door, and grab a newspaper from the stack. Nothing prevents you from grabbing two or more copies, but most people do not. Why? Newspaper boxes work because the marginal utility of newspapers is sharply diminishing. While the first copy of the *Wall Street Journal* permits you to learn what is going on in the markets, subsequent copies are best used to make funny hats or to wrap fish. There are exceptions to the rule, however. Beer is not sold like newspapers, and for good reason: its marginal utility is not diminishing and may even be increasing. As you may have read in a book, after people have had a beer, a second beer frequently seems like an even better idea than the first one did, and so forth. This is why a beer – as in "Let's have a beer" – is a mythical animal not unlike unicorns.

How does this help? Consider the St Petersburg gamble from Section 6.3. Let us assume that the marginal utility for money is diminishing, which seems plausible.

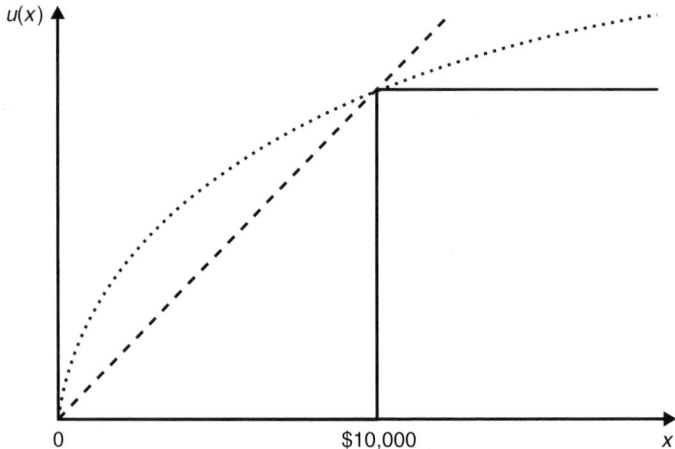

Figure 6.7 The utility of money

Table 6.7 St Petersburg gamble with utilities

	H	TH	TTH	...
St Petersburg gamble	log (2)	log (4)	log (8)	...

Mathematically, the utility of a given amount of money x might equal the logarithm of x, so that $u(x) = \log(x)$. If so, we can transform Table 6.6 into a table in which consequences are expressed in utilities instead of dollars (see Table 6.7). Now, we can compute the **expected utility** of the gamble. The expected utility of a gamble is the amount of utility you can expect to gain *on the average, in the long run,* when you play the gamble. In the case of the St Petersburg gamble, the expected utility is:

$$\frac{1}{2} * \log (2) + \frac{1}{4} * \log (4) + \frac{1}{8} * \log (8) + \ldots \approx 0.602 < \infty.$$

This way, the expected utility of the St Petersburg gamble is well-defined and finite. (In Example 6.35 we will compute what the gamble is worth in dollars and cents.) Formally, this is how we define expected utility.

Definition 6.20 Expected utility *Given a decision problem like Table 6.4, the expected utility* $EU (A_i)$ *of an act* A_i *is given by:*

$$EU (A_i) = \Pr (S_1) * u (C_{i1}) + \Pr (S_2) * u (C_{i2}) + \ldots + \Pr (S_n) * u (C_{in})$$

$$= \sum_{j=1}^{n} \Pr (S_j) u (C_{ij}).$$

Somebody who chooses that option with the greatest expected utility is said to engage in **expected-utility maximization**. Examples like the St Petersburg paradox suggest that expected-utility maximization is both a better guide to behavior, and a better description of actual behavior, than expected-value maximization. That is, the theory of expected utility is a better normative theory, and a better descriptive theory, than the theory of expected value. Computing expected utilities is not much harder than computing expected values, except that you need to multiply each probability with the utility of each outcome.

Example 6.21 Expected utility Consider, again, the gamble from Figure 6.3(c). Suppose that your utility function is $u(x) = \sqrt{x}$. Should you accept or reject the gamble?

The utility of rejecting the gamble is $EU (R) = u (4) = \sqrt{4} = 2$. The utility of accepting the gamble is $EU (A) = 1/2 * u (10) + 1/2 * u (0) = 1/2 * \sqrt{10} \approx 1.58$. The rational thing to do is to reject the gamble.

Exercise 6.22 Expected utility, cont. Suppose instead that your utility function is $u(x) = x^2$.

(a) What is the expected utility of rejecting the gamble?
(b) What is the expected utility of accepting the gamble?
(c) What should you do?

When the curve bends upwards as you move from left to right, like the utility function $u(x) = x^2$ does, the curve is said to be **convex**.

Exercise 6.23 Lotto 6/49, cont. Assume still that your utility function is $u(x) = \sqrt{x}$.

(a) Given your answer to Exercise 4.27 on page 70, what is the expected utility of a Lotto ticket?
(b) What is the expected utility of the dollar you would have to give up in order to receive the Lotto ticket?
(c) Which would you prefer?

Exercise 6.24 Expected value and expected utility Assume again that your utility function is $u(x) = \sqrt{x}$. Compute (i) the expected value and (ii) the expected utility of the following gambles:

(a) G: You have a 1/4 chance of winning $25 and a 3/4 chance of winning $1.
(b) G*: You have a 2/3 chance of winning $7 and a 1/3 chance of winning $4.

Another major advantage of the expected-utility framework is that it can be applied to decisions that do not involve consequences expressed in terms of dollars, lives lost, or the like. The expected-utility formula can be used quite generally, as long as it is possible to assign utilities to all outcomes. That is to say that expected utilities can be calculated whenever you have preferences over outcomes – which you do, if you are rational. Hence, expected-utility theory applies, at least potentially, to all decisions. The following exercises illustrate how expected-utility reasoning applies even when consequences are not obviously quantifiable.

Exercise 6.25 Hearing loss A patient with hearing loss is considering whether to have surgery. If she does not have the surgery, her hearing will get no better and no worse. If she does have the surgery, there is an 85 percent chance that her hearing will improve, and a five percent chance that it will deteriorate. If she does not have the surgery, her utility will be zero. If she does have the surgery and her hearing improves, her utility will be ten. If she does have the surgery but her hearing is no better and no worse, her utility will be minus two. If she does have the surgery and her hearing deteriorates, her utility will be minus ten.

(a) Draw a tree representing the decision problem.
(b) Draw a table representing the problem.
(c) What is the expected utility of not having the operation?
(d) What is the expected utility of having the operation?
(e) What should the patient do?

Exercise 6.26 Thanksgiving indecision Suppose you are contemplating whether to go home for Thanksgiving. You would like to see your family, but you are worried that your aunt may be there, and you genuinely hate your aunt. If you stay in town you are hoping to stay with your roommate, but then again, there is some chance that she will leave town. The probability that your aunt shows up is 1/4, and the probability that your roommate leaves town is 1/3. The utility of celebrating Thanksgiving with your family without the aunt is 12 and with the aunt is minus two. The utility of staying in your dorm without your roommate is three and with the roommate is nine.

(a) Draw a decision tree.
(b) Calculate the expected utility of going home and of staying in town.
(c) What should you do?

One thing to note is that you cannot judge whether a decision was good or bad by examining the outcome alone. A good decision, in this framework, is a decision that maximizes expected utility. Such a decision might lead to adverse outcomes. But that just means that the decision-maker was unlucky, not necessarily that she made a bad decision in the first place.

Exercise 6.27 Pascal's wager   The French seventeenth-century mathematician and philosopher Blaise Pascal suggested the following argument for a belief in God. The argument is frequently referred to as **Pascal's wager**. Either God exists (G), or he does not (¬G). We have the choice between believing (B) or not believing (¬B). If God does not exist, it does not matter if we believe or not: the utility would be the same. If God does exist, however, it matters a great deal: if we do believe, we will enjoy eternal bliss; if we do not believe, we will burn in hell.

(a) Represent the decision problem in table form, making up suitable utilities as you go along.
(b) Let p denote the probability that G obtains. What is the expected utility of B and ¬B?
(c) What should you do?

Notice that it does not matter what p is. B **dominates** ¬B in the sense that B is associated with a higher expected utility no matter what.

Of course, Definition 6.20 can also be used to compute probabilities provided that we know enough about the expected utilities. So, for example, we can ask the following kinds of question.

Example 6.28 Umbrella problem, cont.   This question refers to Table 6.1(b), that is, the umbrella problem from Section 6.2. If the probability of rain is p, what does p need to be for the expected utility of taking the umbrella to equal the expected utility of leaving it at home?

To answer this problem, set up the following equation: EU (Take umbrella) = EU (Leave umbrella). Given the utilities in Table 6.1(b), this implies that $3 = p * 0 + (1 - p) * 5$, which implies that $p = 2/5$.

Exercise 6.29 Indifference   This question refers to Table 6.2. Let p denote the probability that S_1 obtains. (a) If an expected-utility maximizer is indifferent between A and B, what is his p? (b) If another expected-utility maximizer is indifferent between B and C, what is her p? (c) If a third expected-utility maximizer is indifferent between A and C, what is his p?

6.5   Attitudes toward risk

As you may have noticed already, expected-utility theory has implications for attitudes toward risk. Whether you reject a gamble (as in Example 6.21) or accept it (as in Exercise 6.22) depends, at least to some extent, on the shape of your utility function. This means that we can explain people's attitudes toward risk in terms of the character of their utility function.

The theory of expected utility can explain why people often reject a gamble in favor of a sure dollar amount equal to its expected value. We simply have to add to the theory of expected utility the auxiliary assumption of diminishing marginal utility of money.

Example 6.30 Risk aversion Suppose you own $2 and are offered a gamble giving you a 50 percent chance of winning a dollar and a 50 percent chance of losing a dollar. This decision problem can be represented as in Figure 6.8. Your utility function is $u(x) = \sqrt{x}$, so that marginal utility is diminishing. Should you take the gamble?

The problem can be represented as in Table 6.8. Expected-utility calculations show that you should reject the gamble, since $EU\,(\text{Accept}) = 1/2 * \sqrt{3} + 1/2 * \sqrt{1} \approx 1.37$ and $EU\,(\text{Reject}) = \sqrt{2} \approx 1.41$.

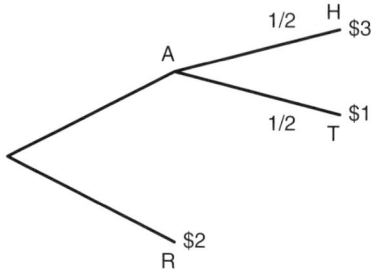

Figure 6.8 Risk aversion

Table 6.8 Another gambling problem

	Win (1/2)	Lose (1/2)
Accept (A)	$\sqrt{3}$	$\sqrt{1}$
Reject (R)	$\sqrt{2}$	$\sqrt{2}$

An expected-value maximizer would have been indifferent between accepting and rejecting this gamble, since both expected values are $2. Trivially, then, if your utility function is $u(x) = x$, you will be indifferent between the two options. For comparison, consider the following problem.

Exercise 6.31 Risk proneness Consider, again, the gamble in Figure 6.8. Now suppose that your utility function is $u(x) = x^2$. Unlike the previous utility function, which gets flatter when amounts increase, this utility function gets steeper. Compute the expected utilities of accepting and rejecting the gamble. What should you do?

As all these examples suggest, the shape of your utility function relates to your attitude toward risk – or your **risk preference** – in the following way. Whether you should reject or accept a gamble with an expected value of zero depends on whether your utility function gets flatter or steeper (bends downwards or upwards). In general, we say that you are **risk averse** if you would reject a gamble in favor of a sure dollar amount equal to its expected value, **risk prone** if you would accept, and **risk neutral** if you are indifferent. Thus, you are risk averse if your utility function bends downwards (as you move from left to right), risk prone if your utility function bends upwards, and risk neutral if your utility function is a straight line.

Notice that the theory itself does not specify what the shape of your utility function should be. Most of the time, economists will assume that utility for money is increasing, so that more money is better. But that is an auxiliary assumption, which is no part of the theory. The theory does not constrain your attitude toward risk; it does not even say that your attitude toward risk has to be the same when you get more (or less money). For instance, you may have a utility function that looks like the solid line in Figure 6.9. Here, you are risk prone in the range below x^* and risk averse in the range above x^*. Or, you may have a utility function that looks like the dashed line. Here, you are risk averse in the range below x^* and risk prone in the range above x^*. The next exercise illustrates the manner in which attitudes toward risk are expressed in a variety of real-world behaviors.

Exercise 6.32 Attitudes to risk As far as you can tell, are the following people *risk prone, risk averse*, or *risk neutral*?

(a) People who invest in the stock market rather than in savings accounts.
(b) People who invest in bonds rather than in stocks.
(c) People who buy lottery tickets rather than holding on to the cash.
(d) People who buy home insurance.
(e) People who play roulette.
(f) People who consistently maximize expected value.
(g) People who have unsafe sex.

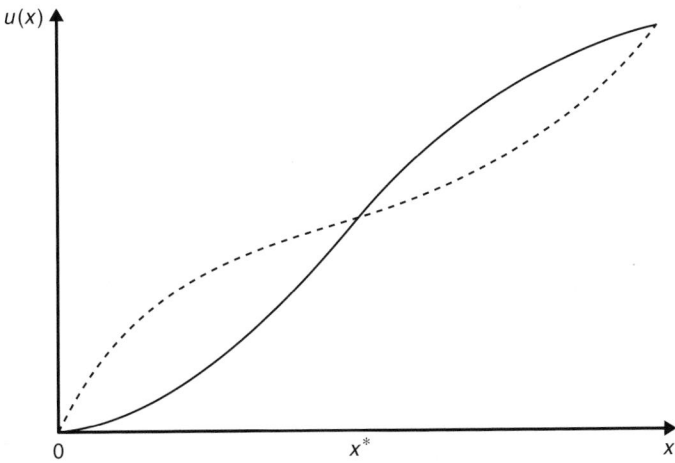

Figure 6.9 S-shaped utility functions

Sometimes it is useful to compute the **certainty equivalent** of a gamble. The certainty equivalent of a gamble is the amount of money such that you are indifferent between playing the gamble and receiving the amount for sure.

Definition 6.33 Certainty equivalent *The certainty equivalent of a gamble G is the number CE that satisfies this equation:* $u(CE) = EU(G)$.

The certainty equivalent represents *what the gamble is worth to you*. The certainty equivalent determines your willingness-to-pay (WTP) and your willingness-to-accept (WTA). In graphical terms, suppose that you have to find the certainty equivalent given a utility function like that in Figure 6.10. Suppose the gamble gives you a 50 percent chance of winning A and a 50 percent chance of winning B.

1. Put a dot on the utility curve right above A. This dot represents the utility of A (on the y-axis).
2. Put another dot on the utility curve right above B. This dot represents the utility of B (on the y-axis).
3. Draw a straight line between the two dots.
4. Put an X half way down the straight line. The X represents the expected utility of the gamble (on the y-axis) and the expected value of the gamble (on the x-axis).
5. Move sideways from the X until you hit the utility curve.
6. Move straight down to the x-axis, and you have the certainty equivalent (on the x-axis).

The procedure is illustrated in Figure 6.10. The same procedure can also be used for gambles where the probabilities are not 50–50. The only thing that changes is the placement of the X on the straight line in Figure 6.10. If there is, say a 3/7 probability of winning A, and a 4/7 probability of winning B, starting from the left, you put that dot four-sevenths of the way up from A to B. As the probability of winning B increases, the X will move right toward B and the expected utility of the gamble will approach the utility of B; as the probability of winning A increases, the X will move

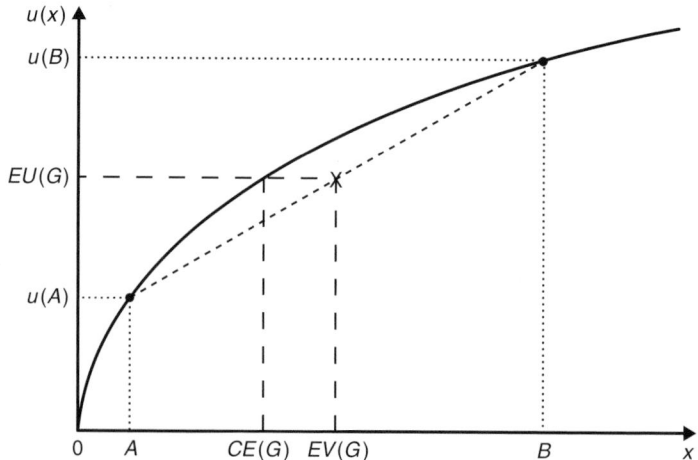

Figure 6.10 Finding the certainty equivalent

left toward A and the expected utility of the gamble will approach the utility of A. This makes sense.

Exercise 6.34 Certainty equivalents Demonstrate how to find the certainty equivalent of the same gamble in the case when the utility function bends upwards. Confirm that the certainty equivalent is greater than the expected value.

Remember: when the utility function bends downwards, you are risk averse, the dashed line falls below the utility function, and the certainty equivalent is less than the expected value. When the utility function bends upwards, you are risk prone, the dashed line falls above the utility function, and the certainty equivalent is greater than the expected value. Read this paragraph one more time to make sure you understand what is going on.

In algebraic terms, you get the certainty equivalent of a gamble by computing the expected utility x of the gamble, and then solving for $u\,(CE) = x$. Thus, you get the answer by computing $CE = u^{-1}(x)$. As long as $u(\cdot)$ is strictly increasing in money, which it ordinarily will be, the inverse function is well defined. Consider the gamble in Table 6.8. We know that the expected utility of this gamble is approximately 1.37. You get the certainty equivalent by solving for $u\,(CE) = 1.37$. Given our utility function $u(x) = \sqrt{x}$, this implies that $CE = 1.37^2 \approx 1.88$. Because you are risk averse, the certainty equivalent of the gamble is lower than the expected value of 2.

Example 6.35 St Petersburg paradox, cont. In Section 6.4 we learned that for an agent with utility function $u(x) = \log(x)$, the expected utility of the St Petersburg gamble is approximately 0.602. What is the certainty equivalent of the gamble?

We compute the certainty equivalent by solving the following equation: $\log\,(CE) = 0.602$. Thus, the certainty equivalent $CE = 10^{0.602} \approx 4.00$. That is, the St Petersburg gamble is worth $4.

Exercise 6.36 Compute the certainty equivalent of the gamble in Figure 6.8, using the utility function $u(x) = x^2$.

We end this section with a series of exercises.

Exercise 6.37 Suppose that you are offered the choice between $4 and the following gamble G: 1/4 probability of winning $9 and a 3/4 probability of winning $1.

(a) Suppose that your utility function is $u(x) = \sqrt{x}$. What is the utility of $4? What is the utility of G? What is the certainty equivalent? Which would you choose?
(b) Suppose instead that your utility function is $u(x) = x^2$. What is the utility of $4? What is the utility of G? What is the certainty equivalent? Which would you choose?

Exercise 6.38 Suppose that your utility function is $u(x) = \sqrt{x}$, and that you are offered a gamble which allows you to win $4 if you are lucky and $1 if you are not.

(a) Suppose, first, that the probability of winning $4 is 1/4 and the probability of winning $1 is 3/4. What is the expected value of this gamble?

(b) Suppose, that the probability of winning $4 is still 1/4 and the probability of winning $1 is 3/4. What is the expected utility of this gamble?

(c) Suppose, that the probability of winning $4 is still 1/4 and the probability of winning $1 is 3/4. What is the certainty equivalent of the gamble, that is, what is the amount of money X such that you are indifferent between receiving $X for sure and playing the gamble?

(d) Imagine now that the probability of winning $4 is p and the probability of winning $1 is $(1-p)$. If the utility of the gamble equals 3/2, what is p?

Exercise 6.39 Suppose that your utility function is $u(x) = \sqrt{x}$, and that you are offered a gamble which allows you to win $16 if you are lucky and $4 if you are not.

(a) Suppose, first, that the probability of winning $16 is 1/4 and the probability of winning $4 is 3/4. What is the expected utility of this gamble?

(b) Suppose, that the probability of winning $16 is still 1/4 and the probability of winning $4 is 3/4. What is the certainty equivalent of the gamble?

(c) Imagine now that the probability of winning $16 is p and the probability of winning $4 is $(1-p)$. If the expected utility of the gamble equals 9/4, what is p?

(d) Are you risk averse or risk prone, given the utility function above?

Exercise 6.40 Lotto 6/49, cont. Compute the certainty equivalent of the Lotto 6/49 ticket from Exercise 4.27 on page 70 if $u(x) = \sqrt{x}$.

6.6 Discussion

In this chapter, we have explored principles of rational choice under risk and uncertainty. As pointed out in the introduction to this chapter, according to the traditional perspective, you face a choice under uncertainty when probabilities are unknown or not even meaningful. In Section 6.2, we explored several principles of rational choice that may apply under such conditions. When it is both meaningful and possible to assign probabilities to the relevant states of the world, it becomes possible to compute expectations, which permits you to apply expected-value and expected-utility theory instead.

The distinction between risk and uncertainty is far from sharp. In real life, it may not be obvious whether to treat a decision as the one or the other. Consider the regulation of new and unstudied chemical substances. Though there are necessarily little hard data on such substances, there is always some probability that they will turn out to be toxic. Some people argue that this means that policy-makers are facing a choice under uncertainty, that the maximin criterion applies, and that new chemicals should be banned or heavily regulated until their safety can be established. Others argue that we can and must assign probabilities to all outcomes, that the probability that new substances will turn out to be truly dangerous is low, and that expected-utility calculations will favor permitting their use (unless or until their toxicity has been established). Whether we treat a decision as a choice under uncertainty or under risk, therefore, can have real consequences. And it is not obvious how to settle such issues in a non-arbitrary way. (We will return to this topic under the heading of ambiguous probabilities in Section 7.5.)

Our study of the theory of choice under risk sheds further light on the economic approach to behavior as understood by Gary Becker, and in particular on what he had in mind when talking about maximizing behavior (see Section 2.8). Recall (from Section 4.7) that the standard approach does not assume that people consciously or not perform calculations in their heads. Notice also that this approach does not assume that people are omniscient, in the sense that they know what state of the world will obtain. What it does assume is that people assign probabilities to states of the world, that these probabilities satisfy the axioms of the probability calculus, that people assign utilities to outcomes, and that they choose that alternative which has the greatest expected utility given the probabilities and utilities.

In the next chapter, we consider some conditions under which these assumptions appear to fail.

Additional exercises

Exercise 6.41 *Deal or No Deal*, cont.   You are on *Deal or No Deal* again, and you are facing three boxes. One of the three contains $1,000,000$, one contains 1000, and one contains 10. Now the dealer offers you $250,000$ if you give up your right to open the boxes.

(a) Assuming that you use expected value as your guide in life, would you choose the sure amount or the right to open the boxes?

(b) Assuming that your utility function $u(x) = \sqrt{x}$, and that you use expected utility as your guide in life, would you choose the sure amount or the right to open the boxes?

(c) Given the utility function, what is the lowest amount in exchange for which you would give up your right to open the boxes?

Exercise 6.42 The humiliation show   You are on a game show where people embarrass themselves in the hope of winning a new car. You are given the choice between pressing a blue button and pressing a red button.

(a) If you press the blue button, any one of two things can happen: with a probability of $2/3$, you win a live frog (utility –1), and with a probability of $1/3$ you win a bicycle (utility 11). Compute the expected utility of pressing the blue button.

(b) If you press the red button, any one of three things can happen: with a probability of $1/9$ you win the car (utility 283), with a probability of $3/9$ you win a decorative painting of a ballerina crying in the sunset (utility 1), and with a probability of $5/9$ you end up covered in green slime (utility –50). Compute the expected utility of pressing the red button.

(c) What should you do?

See also Exercise 7.19 on page 142.

Further reading

The classic definition and discussion of choice under uncertainty is Luce and Raiffa (1957, Ch. 13); Rawls (1971) defends Rawls's theory of justice and Harsanyi (1975) criticizes it. Helpful introductions to expected-utility theory include Allingham (2002) and Peterson (2009).

Chapter 7

Decision-Making under Risk and Uncertainty

Introduction

The theory of expected utility combines the concept of utility from Chapter 2 with the concept of probability from Chapter 4 into an elegant and powerful theory of choice under risk. The resulting theory, which we explored in the previous chapter, is widely used. Yet there are situations in which people fail to conform to the predictions of the theory. In addition, there are situations in which it is seemingly rational to violate it. In this section we explore some such situations. We will also continue to explore what behavioral economists do in the face of systematic deviations from standard theory. To capture the manner in which people actually make decisions under risk, we will make more assumptions about the value function, which we first came across in Section 3.5, and introduce the probability-weighting function. Both these functions are essentials parts of prospect theory, the most prominent behavioral theory of choice under risk.

Framing effects in decision-making under risk

For the next set of problems, suppose that you are a public health official.

Example 7.1 Asian disease problem 1 Imagine that the US is preparing for the outbreak of an unusual Asian disease, which is expected to kill 600 people. Two alternative programs to combat the disease have been proposed. Assume that the exact scientific estimate of the consequences of the programs are as follows: if Program A is adopted, 200 people will be saved; if Program B is adopted, there is 1/3 probability that 600 people will be saved, and a 2/3 probability that no one will be saved. Which of the two programs would you favor?

   When this problem was first presented to participants, 72 percent chose A and 28 percent chose B.

Example 7.2 Asian disease problem 2 Imagine that the US is preparing for the outbreak of an unusual Asian disease, which is expected to kill 600 people. Two alternative programs to combat the disease have been proposed. Assume that the exact scientific estimate of the consequences of the programs are as follows: if Program C is adopted 400 people will die; if Program D is adopted there is 1/3 probability that nobody will die, and 2/3 probability that 600 people will die. Which of the two programs would you favor?

   When this problem was first presented to participants, only 22 percent chose C and 78 percent chose D.

The observed response pattern is puzzling. Superficial differences aside, option A is the same as option C, and option B is the same as option D.

Before discussing what may be going on, let us briefly discuss why this response pattern is hard to reconcile with expected-utility theory. As we learned in the previous chapter, expected-utility theory does not by itself say whether you should choose the safe or the risky option: the theory does not specify what your risk preference should be. But the theory does say that your choice should reflect your utility function. What matters is whether the point marked X in Figure 7.1 falls above or below the utility function itself. If the X falls below the curve, you will choose the safe option. This will occur if your utility function is concave, like the curve marked A, and you are risk averse. If the X falls above the curve, you will choose the gamble. This will occur if your utility function is convex, like the curve marked B, and you are risk prone. If the X falls on the curve, you are indifferent between the two options. This will occur if your utility function is a straight line, like the dashed line in the figure. The point is that as long as you act in accordance with expected-utility theory, you will prefer the safe option no matter how it is described, or you will prefer the risky option no matter how it is described, or you will be indifferent between the two. Your preference should definitely not depend on how the options are described.

So how do we account for the behavior exhibited in the study above? The key is to notice that the behavior can be interpreted in terms of framing. As you will recall from Section 3.5, framing effects occur when preferences and behavior are responsive to the manner in which the options are described, and in particular to whether the options are described in terms of gains or in terms of losses. Options A and B are both framed in a positive way, in terms of the lives that might be saved; that is, they are presented in a gain frame. Options C and D are both framed in a negative way, in terms of the lives that might be lost; that is, they are presented in a loss frame.

The talk about gains versus losses may remind you of our acquaintance with the value function, which we used to model framing effects in Section 3.5. There, we learned that unlike the utility function, which ranges over *total* endowments, the value function ranges over *changes* in the endowment. We already know that many

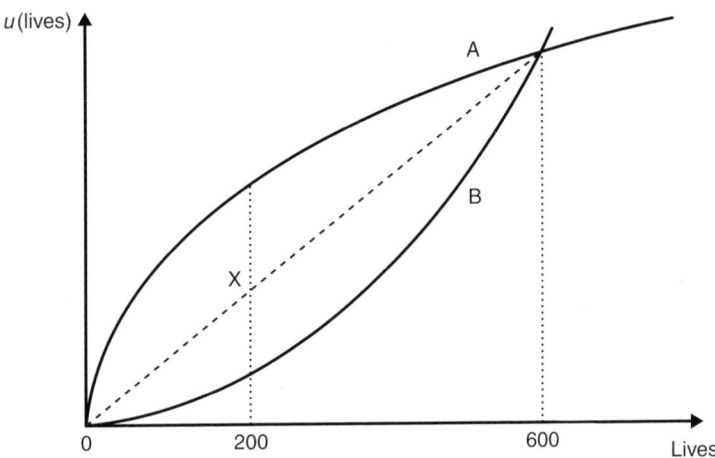

Figure 7.1 The utility of human lives

behavioral phenomena can be modeled by assuming a value function that is steeper for losses than for gains. Now we add the assumption that the value function has different curvatures for losses and for gains. In the realm of losses, we assume that the curve bends upwards (when moving from left to right), so that people are risk prone; in the realm of gains, we assume that the curve bends downwards, so that people are risk averse. In other words, the value function is convex in the realm of losses and concave in the realm of gains. This generates an S-shaped value function, as shown in Figure 7.2.

The curvature of the value function has interesting implications. For one thing, it entails that the absolute difference between $v(\pm0)$ and $v(+10)$ is greater than than the absolute difference between $v(+1000)$ and $v(+1010)$, and that this is true for losses as well as for gains. Consider the following classic example. There are two different versions of this question, one with the original numbers and one with the numbers in square brackets.

Example 7.3 Jacket/calculator problem Imagine that you are about to purchase a jacket for $125 [$15], and a calculator for $15 [$125]. The calculator salesman informs you that the calculator you wish to buy is on sale for $10 [$120] at the other branch of the store, located 20 minutes drive away. Would you make the trip to the other store?

In the original study, 68 percent of respondents were willing to make the drive to save $5 on the $10 calculator. Yet only 29 percent were willing to make the drive to save $5 on the $125.

The observed response pattern is inconsistent with standard theory, which entails that you should make your decision based on the opportunity cost of the 20-minute drive. The opportunity cost does not depend on how you saved the $5. And yet people seem to think of the $5 as more valuable when it is presented as a fraction of $15 than as a fraction of $125. The S-shaped value function can account for this kind of behavior.

We are now in a position to return to the Asian disease problem. The assumption that the value function is convex in the realm of losses and concave in the realm

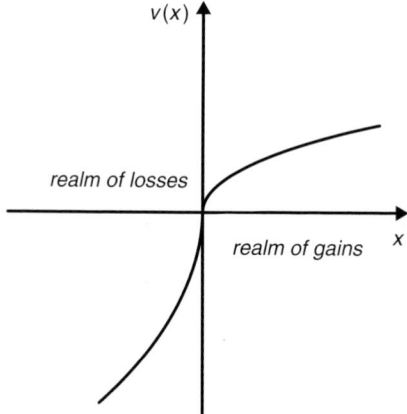

Figure 7.2 The value function

of gains helps account for the behavior of people facing this problem. The essential insight is that participants presented with the gain frame (as in Example 7.1) take their reference point to be the case in which no lives are saved (and 600 lost); participants presented with the loss frame (as in Example 7.2) take their reference point to be the case in which no lives are lost (and 600 saved). We can capture this in one graph by using two value functions to represent the fact that the two groups of participants use different outcomes as their reference point. In Figure 7.3, the concave value function on the top left belongs to people in the gain frame, while the convex value function on the bottom right belongs to people in the loss frame. As you can tell from the figure, people in the gain frame will prefer A to B, but people in the loss frame will prefer D to C.

Exercise 7.4 The ostrich farm   Jen and Joe have an ostrich farm. They have just learned that the farm has been struck by an unusual virus. According to their vet, if they do nothing only 200 of the 600 animals will live. However, the vet offers an experimental drug. If this drug is used, the vet says there is a 2/3 chance that all animals will die, but a 1/3 chance that all animals will live. Jen says: "The drug isn't worth it. It's better to save 200 animals for sure than risk saving none." Joe says: "I think we should use the drug. Even if it's risky, that's the only way we have a chance of losing no animals at all. Taking the risk is better than losing 400 animals for sure." Draw a graph explaining how the two can come to such different realizations even though they have value functions with the same shape.

The following example is another nice illustration of the phenomenon.

Example 7.5 Prospect evaluation   Consider the following two problems: (a) In addition to whatever you own, you have been given $1000. You are now asked to choose between (A) a 50 percent chance of winning $1000 and (B) winning $500 for sure. (b) In addition to whatever you own, you have been given $2000. You are now asked to choose between (C) a 50 percent chance of losing $1000 and (D) losing $500 for sure.

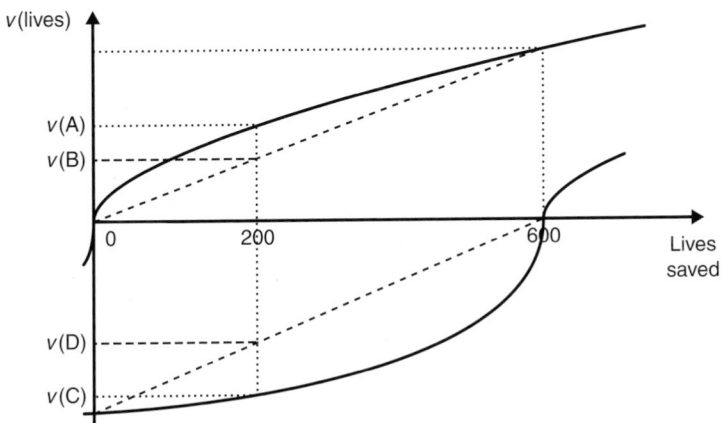

Figure 7.3   The value of human lives

In terms of final outcomes, (A) is obviously equivalent to (C) and (B) to (D). Yet 84 percent of participants chose B in the first problem, and 69 percent chose C in the second.

The difference between Example 7.5(a) and (b) is that in the former, outcomes are described in a gain frame, whereas in the latter, they are described in a loss frame. Consequently, in (a) the gamble represents an opportunity to win the big prize, whereas in (b) the gamble represents an opportunity to prevent a loss. To show how the observed response pattern might emerge we can analyze the problem algebraically.

Exercise 7.6 Prospect evaluation, cont.   This exercise refers to Example 7.5 on the previous page. Suppose that your value function $v(\cdot)$ is defined by:

$$v(x) = \begin{cases} \sqrt{x/2} & \text{for gains } (x \geq 0) \\ -2\sqrt{|x|} & \text{for losses } (x < 0) \end{cases}$$

By the way, $|x|$ is the absolute value of x: that is, x with the minus sign removed (if there is one).

(a) Draw the curve for values between -4 and $+4$. Confirm that it is concave in the domain of gains and convex in the domain of losses.
(b) Assuming that you have integrated the $1000 into your endowment, what is the value of (A)?
(c) Assuming that you have integrated the $1000 into your endowment, what is the value of (B)?
(d) Assuming that you have integrated the $2000 into your endowment, what is the value of (C)?
(e) Assuming that you have integrated the $2000 into your endowment, what is the value of (D)?

Notice how (B) turns out to be better than (A), but (C) better than (D).

The idea that people are risk averse in the domain of gains but risk prone in the domain of losses helps explain a range of phenomena. It can explain why some people are unable to stop gambling: once they find themselves in the red – which they will, soon enough, when playing games like roulette – they enter the domain of losses, where they are even more risk prone than they used to be. There is evidence that people betting on horses, etc., are more willing to bet on long shots at the end of the betting day. This phenomenon is often accounted for by saying that people who have already suffered losses are more prone to risk-seeking behavior. Analogously, the idea can explain why politicians continue to pursue failed projects and generals continue to fight losing wars: as initial efforts fail, the responsible parties enter the domain of losses, in which they are willing to bet on increasingly long shots and therefore take increasingly desperate measures. Here is another algebraic exercise.

Exercise 7.7   A person's value function is $v(x) = \sqrt{x/2}$ for gains and $v(x) = -2\sqrt{|x|}$ for losses. The person is facing the choice between a sure $2 and a 50–50 gamble that pays $4 if she wins and $0 if she loses.

(a) Show algebraically that this person is loss averse, in the sense that she suffers more when she loses $4 than she benefits when she receives $4.

(b) If the outcomes are coded as gains, meaning that she will take the worst possible outcome as her reference point, what is the value of (i) the sure amount and (ii) the gamble? Which would she prefer?

(c) If the outcomes are coded as losses, meaning that she will take the best possible outcome as her reference point, what is the value of (i) the sure amount and (ii) the gamble? Which would she prefer?

Framing effects should not be confused with wealth effects, which occur when people's risk aversion changes when they go from being poor to being rich (or the other way around), and which can be represented using a single utility function. It would be normal, for instance, if your curve got flatter and flatter as your wealth increased, thereby making you less risk averse. Not all the data can be easily accommodated in this framework, however; much of it is better explained by a value function that is convex in the realm of losses and concave in the realm of gains. In the following section, we discuss other applications of these ideas.

7.3 Bundling and mental accounting

The fact that the value function is concave in the domain of gains and convex in the domain of losses has other interesting implications, one being that it matters how outcomes are **bundled**. Suppose that you buy two lottery tickets at a charity event, and that you win $25 on the first and $50 on the second. There are different ways to think of what happened at the event (see Figure 7.4). You can **integrate** the outcomes, and tell yourself that you just won $75, which in value terms would translate into $v(+75)$. Or you can **segregate** the outcomes and tell yourself that you first won $25 and then won $50, which in value terms would translate into $v(+25) + v(+50)$. Bundling can be seen as an instance of framing: at stake is whether you frame the change as one larger gain or as two smaller gains.

According to the standard view, bundling should not matter. The utility function ranges over total endowments, and no matter how you describe the various outcomes you end up with an additional $75 dollars in your pocket. In utility terms, then, if you start off at $u(w)$, you will end up at $u(w + 25 + 50) = u(w + 75)$ either way.

According to prospect theory, however, bundling matters. Suppose that you start off with wealth w and that you take the status quo as your reference point. When the two gains are integrated, the value of winning $75 can be characterized as in Figure 7.5(a). However, when the two gains are segregated, the situation looks different. This is so because you have the time to adjust your reference point before assessing the value of the second gain. When the two gains are segregated, your picture will look more as in Figure 7.5(b), where the dashed line represents your value function relative to the new reference point. It should be clear just from looking at these two figures that the value of a $25 gain plus the value of a $50 gain is greater than the value of a $75 gain; that is, $v(+25) + v(+50) > v(+75)$. This result follows from the value function being concave in the domain of gains. The upshot is that people value two gains more when they are segregated than when they are integrated.

Figure 7.4 Integration vs. segregation of gains. Illustration by Cody Taylor

The fact that gains are valued more when segregated helps explain a variety of phenomena. For example, it explains why people do not put all their Christmas presents in one big box, even though that would save them time on wrapping: the practice of wrapping each present separately encourages the recipient to segregate the gains. The analysis also suggests that it is even better to give separate presents on separate nights, as on Hanukkah, rather than delivering all presents on Christmas, since this would do even more to encourage recipients to separate the gains. The analysis indicates that it is better to give people multiple small presents over the course of the year than to give them one big present once a year. While it is in good taste to give your spouse a present on your anniversary, you may wish to save some of the money and buy smaller presents during the rest of the year too. In addition, the effect of segregating gains explains why workers receive end-of-year bonuses: receiving a $50k salary plus a $5k bonus encourages the segregation of gains in a manner that receiving a $55k salary does not. Finally, the value of segregated gains explains why people on daytime television try to sell pots and pans by offering to throw in lids, knives, cutting boards, and so on, rather than simply offering a basket consisting of all these goods. Again, this practice encourages the segregation of the gains.

Exercise 7.8 Evaluation of gains Yesterday, you had a decent day: you first received a $48 tax refund, and then an old friend repaid a $27 loan you had forgotten about. Suppose that your value function $v(\cdot)$ is defined by:

$$v(x) = \begin{cases} \sqrt{x/3} & \text{for gains } (x \geq 0) \\ -3\sqrt{|x|} & \text{for losses } (x < 0) \end{cases}$$

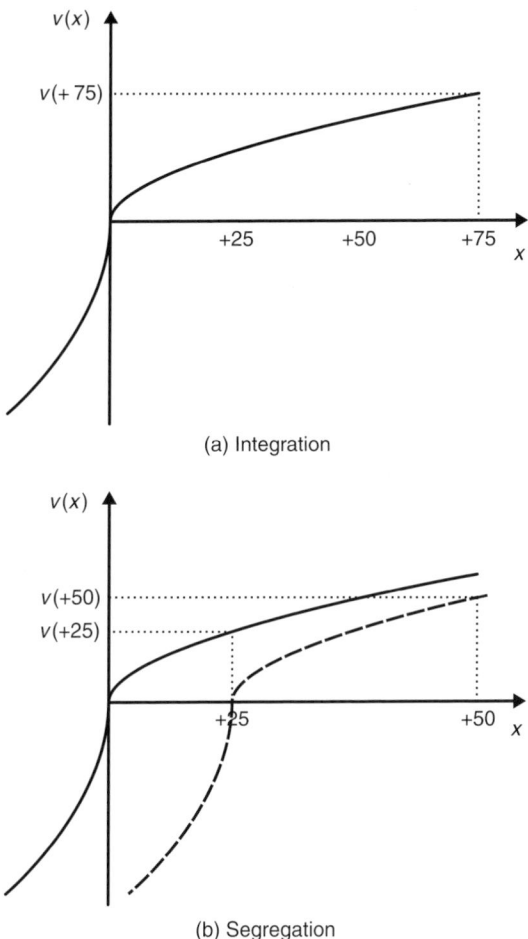

(a) Integration

(b) Segregation

Figure 7.5 Evaluation of two gains

(a) If you integrate the two gains, what is the total value?
(b) If you segregate the two gains, what is the total value?
(c) From the point of view of value, is it better to integrate or to segregate?

Meanwhile, people are less dissatisfied when multiple losses are integrated than when they are segregated. By constructing graphs like those in Figure 7.5, you can confirm that, from the point of view of value, a $25 loss plus an additional $50 loss is worse than a $75 loss; that is, $v(-25) + v(-50) < v(-75)$. This result follows from the fact that the value function is convex in the domain of losses. Notice that if you do purchase the pots and pans from daytime television, and get all the other stuff in the bargain, your credit card is likely to be charged only once, meaning that costs are integrated. This is no coincidence: by encouraging customers to integrate the losses while segregating the gains, marketers take maximum advantage of these effects.

The fact that people experience less dissatisfaction when losses are segregated helps explain a variety of phenomena. It explains why sellers of cars, homes, and other pricey goods often try to sell expensive add-ons. Although you may never pay $1000 for a car radio, when it is bundled with a $25,999 car it may not sound like very much: for reasons explored in the previous section, a loss of $26,999 might not seem that much worse than a loss of $25,999. By contrast, since they are entirely different quantities, you might find it easy to segregate the car from the radio, which would further encourage you to accept the offer. Similarly, the wedding industry makes good use of integration by adding options that individually do not seem very expensive relative to what the hosts are already spending, but which jointly can cause major financial distress. "If you're spending $3000 dollars on a dress, does it matter if you spend an additional $10 on each invitation?" The effects of integrating losses can also explain why so many people prefer to use credit cards rather than paying cash. When you use a credit card, though the monthly bill might be alarming, it only arrives once a month, thereby encouraging you to integrate the losses. By contrast, the satisfaction of receiving the things you buy is distributed throughout the month, thereby encouraging the segregation of gains.

This analysis might also explain why people hold on to cars even though taking cabs may be less expensive in the long run. The actual cost of owning a car for a month (including maintenance, car payments, insurance payments, gasoline, car washes, etc.) is so high that for many people it would make financial sense to sell the car and just hail cabs. The reason why people hesitate to do this (outside the major cities) may be related to the fact that car payments are made monthly or weekly, whereas taxi payments are made at the conclusion of every ride. Consequently, taxi companies could encourage more business by allowing people to run a tab and to pay it off once a month. The analysis can also explain why people prefer to pay a flat monthly fee for cell phone services, internet connections, and gym memberships: doing so permits them to integrate what would otherwise be many separate losses. The chances are you would not dream of joining a gym that charged you by the mile you ran on the treadmill. In part, this is for incentive-compatibility reasons: you do not want to join a gym that gives you a disincentive to exercise. But, in part, this may be because you wish to integrate the losses associated with your gym membership.

Exercise 7.9 Evaluation of losses   Yesterday, you had a terrible day: you got a $144 speeding ticket on your way to the opera, and then had to pay $25 for a ticket you thought would be free. Suppose your value function remains that of Exercise 7.8.

(a) If you integrate the two losses, what is the total value?
(b) If you segregate the two losses, what is the total value?
(c) From the point of view of value, is it better to integrate or to segregate?

Related phenomena occur when experiencing a large loss in combination with a small gain or a small gain in combination with a large loss. People gain more value when they integrate a small loss with a large gain. That way, the pain of the loss is not felt so intensely. This phenomenon is referred to as **cancellation**. Suppose that you win a million dollars, but have to pay a 10 percent tax on your winnings. The theory suggests that you will derive more value from telling yourself that you won $900,000 than by telling yourself that you won $1,000,000 and then lost $100,000.

Meanwhile, people gain more value when they segregate a large loss from a small gain. The small gain is often described as a **silver lining**. This analysis explains why some cars, apartments, and other big-ticket items sometimes come with cash-back offers. A customer may be more likely to buy a car with a $27k price tag and a $1k cash-back offer than to buy the very same car with a $26k price tag: the $1k gain, when segregated, helps offset the pain associated with the $27k loss. The analysis also explains why credit-card companies frequently offer more reward points the more you spend. Though the value of the reward points is small relative to monthly fees and charges, the company hopes that you will segregate and that the reward points therefore will serve to offset the larger loss. Finally, silver-lining phenomena may explain why rejection letters frequently include lines about how impressed the committee was with your submission or job application. The hope is that disingenuous flattery, when segregated, will to some extent offset the perceived loss of the publication or job.

Exercise 7.10 Silver linings   For this question, suppose your value function is $v(x) = \sqrt{x/2}$ for gains and $v(x) = -2\sqrt{|x|}$ for losses. Last night, you lost $9 in a bet. There was a silver lining, though: on your way home, you found $2 lying on the sidewalk.

(a) If you integrate the loss and the gain, what is the total value?
(b) If you segregate the loss and the gain, what is the total value?
(c) From the point of view of value, is it better to integrate or to segregate?

When do people integrate and when do they segregate? One possibility that might come to mind is that people bundle outcomes so as to maximize the amount of value that they experience. This is called the **hedonic-editing hypothesis**. According to this hypothesis, people will (1) segregate gains, (2) integrate losses, (3) cancel a small loss against a large gain, and (4) segregate a small gain from a large loss. Unfortunately, data suggest that the hypothesis is not in general true. In particular, it seems, people frequently fail to integrate subsequent losses. If you think about it, the failure the hedonic-editing hypothesis is unsurprising in light of the fact that we need parents, therapists, boyfriends, and girlfriends to remind us of how to think about things in order not to be needlessly unhappy.

Bundling may be driven in part by **mental accounting**: people's tendency, in their minds, to divide money into separate categories. Mental accounting might cause people to overconsume or underconsume particular kinds of goods: if the mental "entertainment account" is seen as having money left in it, but the mental "clothing account" is seen as overdrawn, people might spend more on entertainment even though they would maximize utility by buying clothes. But mental accounting might also affect the manner in which goods are bundled. For example, coding goods as belonging to the same category is likely to encourage integration, whereas coding goods as belonging to separate categories is likely to encourage segregation.

7.4   The Allais problem and the sure-thing principle

The following decision problem is called the **Allais problem**.

Example 7.11 Allais problem   Suppose that you face the following options, and that you must choose first between (1a) and (1b), and second between (2a) and (2b). What would you choose?

(1a) $1 million for sure
(1b)   An 89% chance of $1 million & a 10% chance of $5 million
(2a)   An 11% chance of $1 million
(2b)   A 10% chance of $5 million

A common response pattern here is (1a) and (2b). For the first pair, people may reason as follows: "Sure, $5 million is better than $1 million, but if I chose (1b) there would be some chance of winning nothing, and if that happened to me I would definitely regret not choosing the million dollars. So I'll go with (1a)." That is, a choice of (1a) over (1b) might be driven by regret aversion (see Section 6.2). For the second pair, people may reason in this way: "Certainly, an 11 percent chance of winning is better than a 10 percent chance of winning, but that difference is fairly small; meanwhile, 5 million dollars is a lot better than 1 million dollars, so I'll go with (2b)." For the second pair, the potential for regret is much less salient.

Unfortunately, this response pattern is inconsistent with expected-utility theory. To see this, consider what it means to prefer (1a) to (1b). It means that the expected utility of the former must be greater than the expected utility of the latter. Thus:

$$u\,(1M) > .89 * u\,(1M) + .10 * u\,(5M) \tag{7.1}$$

Preferring (2b) to (2a) means that the expected utility of the former must exceed the expected utility of the latter. Hence:

$$.10 * u\,(5M) > .11 * u\,(1M) \tag{7.2}$$

But because $.11 * u\,(1M) = (1 - .89) * u\,(1M) = u\,(1M) - .89 * u\,(1M)$, (7.2) is equivalent to

$$.10 * u\,(5M) > u\,(1M) - .89 * u\,(1M) \tag{7.3}$$

Rearranging the terms in (7.3), we get:

$$.89 * u\,(1M) + .10 * u\,(5M) > u\,(1M) \tag{7.4}$$

But (7.4) contradicts (7.1). So the choice pattern that we are analyzing is in fact inconsistent with expected-utility theory.

There is another way of seeing why the choice pattern is inconsistent with expected-utility theory. Suppose that you spin a roulette wheel with 100 slots: 89 black, 10 red, and 1 white. This permits us to represent the four options in table form, as in Table 7.1.

Table 7.1   The Allais problem

	Black (89%)	Red (10%)	White (1%)
(1a)	$1M	$1M	$1M
(1b)	$1M	$5M	$0
(2a)	$0	$1M	$1M
(2b)	$0	$5M	$0

Let us begin by considering the first decision problem: that between (1a) and (1b). The table reveals that when black occurs, it does not matter what you choose; you will get a million dollars either way. In this sense, the million dollars if black occurs is a **sure thing**. The expression $.89 * u$ (1M) appears in the calculation of the expected utility of (1a), of course, but because it also appears in the calculation of the expected utility of (1b), it should not affect the decision. Let us now consider the second decision problem. Again, the table reveals that when black occurs, you receive nothing no matter what you choose. So again, the $0 is a sure thing and should not affect the relative desirability of (2a) and (2b). Thus, what happens in the column marked "Black" should not affect your choices at all. Instead, your choices will be determined by what happens in the other two columns. But once you ignore the column marked "Black," (1a) is identical to (2a) and (1b) is identical to (2b): just compare the two shaded areas in Table 7.1. So if you strictly prefer (1a), you are rationally compelled to choose (2a); if you strictly prefer (1b), you are rationally compelled to choose (2b).

The **sure-thing principle** says that your decisions should not be influenced by sure things. As this discussion indicates, it is implicit in expected-utility theory. The next exercise that may help make the principle clearer.

Exercise 7.12 Sure-thing principle   Suppose that you face the options in Table 7.2 and that you must choose first between (1a) and (1b), and second between (2a) and (2b). What choice pattern is ruled out by the sure-thing principle?

As a normative principle, the sure-thing principle has its appeal, but it is not uncontroversial. Some people argue that violations of the sure-thing principle can be perfectly rational, and that there consequently is something wrong with expected-utility theory as a normative standard. Others insist that the sure-thing principle is a normatively correct principle. What is fairly clear, though, is that it is false as a description of actual behavior; people seem to violate it regularly and predictably. (We will return to this topic in the next section.)

One way to describe the Allais paradox is to say that people overweight outcomes that are certain, in the sense that they occur with a 100 percent probability. This tendency has been called the **certainty effect**. As suggested above, the certainty effect might result from regret aversion: whenever you forego a certain option for a risky one, there is some chance that you will experience regret. Thus, a desire to minimize anticipated regret would lead to the rejection of the option that is not certain.

The certainty effect is apparent in slightly different kinds of context as well, as the following example shows.

Table 7.2   Sure-thing principle

	X	Y	Z
(1a)	80	100	40
(1b)	40	100	80
(2a)	40	0	80
(2b)	80	0	40

Example 7.13 Certainty effect　Which of the following options do you prefer: (A) A sure win of $30; (B) 80 percent chance to win $45? Which of the following options do you prefer: (C) 25 percent chance to win $30; (D) 20 percent chance to win $45?

In this study, 78 percent of respondents favored A over B, yet 58 percent favored D over C.

The observed behavior pattern is an instance of the certainty effect, since a reduction from 100 percent to 25 percent makes a bigger difference to people than a reduction from 80 percent to 20 percent.

Exercise 7.14 Certainty effect, cont.　Show that it is a violation of expected-utility theory to choose (A) over (B) and (D) over (C) in Example 7.13. Notice that (C) and (D) can be obtained from (A) and (B) by dividing the probabilities by four.

Does the certainty effect appear in the real world? It might. In a study of 72 physicians attending a meeting of the California Medical Association, physicians were asked which treatment they would favor for a patient with a tumor, given the choice between a radical treatment such as extensive surgery (options A and C), which involves a greater chance of imminent death, and a moderate treatment such as radiation (options B and D). They were presented with the following options:

    A 80 percent chance of long life
          (20 percent chance of imminent death)
    B 100 percent probability of short life
          (0 percent chance of imminent death)
    C 20 percent chance of long life
          (80 percent chance of imminent death)
    D 25 percent chance of short life
          (75 percent chance of imminent death)

The certainty effect was plainly visible: in violation of expected-utility theory, 65 percent favored B over A, yet 68 percent favored C over D. The fact that medical doctors exhibit the same behavior patterns as other people should not surprise us. It might be helpful to know this, whether or not you are a medical doctor.

7.5　The Ellsberg problem and ambiguity aversion

The following decision problem is referred to as the **Ellsberg problem**. The problem is due to Daniel Ellsberg, a US military analyst otherwise famous for releasing the so-called Pentagon Papers. Ellsberg was the subject of the 2009 documentary *The Most Dangerous Man in America*.

Example 7.15 Ellsberg problem　Suppose that Dan shows you an urn with a total of 90 balls in it. There are three kinds of ball: red, black, and yellow. You know (from a trustworthy authority) that 30 are red, but you do not know how many

Table 7.3   Dan's urn

	Red	Black	Yellow
Number of balls in urn	30	60	

of the remaining 60 are black and how many are yellow: there could be anywhere from 0 black and 60 yellow to 60 black and 0 yellow. The composition of the urn is illustrated by Table 7.3.

Dan invites you to randomly draw a ball from the urn. He gives you the choice between two different gambles: (I) $100 if the ball is red, and (II) $100 dollars if the ball is black. Which one would you choose? Next, Dan gives you a choice between the following two gambles: (III) $100 if the ball is red or yellow, and (IV) $100 if the ball is black or yellow. Which one would you choose?

When faced with the Ellsberg problem, many people will choose (I) rather than (II), apparently because they know that the chances of winning are 1/3; if they choose the other option the chances of winning could be anywhere from 0 to 2/3. Meanwhile, many people will choose (IV) rather than (III), apparently because they know the chances of winning are 2/3; if they choose the other option the chances of winning could be anywhere from 1/3 to 1.

However, and perhaps unfortunately, the choice of (I) from the first pair of options and (IV) from the second pair violates the sure-thing principle introduced in the previous section. The violation may be clearer if we represent the problem as in Table 7.4, which shows the payoffs for all four gambles and the three different outcomes.

As the table shows, what happens when a yellow ball is drawn does not depend on your choices. Whether you choose (I) or (II) from the first pair, when a yellow ball is drawn you will get nothing either way. The $0 when a yellow ball is drawn is a sure thing. Whether you choose (III) or (IV) from the second pair, when a yellow ball is drawn you will get $100 either way. Again, the $100 is a sure thing. Thus, the sure-thing principle says that your choices should not depend on what happens when you draw a yellow ball. That is, your choice should not depend on what is going on in the last column of Table 7.4. Your choice must reflect your evaluation of what is going in the two columns to the left only. Ignoring the column marked "Yellow," however, you will see that (I) and (III) are identical, as are (II) and (IV): just compare the two shaded areas in the table. Hence, unless you are indifferent, you must either choose (I) and (III) or (II) and (IV).

Table 7.4   The Ellsberg problem

	Red (R)	Black (B)	Yellow (Y)
I	100	0	0
II	0	100	0
III	100	0	100
IV	0	100	100

There is another way of showing how the choice pattern (I) and (IV) is inconsistent with expected-utility theory. A strict preference for (I) over (II) entails that EU (I) $>$ EU (II), which means that:

$$\Pr(R) * u(100) + \Pr(B) * u(0) + \Pr(Y) * u(0) >$$
$$\Pr(R) * u(0) + \Pr(B) * u(100) + \Pr(Y) * u(0)$$

Meanwhile, a strict preference for (IV) over (III) entails that EU(IV) $> EU$(III), which means that:

$$\Pr(R) * u(0) + \Pr(B) * u(100) + \Pr(Y) * u(100) >$$
$$\Pr(R) * u(100) + \Pr(B) * u(0) + \Pr(Y) * u(100)$$

Let us assume that $u(0) = 0$ and that $u(100) = 1$, which is only to say that you prefer \$100 over nothing. If so, these two expressions imply that the following two conditions must simultaneously be satisfied:

$$\Pr(R) > \Pr(B)$$
$$\Pr(B) > \Pr(R)$$

But that is obviously impossible. So again, the choice pattern we have been talking about is inconsistent with expected-utility theory.

How do we explain the fact that people exhibit this inconsistency? The two rejected options – (II) and (III) – have something in common, namely, that the exact probability of winning is unclear. We say that these probabilities are **ambiguous**. By contrast, the favored options – (I) and (IV) – are not associated with ambiguous probabilities. The observed choices seem to reflect is an unwillingness to take on gambles with ambiguous probabilities. We refer to this phenomenon as **ambiguity aversion**. Some people have a greater tolerance for ambiguity than others, but any aversion to ambiguity is a violation of expected-utility theory. Insofar as people are in fact ambiguity averse, which they seem to be, expected-utility theory fails to capture their behavior. And insofar as it is rationally permissible to take ambiguity into account when making decisions, expected-utility theory does not capture the manner in which people should make decisions.

Exercise 7.16 Tennis You have been invited to bet on one of three tennis games. In game 1, two extraordinarily good tennis players are up against each other. In game 2, two extraordinarily poor tennis players are up against each other. In game 3, one very good and one very bad player are up against each other, but you do not know which is good and which is bad. As a result, as far as you are concerned, the probability that any given player will win is 50 percent. Suppose that you are ambiguity averse. Which of the three games would you be *least* likely to bet on? Why?

There is no principled reason why people cannot be **ambiguity prone** rather than ambiguity averse. In fact, evidence suggests that people's behavior in the face of ambiguous probabilities depends on the context. According to the **competence hypothesis**, for example, people are less averse to ambiguity in contexts where they consider themselves particularly knowledgeable. Thus, a football fan may be ambiguity averse in the Ellsberg case (where outcomes are completely random) but ambiguity prone when predicting the outcomes of football games (where he or she feels like an expert).

Even so, the Ellsberg paradox and ambiguity aversion have potentially vast implications. What they suggest is that people do not in general assign probabilities satisfying the axioms of the probability calculus to events with ambiguous probabilities. And in the real world, ambiguous probabilities are common. The probability of bankruptcies, oil spills, and nuclear meltdowns can be estimated, but, outside games of chance, some ambiguity almost always remains. Thus, it is highly likely that people's choices *do* reflect the fact that people are ambiguity averse – or prone, as the case may be. And perhaps choices *should* reflect the ambiguity of the probabilities too.

7.6 Probability weighting

The idea that the value function is concave in the domain of gains and convex in the domain of losses helps us to analyze a wide range of behaviors, as we saw in Sections 7.2 and 7.3. Yet there are widely observed behavior patterns that cannot be accommodated within this framework. Consider the fact that some people simultaneously gamble and purchase insurance. This is paradoxical from the point of view of expected-utility theory. If people are risk averse, they should buy insurance but not gamble; if they are risk prone, they should gamble but not buy insurance; and if they are risk neutral, they should do neither. It is theoretically possible that people have inverted-S-shaped utility functions, like the dashed line in Figure 6.9 on page 119, and that the inflection point (marked x^* in the figure) just happens to correspond to their present endowment. Yet it seems too much like a coincidence that this should be true for so many people.

Simultaneous gambling and insurance shopping is equally paradoxical from the point of view of the theory we have studied in this chapter so far. The fact that people are willing to accept a gamble in which they may win a large sum of money suggests that they are risk prone in the domain of gains, while the fact that they are willing to reject a gamble in which they may lose their house suggests that they are risk averse in the domain of losses. This would entail that their value function is convex in the domain of gains and concave in the domain of losses, which is the very opposite of what we have assumed to date. The only way to accommodate this behavior pattern within the framework above is to assume that people take the state when they win the grand prize as their reference point when gambling, and the state in which they lose things as their reference point when buying insurance. This seems artificial, however, in light of the other evidence that people otherwise frequently take their endowment as their reference point.

Another way to understand the observed behavior pattern is to think of those who gamble as well as those who buy insurance as prone to paying too much attention to unlikely events. The more weight you put on the probability of winning the lottery, the more likely you will be to gamble. And the more weight you put on the probability of losing your house, car, life, and limb, the more likely you will be to purchase insurance. This insight suggests a more systematic approach to explaining how people can simultaneously buy lottery tickets and insurance.

Prospect theory incorporates this kind of behavior by introducing the notion of **probability weighting**. We know from Definition 6.20 on page 115 that expected-utility theory says that the agent maximizes an expression of the following form:

$$EU(A_i) = \Pr(S_1) * u(C_{i1}) + \Pr(S_2) * u(C_{i2}) + \ldots + \Pr(S_n) * u(C_{in})$$

By contrast, prospect theory says that the agent maximizes an expression in which the value function $v(\cdot)$ is substituted for the utility function $u(\cdot)$, and in which probabilities are weighted by a **probability-weighting function** $\pi(\cdot)$.

Definition 7.17 Value   *Given a decision problem as in Table 6.4 on page 109, the value (or weighted value) $V(A_i)$ of an act A_i is given by:*

$$V(A_i) = \pi\left[\Pr(S_1)\right] * v(C_{i1}) + \pi\left[\Pr(S_2)\right] * v(C_{i2}) + \ldots + \pi\left[\Pr(S_n)\right] * v(C_{in})$$

$$= \sum_{j=1}^{n} \pi\left[\Pr(S_j)\right] v(C_{ij}).$$

The probability-weighting function $\pi(\cdot)$ assigns weights, from zero to one inclusive, to probabilities. It is assumed that $\pi(0) = 0$ and that $\pi(1) = 1$. But, as shown in Figure 7.6, for values strictly between zero and one, the curve does not coincide with the 45-degree line. For low probabilities, it is assumed that $\pi(x) > x$, and for moderate and high probabilities, that $\pi(x) < x$.

The probability-weighting function can help resolve the paradox that some people simultaneously buy lottery tickets and insurance policies. A well-informed expected-utility maximizer weights the utility of winning the grand prize by the probability of winning it, which as we know from Section 4.4 is low indeed. Thus, expected-utility theory says that such outcomes should not loom very large in our decision-making. Prospect theory makes a different prediction. Winning the lottery and losing house, car, life, and limb are positive- but low-probability events, so the probability-weighting function implies that they would loom relatively large. And when such events loom large, people are willing to purchase lottery tickets and insurance policies. This also explains why people purchase extended warranties on equipment such as computers, in spite of the fact that simple expected-value calculations suggest that for most people extended warranties are not a very good deal (see Exercise 6.18 on page 113).

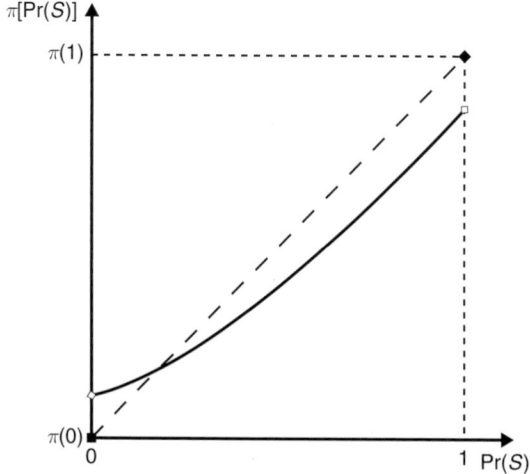

Figure 7.6   The probability-weighting function $\pi(\cdot)$

Table 7.5 Risk attitudes according to prospect theory

	Domain of losses	Domain of gains
Probability low	risk averse	risk prone
Probability moderate	risk prone	risk averse
Probability high	risk prone	risk averse

Example 7.18 Freakonomics The book *Freakonomics* discusses the economics of crack-cocaine. Contrary to what many people think, the vast majority of crack deal-ers make little money – frequently less than the federally mandated minimum wage. They stay in the job, according to the *Freakonomics* authors, because of a small chance of joining the upper stratum of the organization, in which an exclusive "board of directors" makes decent money.

Even so, this does only seem to be part of the explanation. The directors do not make astronomical amounts of money, the probability of joining their group is small, and the probability of getting shot or landing in jail is high. We can augment the explanation by adding that aspiring directors might overweight the low probability of rising through the ranks and joining the board of directors. This is what prospect theory would predict.

As the authors suggest, the same analysis might apply to aspiring models, actors, concert pianists, and CEOs. The probability of succeeding in any one of these endeavors is low, yet people continue to bet that they will be the one who does. Their aspirations may, in part, be driven by the fact that they overweight the probability of success.

The probability-weighting function can also account for the certainty effect: the tendency to overweight outcomes that are certain (see Section 7.4). As Figure 7.6 shows, there is a discontinuity at probabilities approaching one, so that as $x \to 1$, $\lim \pi(x) < \pi(1)$. Thus, events that are not certain (even when their probability is very high) will be underweighted relative to events that are certain.

The upshot is that people's behavior in the face of risk depends not just on whether outcomes are construed as gains or as losses relative to some reference point, but on whether or not the relevant probabilities are low. In the domain of losses, people tend to be risk prone, except for gambles involving a low-probability event of significant (negative) value, in which case they may be risk averse. In the domain of gains, people tend to be risk averse, except for gambles involving a low-probability event of significant (positive) value, in which case they may be risk prone. See Table 7.5 for a summary of these implications.

7.7 Discussion

In this chapter we have discussed situations in which people appear to violate the standard implicit in the theory of expected utility outlined in Chapter 6. The problem is not that people fail to maximize some mathematical utility function in their heads. Rather, the problem is that people's observed choices diverge from the predictions of the theory. Though the divergences are not universal, they are substantial, sys-tematic, and predictable, and they can have real, and sometimes adverse, effects on people's decision-making. Behavioral economists take the existence of divergences to undercut the descriptive adequacy of the theory of expected utility. Obviously, the chapter does not purport to offer a complete list of violations of expected-utility theory. We have also discussed situations where people's firmly held intuitions about the rational course of action differ from the recommendations of expected-utility theory, as in the presence of ambiguous probabilities. This raises deep issues about the nature of rationality.

We have also explored more theoretical tools developed by behavioral economists to capture the manner in which people actually make decisions. Among other things, we studied other components of prospect theory, including the S-shaped value function and the probability-weighting function. This concludes our review of prospect theory. These tools can be used not just to explain and predict but also to influence other people's evaluations. It appears that, under certain conditions, a person's risk preferences can be reversed simply by changing the frame of the relevant options. This gives behavioral economists more levers to use, which is obviously important for therapists, marketers, public health officials, and others who hope to affect people's behavior. But again, knowledge of the tools also permits us to anticipate and prevent other people from employing them.

In Part IV we will add another layer of complexity to the analysis, by introducing the topic of time.

Additional exercises

Exercise 7.19 Savings decisions   You are lucky enough to have million dollars in the bank. You have decided that there are only three serious investment options: putting it in your mattress, investing in stocks, and investing in bonds. Your utility function over total wealth is $u(x) = \sqrt{x}$. There is no inflation.

(a) If you stick your money in the mattress (where we can assume that it will be perfectly safe), how much utility will you have at the end of the year?

(b) Bonds are in general very dependable, but markets have been jittery as of late. You estimate that there is a 90 percent chance that you will gain 4 percent, but there is a 10 percent chance that you will gain nothing (zero percent). What is the expected utility of investing the $1,000,000 in bonds?

(c) Stocks have recently been extremely volatile. If you invest in stocks, there is a 40 percent chance that you will gain 21 percent, a 40 percent chance that you will gain nothing (zero percent), and a 20 percent chance that you will lose ten percent. What is the expected utility of investing the $1,000,000 in stocks?

(d) Given that you are an expected-utility maximizer, what is the sensible thing to do with your money?

(e) If, instead of maximizing expected utility, you were exceedingly loss averse, what would you do?

Exercise 7.20   Match each of the vignettes below with one of the following phenomena: *ambiguity aversion, cancellation, certainty effect, competence hypothesis, silver lining,* and *mental accounting*. If in doubt, pick the best fit.

(a) Abraham is seriously depressed after his girlfriend of several years leaves him for his best friend. His therapist tells him that every time a door closes, another one opens. Abraham thinks about all the other potential girlfriends out there and finally feels a little better.

Additional exercises cont'd

(b) Berit is trying to save money by limiting the amount of money she spends eating out. She tells herself she must never spend more than $100 each week in restaurants. It is Sunday night, and Berit realizes that she has spent no more than $60 eating out during the past week. She does not quite feel like going out, but tells herself that she must not miss the opportunity to have a $40 meal.

(c) Charles is not much of a gambler and rarely accepts bets. The difference is politics. He considers himself a true policy expert and is happy to accept bets when it comes to the outcome of local and national elections. His friends note that he still does not win the bets more than about half of the time.

(d) According to a common saying: "Better the devil you know than the devil you don't."

(e) Elissa very much wants to go to medical school, but cannot stand the thought of not knowing whether she will pass the rigorous curriculum. Instead, she decides to sign up for a less demanding physical therapy curriculum that she is confident that she can pass.

Problem 7.21 *Drawing on your own experience, make up stories like those in Exercise 7.20 to illustrate the various ideas that you have read about in this chapter.*

Further reading

Framing effects and probability weighting, which are part of prospect theory, are discussed in Kahneman and Tversky (1979); see also Tversky and Kahneman (1981), the source of the Asian disease problem (p. 453) and jacket/calculator problem (p. 457). The example from the original prospect-theory paper appears in Kahneman and Tversky (1979, p. 273), and the two examples of the certainty effect in Tversky and Kahneman (1986, pp. S266–9). Bundling and mental accounting are explored in Thaler (1980) and (1985) and hedonic editing in Thaler and Johnson (1990). The Allais problem is due to Allais (1953); the certainty effect is discussed in Tversky and Kahneman (1986). The Ellsberg problem is due to Ellsberg (1961); the competence hypothesis is due to Heath and Tversky (1991). *Freakonomics* is Levitt and Dubner (2005).

Part IV

Intertemporal Choice

Chapter 8
The Discounted Utility Model

Introduction

So far, we have treated decision problems as though all possible consequences of actions were instantaneous. That is, we have assumed that all relevant consequences occur more or less immediately, or at least at one and the same time. There are cases when this is a perfectly reasonable assumption. If you are playing roulette once and have preferences over money, for example, whatever happens will happen more or less at the same time.

Very often, however, time is a factor. When you decide whether to purchase the one-year warranty for your new tablet computer (see Exercise 6.18 on page 113), you are not only choosing between a sure option (investing in the warranty) and a risky option (foregoing the warranty), but you are also choosing between a certain loss now (since the warranty has to be paid for now) and the possibility of suffering a loss later (the possibility of having to pay to replace a broken tablet some time down the road).

It may be that most decisions have consequences that occur at different points in time. Some decisions have immediate benefits and deferred costs: procrastination, for example, is matter of favoring some immediate good (a dinner and movie with friends) over some a later benefit (a clean house). Other decisions have immediate costs and deferred benefits: savings behavior, for example, is a matter of favoring some later benefit (a comfortable retirement) over some immediate good (a new car). In this chapter and the next, we will talk about how to model decisions when time is a factor.

8.2 Interest rates

Before we begin the theory, let us talk about **interest**. Much of this should be familiar, but knowing how to think about interest is so useful that it justifies a review. Evidence from studies like that in Exercise 1.3 on page 8 indicates that many people have a limited grasp of how interest works.

Example 8.1 Interest   Suppose you borrow $100 for a year at an annual interest rate of 9 percent. At the end of the process, how much interest will you owe the lender?

The answer is $100 * 0.09 = $9.

Slightly more formally, let r be the interest rate, P the **principal** (that is, the amount you borrow), and I the interest. Then:

$$I = Pr \tag{8.1}$$

This formula can be used to evaluate credit-card offers. Table 8.1 was adapted from a website offering credit cards to people with bad credit. Given this information,

Table 8.1 Credit-card offers for customers with bad credit

Credit-card offer	APR	Fee
Silver Axxess Visa Card	19.92%	$48
Finance Gold MasterCard	13.75%	$250
Continental Platinum MasterCard	19.92%	$49
Gold Image Visa Card	17.75%	$36
Archer Gold American Express	19.75%	$99
Total Tribute American Express	18.25%	$150
Splendid Credit Eurocard	22.25%	$72

we can compute what it would cost to borrow a given amount by charging it to the card.

Example 8.2 Cost of credit Suppose you need to invest $1000 in a new car for one year. If you charge it to the Silver Axxess Visa Card, what is the total cost of the credit, taking into account the fact that you would be charged both interest and an annual fee?

Given that the Annual Percentage Rate (APR) $r = 19.92\% = 0.1992$, you can compute $I = Pr = \$1000 * 0.1992 = \$199.20$. The annual fee of $48. The total cost would be the interest (I) plus the annual fee: $\$199.20 + \$48 = \$247.20$.

Expressed as a fraction of the principal, this is almost 25 percent. And that is not the worst offer, as the next exercise will make clear.

Exercise 8.3 Cost of credit, cont. What would it cost to borrow $1000 for one year using one of the other credit cards in Table 8.1? What if you need $100 or $10, 000?

Fees and APRs fluctuate; never make decisions about credit cards without looking up the latest figures.

At the end of the year, the lender will want the principal back. In Example 8.1 above, the lender will expect the $100 principal as well as the $9 interest, for a total of $109. Let L be the **liability**, that is, the total amount you owe the lender at the end of the year. Then:

$$L = P + I \tag{8.2}$$

Substituting for I from (8.1) in (8.2), we get:

$$L = P + I = P + (Pr) = P(1 + r) \tag{8.3}$$

It is sometimes convenient to define R as one plus r:

$$R = 1 + r \tag{8.4}$$

Together, (8.3) and (8.4) imply that:

$$L = PR \tag{8.5}$$

Returning to Example 8.1, we can use this formula to compute the liability: $L = \$100 *$ $(1 + 0.09) = \$109$, as expected. These formulas can also be used to compute interest rates given the liability and the principal.

Example 8.4 Implicit interest Suppose that somebody offers to lend you $105 on condition that you pay them back $115 one year later. What is the interest rate (r) implicit in this offer?

We know that $P = \$105$ and $L = \$115$. (8.5) implies that $R = L/P = \$115/\$105 = 1.095$. By (8.4), $r = R - 1 = 1.095 - 1 = 0.095$. Thus, the potential lender is implicitly offering you a loan at an annual interest rate of 9.5 percent.

Exercise 8.5 Payday loans Payday loan establishments offer short-term loans to be repaid on the borrower's next payday. Fees fluctuate, but such an establishment may offer you $400 on the 15th of the month, provided you repay $480 two weeks later. Over the course of the two weeks, what is the interest rate (r) implicit in this offer?

In some US states, the number of payday loan establishments exceeds the number of Starbucks and McDonald's locations combined. The answer to Exercise 8.5 suggests why. (See also Exercise 8.9.)

We can extend the analysis over longer periods of time. Broadly speaking, there are two kinds of scenario that merit our attention. Here is the first:

Example 8.6 Simple interest Imagine that you use a credit card to borrow $100, and that every month the credit-card company will charge you an interest rate of 18 percent of the principal. Every month, you pay only interest, but you pay it off in full. At the end of the year, you also repay the $100 principal. What is the total interest over the course of a year, expressed both in dollars and as a fraction of the principal?

Every month, by (8.1), you have to pay the credit-card company $I = Pr = \$100 *$ $0.18 = \$18$ in interest. Because you have to do this 12 times, the total interest will amount to $\$18 * 12 = \$216$. As a fraction of the $100 principal, this equals $\$216/\$100 = 2.16 = 216$ percent.

This is a case of **simple interest**. You can get the same figure by multiplying 18 percent by 12. Here is the other kind of case.

Example 8.7 Compound interest Imagine, again, that you use a credit card to borrow $100 and that the monthly interest rate is 18 percent. In contrast to the previous example, however, you do not make monthly interest payments. Instead, every month your interest is added to the principal. What is the total interest over the course of a year, expressed both in dollars and as a fraction of the principal?

At the conclusion of the first month, by (8.3) given that $r = 0.18$, you will owe $L = P(1 + r) = \$100 * 1.18 = \$118$. At the conclusion of the second month, your liability will be $L = \$118 * 1.18 = \$139.24$. Notice that you could have gotten the same answer by computing $L = \$100 * 1.18 * 1.18 = \$100 * 1.18^2$. At the conclusion of the third month, your liability will be $L = \$100 * 1.18 * 1.18 * 1.18 = \$100 * 1.18^3 \approx 164.30$. At the conclusion of the 12th month, your liability will be $L = \$100 * 1.18^{12} \approx \$728.76$. The liability at the end of the year includes the $100 principal, so your interest payments, by (8.2), only add up to $I = L - P \approx \$728.76 - \$100 = \$628.76$. As a fraction of the principal, this equals $\$628.76/\$100 = 6.2876 = 628.76$ percent.

The answer to Example 8.7 is so much higher than the answer to Example 8.6 because the former involves **compound interest**. Unlike the case of simple interest, here the interest accumulated during the first period is added to the principal, so that you will end up paying interest on the interest accumulated during previous periods. Notice that in cases of compound interest, you cannot simply multiply the interest accumulated during the first period by the number of periods, as we did in the case of simple interest. Instead, with compound interest your liability after t periods is computed as:

$$L = PR^t \qquad (8.6)$$

This formula gives us the answer to part (c) of Exercise 1.3 on page 8, by the way: $\$200 * (1 + 0.10)^2 = \$242$.

Albert Einstein is sometimes quoted as having said that compound interest is one of the most powerful forces in the universe. This would have been a wonderful quote, had he actually said it, which there is no evidence that he did. Even so, you can get the power of compounding to work in your favor by saving your money and allowing the interest to accumulate.

Exercise 8.8 Savings Suppose that you put \$100 into a savings account today and that your bank promises a 5 percent annual interest rate. (a) What will your bank's liability be after 1 year? (b) After 10 years? (c) After 50 years?

Finally, let us return to the payday loan establishments.

Exercise 8.9 Payday loans, cont. Imagine that you borrow \$61 from a payday loan establishment. After one week, it wants the principal plus 10 percent interest back. But you will not have that kind of money; so, instead, you go to another establishment and borrow the money you owe the first one. You do this for one year. Interest rates do not change from one establishment to another, or from one week to another.

(a) How much money will you owe at the end of the year?
(b) What is the total amount of interest that you will owe at the end of the year, in dollar terms?
(c) What is the total amount of interest that you will owe at the end of the year, expressed as a fraction of the principal?
(d) What does this tell you about the wisdom of taking out payday loans?

Payday loan establishments have generated controversy, with some state legislatures capping the interest rates they may charge. Such controversy is not new. For much of the Christian tradition, it was considered a crime against nature to charge interest on loans, that is, to engage in **usury**. According to Dante's *Divina Commedia*, usurers are condemned to eternal suffering in the seventh circle of hell, in the company of blasphemers and sodomites; you know where Dante would have expected to find payday loan officers. On the other hand, payday loan establishments provide a service that (rational and well-informed) people may have reason to demand. Parents may be willing to pay a premium to have money for Christmas presents at Christmas rather than in January, for example.

Either way, as these exercises show, knowing the basics about interest rates can be enormously useful. Now, let us return the theory of decision.

8.3 Exponential discounting

Which is better, $100 today or $100 tomorrow? $1000 today or $1000 next year? The chances are you prefer your money today. There are exceptions – and we will discuss some of these in the next chapter – but typically people prefer money sooner rather than later. This is not to say that tomorrow you will enjoy a dollar any less than you would today. But it is to say that, *from the point of view of today,* the utility of a dollar today is greater than the utility of a dollar tomorrow.

There are many reasons why you might feel this way. The earlier you get your money, the more options will be available to you: some options may only be available for a limited period, and you can always save your money and go for a later option. In addition, the earlier you get your money, the longer you can save it, and the more interest you can earn. Whatever the reason, when things that happen in the future do not give you as much utility, from the point of view of today, as things that happen today, we say that you **discount the future**. The general term is **time discounting**. The extent to which you discount the future will be treated as a matter of personal preference, specifically, what we call **time preference**.

There is a neat model that captures the basic idea that people prefer their money sooner rather than later: the model of **exponential discounting**. Suppose that $u > 0$ is the utility you derive from receiving a dollar today. From your current point of view, as we established, the utility of receiving a dollar tomorrow is less than u. We capture this by multiplying the utility of receiving a dollar now by some fraction. We will use the Greek letter delta (δ) to denote this fraction, which we call the **discount factor**. Thus, from your current point of view, a dollar tomorrow is worth $\delta * u = \delta u$. As long as $0 < \delta < 1$, as we generally assume, this means that $\delta u < u$. Hence, today you will prefer a dollar today to a dollar tomorrow, as expected. From the point of view of today, a dollar the day after tomorrow will be worth $\delta * \delta * u = \delta^2 u$. Because $\delta^2 u < \delta u$, today you prefer a dollar tomorrow to a dollar the day after tomorrow, again as expected.

In general, we want to be able to evaluate a whole sequence of utilities, that is, a **utility stream**. Letting t represent time, we will use $t = 0$ to represent today, $t = 1$ to represent tomorrow, and so on. Meanwhile, we let u_t denote the utility you receive at time t, so that u_0 represents the utility you receive today, u_1 represents the utility you receive tomorrow, and so on. We write $U^t(\mathbf{u})$ to denote the utility of stream $\mathbf{u}$ from time t. The number we seek is the utility $U^0(\mathbf{u})$ of the entire utility stream $\mathbf{u} = \langle u_0, u_1, u_2, \ldots \rangle$.

Definition 8.10 The delta function *According to the **delta function**, the utility $U^0(\mathbf{u})$ of utility stream $\mathbf{u} = \langle u_0, u_1, u_2, \ldots \rangle$ from the point of view of $t = 0$ is:*

$$U^0(\mathbf{u}) = u_0 + \delta u_1 + \delta^2 u_2 + \delta^3 u_3 + \ldots$$

$$= u_0 + \sum_{i=1}^{\infty} \delta^i u_i$$

Table 8.2 Simple time-discounting problem

	$t=0$	$t=1$	$t=2$
a	1		
b		3	
c			4
d	1	3	4

Thus, you evaluate different utility streams by adding the utility you would receive now, δ times the utility you would receive the next round, δ^2 times the utility you would receive in the round after that, and so on. The resulting model is called the **delta model**.

Utility streams can be represented in table form, as in Table 8.2. An empty cell means that the utility received at that time is zero. In order to compute the utility from the point of view of time zero, or any other point in time, you just need to know the discount factor δ. As soon as we are given the discount factor, we can use Definition 8.10 to determine which option you should choose.

Example 8.11 Exponential discounting Suppose that $\delta = 0.9$, and that each utility stream is evaluated from $t = 0$. If so, $U^0(\mathbf{a}) = u_0 = 1$, $U^0(\mathbf{b}) = \delta u_1 = 0.9 * 3 = 2.7$, $U^0(\mathbf{c}) = \delta^2 u_2 = 0.9^2 * 4 = 3.24$, and $U^0(\mathbf{d}) = u_0 + \delta u_1 + \delta^2 u_2 = 1 + 2.7 + 3.24 = 6.94$. Hence, if given the choice between all four alternatives, you would choose **d**. If given the choice between **a**, **b**, and **c**, you would choose **c**.

Exercise 8.12 Exponential discounting, cont. Suppose instead that $\delta = 0.1$. (a) Compute the utility of each of the four utility streams from the point of view of $t = 0$. (b) What would you choose if given the choice between all four? (c) What if you had to choose between **a**, **b**, and **c**?

As these calculations show, your discount factor can have a dramatic impact on your choices. If your discount factor is high (that is, close to one) what happens in future periods matters a great deal. That is to say that you exhibit **patience**: you do not discount your future very much. If your discount factor is low (that is, close to zero) what happens in the future matters little. That is to say that you exhibit **impatience**: you discount your future heavily. It should be clear how the value of δ captures your time preference.

Economists believe discount factors can be used to explain a great deal of behavior. If your discount factor is low, you are more likely to spend money, procrastinate, do drugs, and have unsafe sex. If your discount factor is high, you are more likely to save money, plan for the future, say no to drugs, and use protection. Notice that this line of thought makes all these behaviors at least potentially rational. For somebody who discounts the future enough, there is nothing irrational about nurturing a crack-cocaine habit. In fact, Gary Becker (whom we came across in Section 2.8) is famous, among other things, for defending a theory of **rational addiction**.

Exercise 8.13 Discount factors For each of the following, identify whether the person's δ is likely to be high (as in close to one) or low (as in close to zero):

(a) A person who raids his trust fund to purchase a convertible.
(b) A person who enrolls in a MD/PhD program.
(c) A person who religiously applies sunscreen before leaving the house.
(d) A person who skips her morning classes to go rock climbing.
(e) The Iroquois Native American who requires that every deliberation must consider the impact on the seventh generation.

Discounting can usefully be represented graphically. We put time on the x-axis and utility on the y-axis. A bar of height u at time t represents a reward worth u utiles to you when you get it at time t. A curve represents how much receiving the reward at t is worth to you from the point of view of times before t. As we know from Definition 8.10, that is δu at $t - 1$, $\delta^2 u$ at $t - 2$, and so on. As a result, we end up with a picture like Figure 8.1. As you move to the left from t, the reward becomes increasingly distant, and therefore becomes worth less and less to you in terms of utility.

We can use this graphical device to represent the difference between people with high and low δ's. If δ is high, δu will not differ much from u, and the curve will be relatively flat: it will only approach the x-axis slowly as you move to the left in the diagram, like the dashed curve in Figure 8.1. If δ is low, δu will be much lower than u, and the curve will be relatively steep: it will approach the x-axis quickly as you move to the left in the diagram, like the dot-dashed curve in the figure. Again, if δ is high, the person does not discount the future very much, and the curve is flat; if δ is low, the person does discount the future a great deal, and the curve is steep.

So far, we have used our knowledge of δ to determine a person's preferences over utility streams. Definition 8.10 also permits us to go the other way, as it were. Knowing the person's preferences over utility streams, we can determine the value of her discount factor.

Example 8.14 Indifference Suppose that Alexandra, at time zero, is indifferent between utility streams **a** (2 utiles at $t = 0$) and **b** (6 utiles at $t = 1$). What is her discount factor δ?

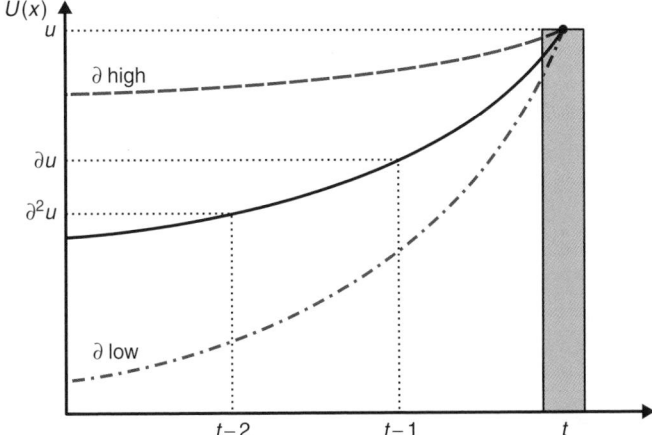

Figure 8.1 Exponential discounting

Given that Alexandra is indifferent between **a** and **b** at time zero, we know that $U^0(\mathbf{a}) = U^0(\mathbf{b})$, which implies that $2 = 6\delta$ which is to say that $\delta = 2/6 = 1/3$.

When experimental economists study time discounting in the laboratory, they rely heavily on this kind of calculation. As soon as a laboratory subject is indifferent between an immediate and a delayed reward, his or her discount factor can easily be estimated.

Indifference can be represented graphically as in Figure 8.1. Graphically, indifference between options **a** and **b** in Example 8.14 means that the picture would look like Figure 8.2. It can easily be ascertained that a strict preference for **a** over **b** would imply that $\delta < 1/3$ and that a strict preference for **b** over **a** would imply that $\delta > 1/3$.

Exercise 8.15 Use Figure 8.2 to answer the following questions: (a) If $\delta < 1/3$, what would the curve look like? (b) What if $\delta > 1/3$?

Exercise 8.16 This exercise refers to the utility streams in Table 8.2. For each of the following people, compute δ.

(a) At $t = 0$, Ahmed is indifferent between utility streams **a** and **b**.
(b) At $t = 0$, Bella is indifferent between utility streams **b** and **c**.
(c) At $t = 0$, Cathy is indifferent between utility streams **a** and **c**.
(d) At $t = 1$, Darrence is indifferent between utility streams **b** and **c**.

Exercise 8.17 For each of the three decision problems in Table 8.3, compute δ on the assumption that a person is indifferent between **a** and **b** at time zero.

All the decision problems we have encountered so far in this chapter were defined by matrices of utilities. Very often, however, the relevant outcomes are given in dollars, lives saved, or the like. Given the appropriate utility function, however, we know how to deal with those problems too.

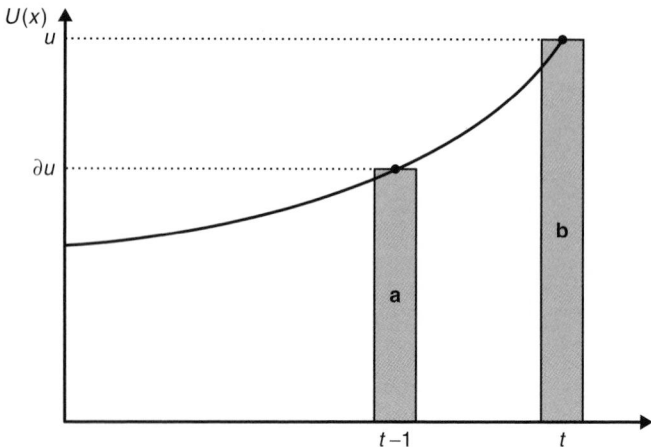

Figure 8.2 Exponential discounting with indifference

Table 8.3 Time-discounting problems

	$t=0$	$t=1$
a	3	4
b	5	1

(a)

	$t=0$	$t=1$	$t=2$		$t=0$	$t=1$	$t=2$
a		6	1	a	1		1
b		3	4	b			5

(b)   (c)

Example 8.18 Suppose you are indifferent between utility streams **a** and **b** in Table 8.4(a). Your utility function is $u(x) = \sqrt{x}$. What is your δ?

Given the utility function, Table 8.4(a) can be converted into a matrix of utilities as in Table 8.4(b). We can compute δ by setting up the following equation: $3 + \delta 2 = 1 + \delta 5$. Or we can simply set up the following equation: $\sqrt{9} + \delta\sqrt{4} = \sqrt{1} + \delta\sqrt{25}$. Either way, the answer is $\delta = 2/3$.

Exercise 8.19 Suppose instead that the utility function is $u(x) = x^2$. What would Table 8.4(b) look like, and what would δ be?

Table 8.4 Time-discounting problem (in dollars and utiles)

	$t=0$	$t=1$		$t=0$	$t=1$
a	$9	$4	a	3	2
b	$1	$25	b	1	5

(a) In dollar terms   (b) In utility terms

Discount rates

Sometimes discounting is expressed in terms of a **discount rate** r rather than a discount factor δ. The conversion is easy:

$$r = \frac{1 - \delta}{\delta}.$$

You can confirm that when $\delta = 1$, $r = 0$ and that as δ approaches zero, r increases. Knowing r, you can compute δ as follows:

$$\delta = \frac{1}{1 + r}.$$

In this text, I favor discount rates over discount factors. But it is useful to know what both are.

8.4   Discussion

In this chapter we have explored exponential discounting. The model of exponential discounting has a remarkable feature in that it is the only model of discounting that entails time consistency. Consistency is an important topic in intertemporal decision-making, and we will return to it in Section 9.2. Though relatively simple, exponential discounting offers an extraordinarily powerful model. For this reason, it is critical to a variety of fields, including in cost–benefit analysis, to assess the costs and benefits of deferred outcomes, and, in finance, to determine the present value of alternative investments. While the model might seem intuitively appealing and uncontroversial from both a descriptive and a normative perspective, as the next chapter will show, it is anything but.

As is common practice these days, I have treated the value of δ (and r) as a matter of personal preference. Yet historically, time discounting (with $\delta < 1$ and $r > 0$) has been thought to arise from intellectual or moral deficiency. The economist A. C. Pigou, commonly considered the father of welfare economics, wrote that "this preference for present pleasures ... implies only that our telescopic faculty is defective, and that we, therefore, see future pleasures, as it were, on a diminished scale." The philosopher Frank P. Ramsey, who made path-breaking contributions to philosophy, statistics, and economics – his theory of saving is still taught in graduate-level macroeconomics courses – before dying at the age of 26, called time discounting "a practice which is ethically indefensible and arises merely from the weakness of the imagination."

More recently, the topic has come up in the discussion of climate change. On the assumption that taking action to prevent or mitigate the negative consequences of climate change would be costly in the short term but (at least potentially) beneficial in the long term, cost–benefit analysis with a high enough δ will favor taking action, but cost–benefit analysis with a low enough δ will favor not taking action. Thus, the rationality of taking action to prevent or mitigate the effects of climate change depends on the value of δ – and there is no agreement whatsoever about the appropriate value of the parameter.

In the next chapter, we will discuss to what extent the exponential model of time discounting captures the manner in which people make decisions and whether it is appropriate as a normative standard.

Additional exercises

Exercise 8.20 Time discounting and interest rates   Whether you should spend or save will depend not just on your time preference, but on the interest you can get when putting your money in a savings account. Suppose you have the option of spending $\$w$ now or saving it until next year. If you save it, the bank will pay you interest rate i.

(a) Suppose that your utility function is $u(x) = x$. What does your discount factor δ need to be for you to be indifferent between spending it now and saving it? What about your discount rate r (see text box on the previous page)?

(b) Suppose that your utility function is $u(x) = \sqrt{x}$. What does your discount factor δ need to be for you to be indifferent between spending it now and saving it? What about your discount rate r?

Further reading

Mas-Colell et al. (1995, Chapter 20) contains a more advanced discussion of intertemporal utility. The battle over payday loan establishments is covered by *the Wall Street Journal* (Anand, 2008). Pigou (1952 [1920], p. 25) discusses our flawed telescopic faculty and Ramsey (1928, p. 543) our weakness of imagination.

Chapter 9

Intertemporal Choice

9.1 Introduction

As the many examples in the previous chapter suggest, the model of exponential discounting can be used to accommodate a variety of behavior patterns. For this reason, and because of its mathematical tractability, the model is heavily relied upon in a variety of disciplines. Yet it fails to capture some of the things people do. In this chapter we focus on two phenomena that are not easily described in using the standard model. One is that people are time inconsistent; that is, their preferences appear to change for no reason other than the passing of time, as when a drug addict who woke up in the morning completely determined to clean up his act gives in and takes more drugs in the afternoon. Because people sometimes anticipate time-inconsistent behavior, they *choose not to choose*; that is, they take action intended to prevent themselves from taking action. Another phenomenon is the fact that people seem to have preferences over utility profiles; that is, they care about the shape of their utility stream, and not just about the (discounted) individual utilities. We will also study how behavioral economists go about capturing these phenomena. Time inconsistency will be captured by means of a model of hyperbolic discounting, a highly versatile model. We will see that the model of hyperbolic discounting does a good job of capturing time inconsistency, but that it is inadequate to account for preferences over profiles.

9.2 Hyperbolic discounting

As we saw in the previous chapter, the exponential discounting model can capture a great deal of behavior, including – perhaps surprisingly – forms of addiction. Yet the image of the rational addict does not sit well with observed behavior and first-person reports of many addicts. As the beat poet William S. Burroughs writes in the prologue to his autobiographical novel *Junky*:

> The question is frequently asked: Why does a man become a drug addict? The answer is that he usually does not intend to become an addict. You don't wake up one morning and decide to be a drug addict...One morning you wake up sick and you're an addict.

Later in this chapter, we will discuss other behaviors that are hard to reconcile with the model of exponential discounting.

Exponential discounting implies the agent's behavior is **time consistent**, meaning that his or her preferences over two options do not change simply because time passes. If you are time consistent and feel (today) that **a** is better than **b**, then you felt the same way about **a** and **b** yesterday, and you will feel the same way about them tomorrow.

It is relatively easy to prove that anybody who discounts the future exponentially will be time consistent. But first we will need to review some notation. We continue to let $U^t(\mathbf{a})$ denote the utility from the point of view of time t of receiving some utility stream $\mathbf{a}$. Let u_t refer to the utility received at time t. Then, $U^t(u_{t'})$

Figure 9.1 Time inconsistency. Illustration by Cody Taylor

refers to the utility, from the point of view of t, of receiving $u_{t'}$ at time t'. As an example, if $u_{tomorrow}$ refers to the utility you will receive tomorrow from eating ice-cream tomorrow, then $U^{today}(u_{tomorrow})$ is the utility, from the point of view of today, of eating ice-cream tomorrow. This number would normally be high, but not as high as $U^{tomorrow}(u_{tomorrow})$, which is the utility you will receive tomorrow when you eat ice-cream tomorrow.

Suppose you are facing two rewards **a** and **b**, as in Figure 8.2 on page 154. Let us say that **a** gives you u_t at time t, and that **b** gives you u_{t+1} at time $t + 1$. Imagine that, from the point of view of time t, you strictly prefer **a** to **b**; that is, $U^t(\mathbf{a}) > U^t(\mathbf{b})$. If so, given that you are an exponential discounter, $U^t(\mathbf{a}) > U^t(\mathbf{b})$ implies that $u_t > \delta u_{t+1}$. Now let us look at what is going on before t, for example, at time $t - 1$. Would it be possible to weakly prefer **b** to **a**? If you did, $U^{t-1}(\mathbf{b}) \geq U^{t-1}(\mathbf{a})$, and $\delta^2 u_{t+1} \geq \delta u_t$. Since $\delta > 0$, we can divide by δ on both sides, which gives us $\delta u_{t+1} \geq u_t$, which is a contradiction. So at $t - 1$, you must strictly prefer **a** to **b**. What about $t - 2$? The same conclusion obtains and for the same reason. What about $t - 3$? We could go on.

In brief, if you discount the future exponentially, you must be time consistent. Graphically, what this means is that you either prefer **a** to **b** at all times (as in the dotted line in Figure 9.2), or you prefer **b** to **a** at all times (as in the dashed line in Figure 9.2), or you are indifferent between the two options (as in Figure 8.2 on page 154). At no point will the two lines cross. Your preference over **a** and **b** will never change simply because time passes.

The bad news, from the point of view of this model, is that people violate time consistency with alarming regularity (Figure 9.1). In the morning, we swear never to touch alcohol again; yet, by the time happy hour comes around, we gladly order another martini. On January 1, we promise our partners that we will stop smoking and start exercising; yet, when opportunity arises, we completely ignore our promises. If this is unfamiliar, good for you! Otherwise, you will probably agree that

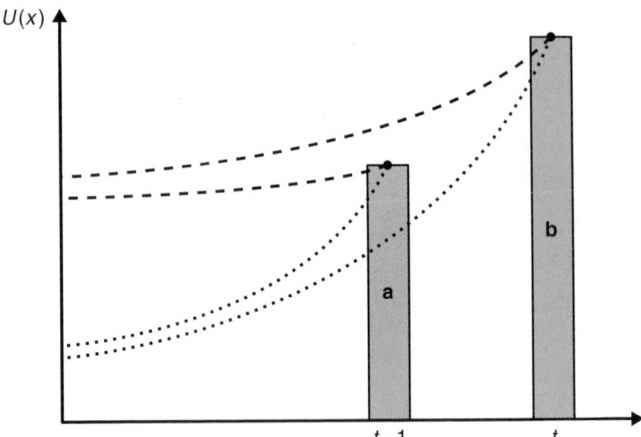

Figure 9.2 Time-consistent preferences

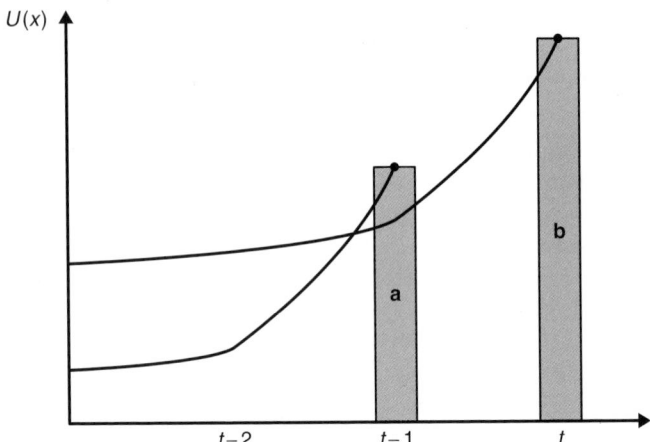

Figure 9.3 Time-inconsistent preferences

time inconsistency is common. Graphically, we seem to discount the future in accordance with Figure 9.3. That is, at time $t-1$ (and possibly right before it), we want the smaller, more immediate reward; earlier than that, we want the larger, more distant reward.

It turns out that this kind of behavior can be usefully modeled with a slight variation of Definition 8.10 on page 151.

Definition 9.1 The beta–delta function *According to the **beta–delta function**, the utility $U^0(\mathbf{u})$ of utility stream $\mathbf{u} = \langle u_0, u_1, u_2, \ldots \rangle$ from the point of view of $t = 0$ is:*

$$U^0(\mathbf{u}) = u_0 + \beta \delta u_1 + \beta \delta^2 u_2 + \beta \delta^3 u_3 + \ldots$$

$$= u_o + \sum_{i=1}^{\infty} \beta \delta^i u_i$$

If you act in accordance with this formula, you evaluate utility streams by adding the utility you would receive now $\beta\delta$ times the utility you would receive the next round, $\beta\delta^2$ times the utility you would receive in the round after that, and so on. The only difference relative to the exponential discounting function is that all utilities except u_0 are multiplied by an additional β, which is assumed to be a number such that $0 < \beta \leqslant 1$. Notice that while δ is raised to higher powers $(\delta, \delta^2, \delta^3, \ldots)$ for later rewards, β is not. This form of discounting is called **quasi-hyperbolic discounting**. Here, I loosely refer to it as **hyperbolic discounting**. The resulting model is called the **beta–delta model**.

The introduction of the parameter β makes an interesting difference. When $\beta = 1$, an agent who discounts the future hyperbolically will behave exactly like an agent who discounts the future exponentially. For, if $\beta = 1$, the hyperbolic discounter will maximize the following expression:

$$U^0(\mathbf{u}) = u_0 + \beta\delta u_1 + \beta\delta^2 u_2 + \ldots = u_0 + \delta u_1 + \delta^2 u_2 + \ldots,$$

which is identical to the delta function (Definition 8.10). When $\beta < 1$, however, things are different. In this case, all outcomes beyond the present time get discounted more than under exponential discounting, as shown in Figure 9.4. Compare this figure with Figure 8.1 on page 153. As you can tell, the hyperbolic curve is relatively steep between t and $t-1$, and relatively flat before $t-1$.

When an agent discounts the future hyperbolically, if given a choice between a smaller, earlier reward and a bigger, later reward, the picture may well end up looking like Figure 9.3. The fact that hyperbolic discounting may lead to time-inconsistent behavior can be shown algebraically, too.

Example 9.2 Hyperbolic discounting Suppose that you are on a diet, but have to decide whether to have a slice of red-velvet cake at a party some random Saturday. Eating the cake would give you a utility of 4. If you have the cake, however, you will have to exercise for hours on Sunday, which would give you a utility of 0. The other option is to skip the cake, which would give you a utility of 1, and to spend

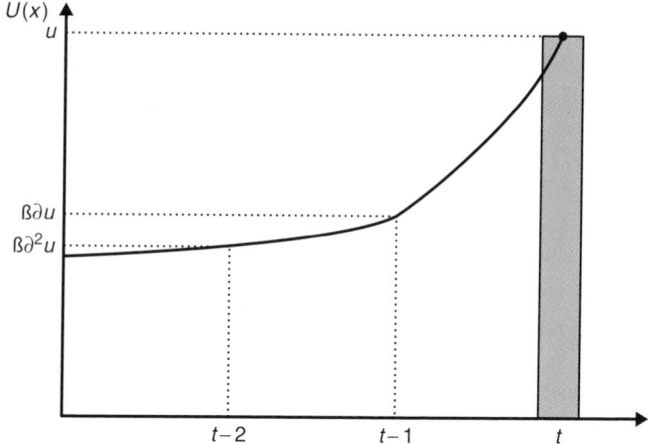

Figure 9.4 Hyperbolic discounting

Table 9.1 Red-velvet problem

	Saturday	Sunday
c	4	0
d	1	6

Sunday relaxing in front of the television, for a utility of 6. Thus, you are facing the choice depicted in Table 9.1. You discount the future hyperbolically, with $\beta = 1/2$ and $\delta = 2/3$. Questions: (a) From the point of view of Friday, what is the utility of eating the cake (c) and of skipping it (d)? Which would you prefer? (b) From the point of view of Saturday, what is the utility of eating the cake and of skipping it? Which would you prefer?

(a) From the point of view of Friday, Friday is $t = 0$, Saturday is $t = 1$, and Sunday is $t = 2$. From this point of view, eating the cake is associated with utility stream $c = \langle 0, 4, 0 \rangle$ and not eating the cake is associated with utility stream $d = \langle 0, 1, 6 \rangle$. Consequently, from the point of view of Friday, the utility of eating the cake is:

$$U^0(c) = 0 + 1/2 * 2/3 * 4 + 1/2 * (2/3)^2 * 0 = 4/3.$$

Meanwhile, from the point of view of Friday, the utility of skipping the cake is:

$$U^0(d) = 0 + 1/2 * 2/3 * 1 + 1/2 * (2/3)^2 * 6 = 5/3.$$

From the point of view of Friday, therefore, you will prefer to skip the cake and stick to your diet.

(b) From the point of view of Saturday, Saturday is $t = 0$ and Sunday is $t = 1$. From this point of view, eating the cake is associated with utility stream $c = \langle 4, 0 \rangle$ and not eating the cake is associated with utility stream $d = \langle 1, 6 \rangle$. Consequently, from the point of view of Saturday, the utility of eating the cake is:

$$U^0(c) = 4 + 1/2 * 2/3 * 0 = 4.$$

Meanwhile, from the point of view of Saturday, the utility of skipping the cake is:

$$U^0(d) = 1 + 1/2 * 2/3 * 6 = 3.$$

From the point of view of Saturday, therefore, you will prefer to eat the cake.

This example shows time inconsistency at work. Ahead of time, you prefer to stick to your diet and resolve to refrain from having the cake. And yet, when the opportunity arises, you prefer to ignore the diet and eat the cake. This means that you are exhibiting **impulsivity**. If impulsivity is not familiar to you, you belong to a small and lucky subsample of humanity. As the example shows, you can be impulsive and impatient at the same time. The next exercise illustrates the interaction between the two.

Exercise 9.3 Impulsivity and impatience Suppose you are offered the choice between option **a** (8 utiles on Thursday) and **b** (12 utiles on Friday).

(a) Assume that $\beta = 1$ and that $\delta = 5/6$. From the point of view of Thursday, which one would you choose? From the point of view of Wednesday, which one would you choose?

(b) Assume that $\beta = 1$ and that $\delta = 1/6$. From the point of view of Thursday, which one would you choose? From the point of view of Wednesday, which one would you choose?

(c) Assume that $\beta = 1/2$, and that $\delta = 1$. From the point of view of Thursday, which one would you choose? From the point of view of Wednesday, which one would you choose?

(d) Assume that $\beta = 1/2$, and that $\delta = 2/3$. From the point of view of Thursday, which one would you choose? From the point of view of Wednesday, which one would you choose?

Hyperbolic discounting can account not just for the fact that people emphasize their present over their future well-being, but also that they change their minds about how to balance the present versus the future. Thus, it can account for the fact that people fully intend to diet, stop smoking, do homework, and quit drugs, and then completely fail to do so. Here is another example.

Exercise 9.4 Cancer screening Most colon cancers develop from polyps. Because early screening can detect polyps before they become cancerous and colon cancer in its early stages, many doctors advise patients over a certain age to have a colonoscopy. Unfortunately, colonoscopies are experienced as embarrassing and painful. The typical person, when young, resolves to have a colonoscopy when older, but changes his or her mind as the procedure approaches. Assume that two patients, Abelita and Benny, have the choice between the following: (a) having a colonoscopy at time 1 (utility $= 0$) and being healthy at time 2 (utility $= 18$); and (b) avoiding the colonoscopy at time 1 (utility $= 6$) and be unhealthy at time 2 (utility $= 0$).

Abelita discounts the future exponentially. Her $\delta = 2/3$.

(a) At $t = 0$: What is her utility of **a**? What is her utility of **b**?
(b) At $t = 1$: What is her utility of **a**? What is her utility of **b**?

Benny discounts the future hyperbolically. His $\beta = 1/6$ and his $\delta = 1$.

(c) At $t = 0$: What is his utility of **a**? What is his utility of **b**?
(d) At $t = 1$: What is his utility of **a**? What is his utility of **b**?
(e) Who acts more like the typical patient?
(f) Who is more likely to end up with health issues?

The beta–delta function also permits you to go the other way. Knowing a person's preferences the function permits you to compute their beta and/or delta. Consider the following exercise.

Exercise 9.5 Suppose that you discount the future hyperbolically, that is, in accordance with the beta–delta function, and that from the point of view of Thursday you are indifferent between options **a** (1 utile on Thursday) and **b** (3 utiles on Friday). (a) If $\beta = 1/2$, what is δ? (b) If $\delta = 4/9$, what is β?

Exercise 9.6 Suppose that you discount the future hyperbolically. Assume that both β and δ are strictly greater than zero but strictly smaller than one. At $t = 0$, you are given the choice between the following three options: **a** (1 utile at $t = 0$), **b** (2 utiles at $t = 1$), and **c** (3 utiles at $t = 2$). As a matter of fact, at at $t = 0$ you are indifferent between **a** and **b** and between **b** and **c**. (a) Compute β and δ. (b) Suppose, in addition, that at $t = 0$ you are indifferent between **c** and **d** (x utiles at $t = 3$). What is x?

Exercise 9.7 Suppose that you discount the future hyperbolically. Assume that both β and δ are strictly greater than zero but strictly smaller than one. At $t = 0$, you are given the choice between the following three options: **a** (2 utiles at $t = 0$), **b** (5 utiles at $t = 1$), and **c** (10 utiles at $t = 2$). As a matter of fact, at $t = 0$ you are indifferent between **a** and **b** and between **b** and **c**. Compute β and δ.

The next two sections contain more exercises on hyperbolic discounting.

9.3 Choosing not to choose

Another feature of human behavior is that we sometimes choose not to choose, in the sense that we take action to prevent ourselves from taking action. We are willing to pay a premium to buy snacks in small packages, soft drinks from overpriced vending machines, and beer in small quantities. Though we know that we could save money by buying in bulk, we fear that doing so would lead to overindulgence, leaving us fat, drunk, and no better off financially.

This kind of behavior is theoretically puzzling. From the point of view of exponential discounting, choosing not to choose makes no sense. According to this model, if you do not want to indulge now, you will not want to indulge later either. But such behavior is not obviously entailed by the hyperbolic discounting model either. If you discount your future hyperbolically, you may very well plan not to overindulge but then overindulge anyway. Thus, neither one of the models that we have explored so far is appropriate for capturing common behaviors such as those above.

Behavioral economists approach the issue by drawing a distinction between **naive** and **sophisticated** hyperbolic discounters. When people are time inconsistent – meaning that they prefer x to y ahead of time, but y to x when the time arrives – they are said to have **self-control problems**. Naive time-inconsistent individuals – or *naifs*, for short – are unaware of their self-control problems. Naifs make their choices based on the inaccurate assumption that their future preferences will be identical to their current preferences. Sophisticated time-inconsistent individuals – or *sophisticates*, for short – are aware of their self-control problems. Sophisticates make their choices based on accurate predictions of their future behavior.

The following example illustrates the forms of behavior exhibited by an exponential discounter, a naive hyperbolic discounter, and a sophisticated hyperbolic discounter.

Example 9.8 Johnny Depp 1 Your local cinema theater offers a mediocre movie this week ($u_0 = 3$), a good movie next week ($u_1 = 5$), a great movie in two weeks

($u_2 = 8$), and a fantastic Johnny Depp movie in three weeks ($u_3 = 13$). Unfortunately, you must skip one of the four. For all questions below, suppose that $\delta = 1$ and $\beta = 1/2$. Will you skip **a** the mediocre, **b** the good, **c** the great, or **d** the fantastic movie?

If you are an exponential discounter, you will skip the worst movie. At $t = 0$, you know that $U^0(\mathbf{a}) = 5 + 8 + 13 = 26$ is better than $U^0(\mathbf{b}) = 3 + 8 + 13 = 24$, which is better than $U^0(\mathbf{c})$, and so on. Because you are an exponential discounter, and therefore time consistent, you stick to your plan.

If you are a naive hyperbolic discounter, you will procrastinate until the very last moment and miss the fantastic movie. At $t = 0$, you choose between $U^0(\mathbf{a}) = 1/2(5 + 8 + 13) = 13$, $U^0(\mathbf{b}) = 3 + 1/2(8 + 13) = 13.5$, $U^0(\mathbf{c}) = 3 + 1/2(5 + 13) = 12$, and $U^0(\mathbf{d}) = 3 + 1/2(5 + 8) = 9.5$. You watch the mediocre movie, fully intending to skip the good one. But at $t = 1$, everything looks different. From there, you no longer have the option to skip the mediocre movie. You choose between $U^1(\mathbf{b}) = 1/2(8 + 13) = 10.5$, $U^1(\mathbf{c}) = 5 + 1/2 * 13 = 11.5$, and $U^1(\mathbf{d}) = 5 + 1/2 * 8 = 9$. You watch the good movie, fully intending to skip the great movie. At $t = 2$, though, you choose between $U^2(\mathbf{c}) = 1/2 * 13 = 6.5$ and $U^2(\mathbf{d}) = 8$. Thus, you watch the great movie and at $t = 3$ have no choice but to skip the fantastic movie.

If you are a sophisticated hyperbolic discounter, by contrast, you will skip the good movie. Your sophistication allows you to predict that self-control problems at $t = 2$ would prevent you from watching the fantastic movie. Consequently, the choice at $t = 1$ is between skipping the good movie for a utility of $U^1(\mathbf{b}) = 10.5$ or else end up with $U^1(\mathbf{d}) = 9$. So you know at $t = 0$ that at $t = 1$ you will choose **b**. At $t = 0$, therefore, the choice is between $U^0(\mathbf{a}) = 13$ and $U^0(\mathbf{b}) = 13.5$. Thus, you will watch the mediocre movie, skip the good one, and watch the great and fantastic ones.

This example shows how sophistication helps people anticipate the problems posed by time-inconsistent behavior. Behavior of this kind is probably common. At night, many people are determined to get up early the next morning, even though they anticipate that tomorrow morning they will want to sleep late. In order to prevent their morning self from sleeping late, therefore, they set alarms and put them on a window ledge across the room, behind a cactus. There are even alarms that, when they go off, roll off the bedside table and under the bed or across the room, forcing your morning self to get up and chase it down, by which time (the idea is) you will be too awake to go back to bed. If this sounds familiar, you are a sophisticated hyperbolic discounter.

Bizarrely, however, sophistication can also exacerbate self-control problems, as the following exercise shows.

Exercise 9.9 Johnny Depp 2   This exercise refers to Example 9.8. Suppose instead that you can only watch one of the four movies. Will you watch **a** the mediocre, **b** the good, **c** the great, or **d** the fantastic movie? (a) Show that an exponential discounter will watch **d** the fantastic movie. (b) Show that a naive hyperbolic discounter will watch **c** the great movie. (c) Show that a sophisticated hyperbolic discounter will watch **a** the mediocre movie.

The problem is that sophisticated hyperbolic discounters tend to **preproperate**, that is, doing something now when it would be better to wait. Preproperation in one sense is the very opposite of procrastination, which is a problem that naive hyperbolic discounters have. Consequently, there are situations in which naifs are better off than sophisticates. Perhaps individuals who are well aware of their self-control problems would do better if they did not try to anticipate their future behavior to the extent that they do.

9.4 Preferences over profiles

The model of hyperbolic discounting, especially when augmented with a story about naifs and sophisticates, can capture a number of phenomena that are simply inconsistent with the model of exponential discounting. Yet, there are many conditions under which both exponential and hyperbolic discounting fail to accurately capture people's actual behavior. The following exercise makes this clear.

Exercise 9.10 Cleaning the house It is Sunday morning ($t=0$), and you are determined to accomplish two things today: cleaning the apartment and going to the movies. You can either clean during the morning (at $t=0$), and go to the movies during the afternoon (at $t=1$) or go to the movies during the morning (at $t=0$) and clean in the afternoon (at $t=1$). You hate cleaning: it only gives you a utility of 2. You love the movies: it gives you as much as 12.

For the first two questions, assume that you discount the future exponentially with $\delta=1/2$. From the point of view of $t=0$:

(a) What is the utility of cleaning first and going to the movies later?
(b) What is the utility of going to the movies first and cleaning later?

For the last two questions, assume that you discount the future hyperbolically with $\beta=1/3$ and $\delta=1/2$. From the point of view of $t=0$:

(c) What is the utility of cleaning first and going to the movies later?
(d) What is the utility of going to the movies first and cleaning later?

What this exercise suggests is that whether you discount the future exponentially or hyperbolically, you will always schedule the pleasant experience first and the unpleasant one later.

This implication contrasts sharply with people's observed behavior. Personal experience suggests that, when choosing between sequences of events, people will make a point of scheduling the unpleasant experience first and the pleasant one later. In this case, personal experience is supported by evidence. In one study, the researchers presented people with verbal descriptions and graphical representations of increasing and decreasing salary profiles, and elicited preferences over the profiles. The authors conclude that all things equal, by and large, a large majority of workers prefer increasing wage profiles over flat or decreasing ones.

Such a **preference for increasing utility profiles** could in principle be captured by relaxing the assumption (which we made tentatively in Chapter 8) that δ is less than one. If δ exceeds one, a rational discounter will postpone pleasant events as much as possible. When $\delta>1$, it follows that $r<0$, which is why the resulting preference is called **negative time preference**. Yet, this solution is awkward, because the very same people who clean in the morning and go to the movies in the afternoon simultaneously discount the future with $\delta<1$ and $r>0$ – that is, exhibit **positive time preference** – in other contexts.

In addition, there is evidence that people also exhibit a **preference for spread**. That is, people sometimes like to distribute multiple desirable events over time. While some children eat all their Halloween candy in one sitting, others prefer to distribute the eating evenly over days or weeks. This kind of preference cannot be accounted for either by positive or negative time preference.

All this suggests that people have **preferences over profiles**: they care about the *shape* of the utility stream as well as about (discounted) individual utilities. People often save the best for last: perhaps they want to end on a high note, hope to get the unpleasant experience over with, or rely on the prospect of a pleasant experience to motivate themselves to take care of the unpleasant one. People also wish to distribute pleasant and unpleasant events over time. Such preferences over profiles cannot be captured in the context of either one of the discounting models we have discussed so far. Yet preferences over profiles seem to be an important phenomenon.

Example 9.11 Economics professors Rumor has it that even economics professors frequently elect to receive their annual salary in twelve rather than nine installments, even though they would maximize their discounted utility by asking to be paid in nine. Obviously, they have the option of saving some of their money to smooth out consumption. A preference for a smooth income profile would explain this phenomenon.

The shape of utility profiles has received a lot of attention in the literature on the **peak–end rule**, which is used to assess the desirability of utility streams or "episodes." When people follow this rule, they consciously or unconsciously rank utility streams based on the average of the peak (that is, the maximum utility during the episode) and the end (that is, the utility near the end of the episode) and choose accordingly. Insofar as people act in accordance with the peak–end rule, the shape of the utility profile – and not just the (discounted) sum of utilities – will be critically important.

The peak–end rule has some interesting implications. Consider Figure 9.5. A person who applies the peak–end rule will assess episode (a) as superior to episode (b). If this is not immediately obvious, notice that the peak utility of the two episodes is identical and that episode (a) has a higher end utility than episode (b). If you apply the peak–end rule to make the choice between (a) and (b), therefore, you will choose (a). But there is something odd about this ranking: episode (b) has all the utility of episode (a) and then some. The peak–end rule entails **duration neglect**, meaning that the *length* of an episode will be relatively unimportant, contrary to exponential and hyperbolic discounting models.

Would anyone apply the peak–end rule? In famous study of patients undergoing a colonoscopy – as in Exercise 9.4 – the researchers confirmed that retrospective evaluations reflect the peak and end utility and that the length of the episode was relatively unimportant. Bizarrely, *adding* a painful tail to an already painful episode made people think of the episode as a whole as *less* painful.

Exercise 9.12 The peak–end rule Suppose you add a pleasant tail to an already pleasant episode. If people assess the episode as a whole in accordance with the peak–end rule, will this make people think of the episode as a whole as more or less pleasant?

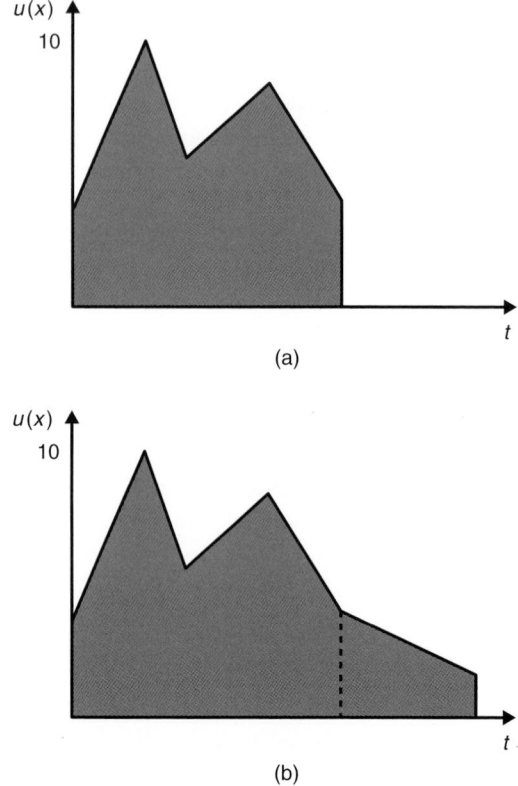

(a)

(b)

Figure 9.5 The peak–end rule

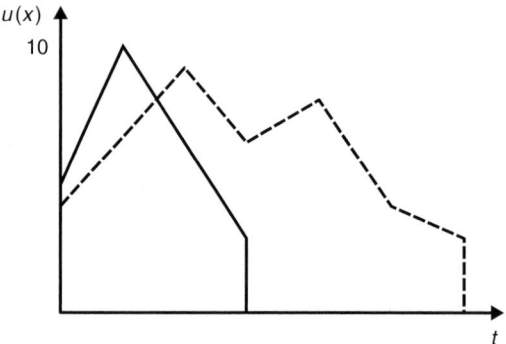

Figure 9.6 The peak–end rule, cont.

Exercise 9.13 The peak–end rule, cont. This exercise refers to Figure 9.6. Would a person who follows the peak–end rule choose the episode described represented by the solid line or the episode represented by the dashed line?

The peak–end rule can perhaps explain why people keep having children, even though systematic data suggest that parents are on the average less happy than non-parents, and that parents on the average are less happy when taking care of their children than when they are engaged in many other activities. As long as the most intense joy generated by children exceeds the most intense joy from other sources, and holding end experience constant, people will rank having children above other experiences. Duration neglect entails that long sleepless nights and the like will be relatively unimportant in the final analysis.

There are choices that superficially look as if they must be the result of a preference over profiles but that really are not. For one thing, insofar as the anticipation of a pleasant event is itself pleasurable, you can rationally postpone the pleasant event. Suppose that it is Saturday, and that you are choosing whether to eat candy today or tomorrow. If you eat it today, you get 6 utiles today and 0 utiles tomorrow; if you postpone eating it until tomorrow, you get 2 utiles today (from the anticipation of the pleasant event) and 6 tomorrow (from the pleasant event itself). Given this sort of scenario, a rational discounter can postpone the eating of the candy until Sunday, even if he or she discounts the future somewhat. And this kind of narrative is consistent with standard theory.

9.5 Discussion

In this chapter, we have discussed the manner in which people make choices when time is a factor. We discovered several phenomena that are difficult to reconcile with the model of exponential discounting which we explored in Chapter 8. For many of these phenomena, the divergence appears significant and systematic, and therefore predictable. Again, knowledge of these phenomena permits us not only to explain and predict other people's behavior, but also to influence it, and to resist other people's efforts to influence ours.

There are many other phenomena that are at odds with the exponential discounting model we learned in Section 8.3. The **sign effect** says that gains are discounted at a higher rate than losses. The **magnitude effect** says that large outcomes are discounted at a lower rate than small ones. Consider also the likelihood that preferences change as a result of becoming sleepy, hungry, thirsty, excited, or old. Such changes are important not just because they mean that people's behavior can be expected to change over time in predictable ways, but also because people can be expected to respond to their own predictions about how their preferences will change. For example, many people know that they will buy too much food when shopping on an empty stomach and try to modulate their behavior accordingly. Economists have built models in which preference change is endogenous, but it may be more parsimonious to postulate the existence of a preference relation that evolves over time.

Behavioral economists take these phenomena to provide evidence that the exponential-discounting model and the assumption of stable preferences are descriptively inadequate. Some of these phenomena also cast doubt on the normative correctness of the model. It is true that some violations of exponential discounting – involving serious procrastination, extreme impulsivity, or similar – can harm the individual. While some degree of sophistication can help mitigate the effects of hyperbolic discounting, it can also hurt, as Exercise 9.9 showed. But then, there is real disagreement about the rationality of time discounting (see Section 8.4). The discussion about utility profiles in the previous section helps underscore these concerns. It can be argued that it is perfectly rational to desire a life of increasing utility, of ups-and-downs, or any other shape of the utility profile. If so, models of exponential and hyperbolic discounting both fail as a normative standard. And if exponential discounting is not the uniquely rational way to assess deferred outcomes, this would put in question its widespread use in disciplines such as cost–benefit analysis and finance.

In Part V we will consider strategic interaction, which will add yet another layer of complexity to the analysis.

Additional exercises

Exercise 9.14 Retirement savings   When young, many people fully intend to save for retirement. However, when they start making money after college, they are often tempted to spend it immediately. Assume that Ximena and Yves have the choice between the following two options: (a) saving for retirement at time 1 ($u_1 = 0$) and retiring in style at time 2 ($u_2 = 12$); and (b) having more disposable income at time 1 ($u_1 = 6$) and retiring poor at time 2 ($u_2 = 0$).

Ximena is an exponential discounter. Her $\delta = 2/3$.

(a) At $t = 0$: What is her utility of **a**? What is her utility of **b**?
(b) At $t = 1$: What is her utility of **a**? What is her utility of **b**?

Yves is a naive hyperbolic discounter. His $\beta = 1/3$ and his $\delta = 1$.

(c) At $t = 0$: What is his utility of **a**? What is his utility of **b**?
(d) At $t = 1$: What is his utility of **a**? What is his utility of **b**?
(e) Who is more likely to experience regret?
(f) Who is more likely to retire in style?

Exercise 9.15   Match each of the vignettes below with one of the following phenomena: *hyperbolic discounting*, *preference over profiles*, and *choosing not to choose*. If in doubt, pick the best fit.

(a) Allie goes to bed at night fully intending to get up at 5 am and study hard before noon. When the alarm goes off, she smacks it hard and goes straight back to sleep.
(b) Bert wants to save more, but simply does not feel that he has enough money left at the end of the month. To encourage himself to save, he sets up an automatic transfer – on the first of each month – from his checking account to a savings account from which withdrawing money is a pain.
(c) Cherry can only afford a really nice meal at a restaurant once every semester. She makes sure to schedule it at the very end of the semester, so that she has something to look forward to when eating her Ramen noodles.
(d) Darius knows that his wife would be so much happier, and his marriage so much healthier, if he spent more time cleaning the house. He keeps thinking that it would be great to clean the house. Yet, when it comes down to it, there is always something on TV that prevents him from doing his part.
(e) Unlike some people she knows, Ellie will not finish a whole tub of ice-cream in one sitting. Rather, she will allow herself exactly one spoonful every day.

Problem 9.16   *Drawing on your own experience, make up stories like those in Exercise 9.15 to illustrate the various ideas that you have read about in this chapter.*

Further reading

The quote from *Junky* at the beginning of Section 9.2 is from Burroughs (1977 [1953], p. xv). A helpful review of violations of the exponential discounting model is Frederick et al. (2002), reprinted as Chapter 1 of Loewenstein et al., eds (2003). The hyperbolic discounting model is due to Ainslie (1975). Naive versus sophisticated hyperbolic discounting is discussed in O'Donoghue and Rabin (2000), from which the Johnny Depp-related example and exercise were adapted (pp. 237–8). The study of workers' preferences is Loewenstein and Sicherman (1991); the peak–end rule is discussed in Kahneman et al. (1997) and the colonoscopy study in Redelmeier and Kahneman (1996). Loewenstein and Angner (2003) examines preference change from a descriptive and normative perspective.

Part V

Strategic Interaction

Chapter 10

Analytical Game Theory

10.1 Introduction

So far, we have assumed that the outcomes that you enjoy or suffer are determined jointly by your choices and the state of the world, which may be unknown to you at the time of the decision. For many real-time decisions, however, this is far from the whole story. Instead, many of the decision problems that you face in real life have an *interactive* or *strategic* nature. This means that whatever happens depends not just on what you do but also on what other people do. If you play chess, whether you win or lose is determined not just by what you do but also on what your opponent does. If you invest in stock, whether or not you make money depends not only on your choice of stock but also on whether the stock goes up or down. And that is a function of supply and demand, which is a function of whether other people buy or sell the stock.

The presence of strategic interaction adds a whole new layer of complexity to the analysis. If you are a defense attorney, the outcome of your case depends not only on your actions but on the actions of the prosecutor. Since you are well aware of this, you do your best to anticipate her decisions. Thus, your decisions will depend on what you think her decisions will be. Her decisions will reflect, in part, what she thinks you will do. So your decisions will depend on what you think she thinks you will do. But what she thinks you will do depends in part on what she thinks you think she will do...and so on. It is obvious that the correct analysis of strategic interaction is not obvious at all.

The analysis of strategic interaction is the province of **game theory**. In this chapter, I offer a brief overview of the standard theory, sometimes referred to as **analytical game theory**.

10.2 Nash equilibrium in pure strategies

The following story is a true internet legend.

Example 10.1 The makeup exam   One year there were two students taking Chemistry. They both did so well on quizzes, midterms, and labs that they decided to leave town and go partying the weekend before the exam. They mightily enjoyed themselves. However, much like a scene in *The Hangover: Part III*, they overslept and did not make it back to campus in time for the exam.

So they called their professor to say that they had got a flat tire on the way to the exam, did not have a spare, and had to wait for a long time. The professor thought about it for a moment, and then said that he was glad to give them a makeup exam the next day. The two friends studied all night.

At the assigned time, the professor placed them in separate rooms, handed them the exams, and asked them to begin. The two friends looked at the first problem, which was a simple one about molarity and solutions and was worth 5 points.

"Easy!" they thought to themselves. Then, they turned the page and saw the second question: "(95 points) Which tire?"

This example illustrates the interactive or strategic nature of many decision problems. Here, the final grade of either friend will depend not just on his answer to the question, but on the other friend's answer too. The two will get As whenever they give the same answer to the question and Fs whenever they do not.

More formally speaking, you are playing a **game** whenever you face a decision problem in which the final outcome depends not just on your action, and on whatever state of the world obtains, but also on the actions of at least one other agent. According to this definition, the two friends are in fact playing a game against each other. And this is true whether or not they think of it as a game. Notice that you can play a game in this sense without competing *against* each other. Here, the name of the game is cooperation – and coordination. The agents involved in games are called **players**. A **strategy** is a complete plan of action that describes what a player will do under all possible circumstances. In the case of the makeup exam, each friend has four strategies to choose from: he can write "Front Left (FL)," "Front Right (FR)," "Rear Left (RL)," or "Rear Right (RR)."

Given a number of players, a set of strategies available to each player, and a set of payoffs (rewards or punishments) corresponding to each possible combination of strategies, a game can be represented using a **payoff matrix**. A payoff matrix is a table representing the payoffs of the players for each possible combination of strategies. The payoff matrix of the game played by the two friends can be represented as in Table 10.1. A **strategy profile** is a vector of strategies, one for each player. ⟨FL, RR⟩ is a strategy profile; so is ⟨RL, RL⟩. Thus, the payoff matrix shows the payoffs resulting from each strategy profile. Of course, the payoff matrix looks much like the tables representing non-strategic decision problems, except for the fact that each column represents a choice by the other player rather than a state of the world.

Analytical game theory is built around the concept of an equilibrium. The most prominent equilibrium concept is that of **Nash equilibrium**.

Definition 10.2 Nash equilibrium   *A Nash equilibrium is a strategy profile such that each strategy in the profile is a best response to the other strategies in the profile.*

In the makeup-exam game from Example 10.1, ⟨FL, FL⟩ is a Nash equilibrium: given that Player I plays FL, FL is a best response for Player II, and given that Player II plays FL, FL is a best response for Player I. In equilibrium, given the other players' strategies, no one player can improve his or her payoff by unilaterally changing to

Table 10.1   The makeup exam

	FL	FR	RL	RR
FL	A	F	F	F
FR	F	A	F	F
RL	F	F	A	F
RR	F	F	F	A

another strategy. By contrast, ⟨FL, RR⟩ is not a Nash equilibrium: given that Player I plays FL, Player II can do better than playing RR, and given that Player II plays RR, Player I can do better than playing FL. In this section, we will limit our analysis to Nash equilibria in pure strategies: Nash equilibria in which each player simply plays one of the individual strategies available to him or her (compare Section 10.3). In all, there are four Nash equilibria in pure strategies, one for each tire.

Example 10.3 Coffee shops   You and your study partner are planning to meet at noon at one of two coffee shops, Lucy's Coffee and Crestwood Coffee. Unfortunately, you failed to specify which one, and you have no way of getting in touch with each other before noon. If you manage to meet, you get a utility of 1; otherwise, you get a utility of 0. Draw the payoff matrix and find the Nash equilibria in pure strategies.

The payoff matrix is Table 10.2. The convention is for the first number in each cell to represent the payoff of Player I, whose strategies are listed in the left-most column; the second number in each cell represents the payoff of Player II, whose strategies are listed in the top row. The Nash equilibria in pure strategies are ⟨Lucy's, Lucy's⟩ and ⟨Crestwood, Crestwood⟩.

Table 10.2   A pure coordination game

	Lucy's	Crestwood
Lucy's	1,1	0,0
Crestwood	0,0	1,1

The coffee-shop game is an example of a **pure coordination game**: a game in which the players' interests are perfectly aligned. The makeup-exam game, obviously, is also a pure coordination game. In some coordination games, however, interests fail to align perfectly. The point is typically made by means of the politically-incorrectly named **battle of the sexes**.

Example 10.4 Battle of the sexes   A husband and wife must decide whether to have dinner at the steak house or at the crab shack. All things equal, both would rather dine together than alone, but the man (Player I) prefers the steak house and the woman (Player II) prefers the crab shack. The man gets 2 units of utility if both dine at the steak house, 1 if both dine at the crab shack, and 0 if they dine apart; the woman gets 2 units of utility if both dine at the crab shack, 1 if both dine at the steak house, and 0 if they dine apart. Draw the payoff matrix and find the Nash equilibria in pure strategies.

The payoff matrix is Table 10.3. There are two Nash equilibria in pure strategies. ⟨Steak House, Steak House⟩ is one. Because this is Player I's best outcome, he cannot improve his payoff by changing strategies. Although Player II would prefer it if *both* switched to Crab Shack, she cannot improve her payoff by *unilaterally* deviating: if she plays Crab Shack when Player I plays Steak House, she will end up with a payoff of 0 rather than 1. Of course ⟨Crab Shack, Crab Shack⟩ is the other Nash equilibrium in pure strategies.

Table 10.3 An impure coordination game

	Steak House	Crab Shack
Steak House	2,1	0,0
Crab Shack	0,0	1,2

Because Player I prefers the one equilibrium and Player II prefers the other, the battle of the sexes, sometimes euphemistically called "Bach or Stravinsky," is an example of an **impure coordination game**. Here are some exercises.

Exercise 10.5 Nash equilibrium in pure strategies Find all Nash equilibria in the games in Table 10.4, where Player I chooses between Up (U), Middle (M), and Down (D) and Player II chooses between Left (L), Middle (M), and Right (R).

Table 10.4 Nash equilibrium exercises

	L	R		L	R		L	M	R
U	2,2	0,0	U	5,1	2,0	U	6,2	5,1	4,3
D	0,0	1,1	D	5,1	1,2	M	3,6	8,4	2,1
						D	2,8	9,6	3,0
	(a)			(b)			(c)		

Notice that in Exercise 10.5(a), there are two Nash equilibria in pure strategies, though one is clearly inferior to the other from the point of view of both players. In Exercise 10.5(b), ⟨U, L⟩ and ⟨D, L⟩ are not both Nash equilibria although they are "just as good" in the sense that they lead to the same payoffs. And in Exercise 10.5(c), there are outcomes that are better for both players than the Nash equilibrium.

As these games illustrate, there is no straightforward connection between Nash equilibria and "best" outcomes for the players. As a result, it would be a mistake to try to identify the former by searching for the latter. An even more striking example of the general phenomenon is the **prisoners' dilemma** (Figure 10.1).

Example 10.6 Prisoners' dilemma Two criminals are arrested on suspicion of two separate crimes. The prosecutor has sufficient evidence to convict the two on the minor charge, but not on the major one. If the two criminals *cooperate* (C) with each other and stay mum, they will be convicted on the minor charge and serve two years in jail. After separating the prisoners, the prosecutor offers each of them a reduced sentence if they *defect* (D), that is, they testify against each other. If one prisoner defects but the other one cooperates, the defector goes free whereas the cooperator serves 20 years in jail. If both defect, both get convicted on the major charge but (as a reward for testifying) only serve ten years. Assume that each prisoner cares about nothing but the number of years he himself spends in jail. What is the payoff matrix? What is the Nash equilibrium?

The payoff matrix in terms of jail sentences is Table 10.5(a); in terms of utilities, the payoff matrix can be represented as Table 10.5(b). Let us consider Player I first. If Player II cooperates, Player I has the choice between cooperating and defecting; by defecting, he can go free instead of serving two years in jail. If Player II defects,

Figure 10.1 The suspects. Illustration by Cody Taylor

Table 10.5 The prisoners' dilemma

	C	D
C	2 years, 2 years	20 years, 0 years
D	0 years, 20 years	10 years, 10 years

(a)

	C	D
C	3,3	0,5
D	5,0	1,1

(b)

Player I still has the choice between cooperating and defecting; by defecting, he can serve 10 instead of 20 years in jail. In brief, Player I is better off defecting no matter what Player II does. But the same thing is true for Player II. Thus, there is only one Nash equilibrium. Both defect and serve 10 years in jail.

One way to identify the unique Nash equilibrium in the prisoners' dilemma is to eliminate all strictly dominated strategies. A strategy X is said to strictly dominate another strategy Y if choosing X is better than choosing Y no matter what the other player does. Because no rational agent will play a strictly dominated strategy, such strategies can be eliminated from consideration when searching for Nash equilibria. In the prisoners' dilemma, defection strictly dominates cooperation, so cooperation can be eliminated. No rational player will cooperate, and both will defect.

Notice that the result holds even though both prisoners agree that it would have been better if they had both cooperated. An outcome X is said to **Pareto dominate** another Y if all players weakly prefer X to Y and at least one player strictly prefers X to Y. An outcome is **Pareto optimal** if it is not Pareto dominated by any other outcome. In the prisoners' dilemma, the cooperative outcome $\langle C, C \rangle$ Pareto dominates the Nash equilibrium $\langle D, D \rangle$. In fact, both players strictly prefer the former to the latter. Still, rational players will jointly choose an outcome which is not Pareto optimal. For this reason, the prisoners' dilemma is sometimes presented – for example, in the film *A Beautiful Mind*, about game theory inventor and Nobel laureate John Nash – as refuting Adam Smith's insight that the rational pursuit of individual self-interest leads to socially desirable outcomes.

Many real-world interactions have features that are reminiscent of the prisoners' dilemma. Arms races are classic examples. Consider the nuclear buildup in India and Pakistan. Whether or not India has nuclear arms, Pakistan wants them. If India has them, Pakistan needs them to preserve the balance of power; if India does not have them, Pakistan wants them to get the upper hand. For the same reason, India wants nuclear arms whether or not Pakistan has them. Thus, both countries acquire nuclear arms, neither country has the upper hand, and both countries are worse off than if neither had them. Overfishing, deforestation, pollution, and many other phenomena are other classic examples. The idea is that no matter what other players do, each player has an incentive to fish, cut down forests, and pollute, but, if everyone does, everyone is worse off than if nobody had acted.

A number of different solutions might occur to you. What if the two prisoners, before committing the crime, got together and promised to cooperate in the event that they are caught? Surely, you might think, a gentleman's agreement and a handshake would do the trick. The solution fails, however, because whatever verbal agreement the prisoners might have entered into before getting caught will not be binding. At the end of the day, each has to make a choice in isolation, defection strictly dominates cooperation, and a rational agent has no choice but to defect. "Talk is cheap," the saying goes, which is why game theorists refer to non-binding verbal agreements as **cheap talk**.

What if the game could be repeated? Repetition, you might think, should afford a prisoner the opportunity to punish defection by defecting. But suppose the two prisoners play ten prisoners' dilemma games against each other. To find the equilibrium in the repeated game, we start at the end and use a procedure called **backward induction**. In the last round, no rational prisoner will cooperate, because his opponent has no way to retaliate against defection; so in round ten, both prisoners will defect. In the next to last round, a rational prisoner already knows that his opponent will defect in round ten, which means that it does not matter whether he cooperates or defects; so in round nine, both prisoners will defect. The same thing is true for round eight, round seven, and so on. In this way, the prospect of rational cooperation in the repeated prisoners' dilemma unravels from the end. Repetition does not necessarily solve the problem.

Cooperation can be sustained if there is no last round, that is, if the game is repeated indefinitely. In the indefinitely repeated prisoners' dilemma, there is a Nash equilibrium in which both prisoners cooperate throughout but are prepared to punish defection by defecting. The cooperative solution presupposes that the players do not discount the future too much: if they do, no amount of repetition will save the prisoners. And there is no guarantee that rational individuals will play that particular equilibrium. In fact, there is an *infinite* number of equilibria in the indefinitely repeated prisoners' dilemma, and in one of those equilibria prisoners always defect. In brief, indefinite repetition upholds the prospect of rational cooperation in the prisoners' dilemma, but cooperation is far from guaranteed.

There is only one sure-fire way for rational agents to avoid defection, and it is to make sure they are not playing a prisoners' dilemma at all. Suppose that the two criminals, before committing their crimes, go to the local contract killer and instruct him to kill anyone who defects in the event that he is caught. If death at the hands of a contract killer is associated with a utility of $-\infty$, the payoff matrix of the two prisoners will now look like Table 10.6. Here, cooperation strictly dominates defection

Table 10.6 The modified prisoners' dilemma

	C	D
C	3,3	$0,-\infty$
D	$-\infty,0$	$-\infty,-\infty$

for both players and $\langle C,C \rangle$ is the unique Nash equilibrium. You might think that it would never be in a person's interest to ask to be killed by a contract killer, no matter what the conditions; yet, by proceeding in this way, the prisoners can guarantee themselves a much better payoff than if they had not. But notice that cooperation is the uniquely rational strategy only because the two prisoners are no longer playing a prisoners' dilemma.

Example 10.7 The Leviathan The seventeenth-century political philosopher Thomas Hobbes offered a justification of political authority by imagining what life would be like without it. In one of the most famous lines in the history of Western philosophy, Hobbes described this "state of nature" as follows:

> [During] the time men live without a common power to keep them all in awe, they are in that condition which is called war, and such a war as is of every man against every man ... In such condition there is ... continual fear and danger of violent death, and the life of man, solitary, poor, nasty, brutish, and short.

The solution, according to Hobbes, is a covenant according to which people give up their right to kill and maim other people in exchange for the right not to be killed and maimed, and which at the same time establishes an overwhelming power – a *Leviathan* – to ensure that people adhere to the terms of the covenant (see Figure 10.2).

Game theory offers a new way to interpret the nature of this "war of all against all." These days, many people think of Hobbes's story as a vivid description of a scenario in which people are forced to play prisoners' dilemmas against each other, and in which the pursuit of rational self-interest therefore leads to the worst possible outcome for all involved. The Leviathan in Hobbes's story serves the same function as the contract killer in the scenario above: by holding people to their promises, he ensures that rational self-interest coincides with social desirability.

10.3 Nash equilibrium in mixed strategies

Some games have no Nash equilibria in pure strategies. But that does not mean that they do not have Nash equilibria.

Example 10.8 Coffee shops, cont. Suppose that you still have to go to one of the two coffee shops in Example 10.3 and that your ex has to also. You do not want to run into your ex, but your ex wants to run into you. What kind of game would you be playing against each other?

If a player gets a utility of 1 whenever his or her goal is attained and 0 otherwise, the payoff matrix is Table 10.7.

Non est potestas Super Terram quæ Comparetur ei Iob qu 24

Figure 10.2 The Leviathan. Detail of the frontispiece from the 1651 edition

Table 10.7 A pure coordination game

	Lucy's	Crestwood
Lucy's	1,0	0,1
Crestwood	0,1	1,0

This game has no Nash equilibria in pure strategies. If you go to Lucy's, your ex will want to go there too, but then you want to go to Crestwood, in which case your ex wants to do so too. This coffee shop game, by the way, has the same payoff structure as a game called **matching pennies**. When two people play matching pennies, each flips a penny. If both coins come up heads, or if both coins come up tails, Player I wins; otherwise, Player II wins. This also happens to be an example of a **zero-sum game**, a game in which whenever one player wins, another player loses.

The game does, however, have a **Nash equilibrium in mixed strategies**. Suppose that you figure out where to go by flipping a coin, and that your ex does the same. Given that you have a 50 percent chance of ending up at Lucy's and a 50 percent chance of ending up at Crestwood, your ex is indifferent between Lucy's and Crestwood and can do no better than flipping a coin. And given that your ex has a 50 percent chance of ending up at Lucy's and a 50 percent chance of ending up at Crestwood, you are indifferent between Lucy's and Crestwood and can do no better than flipping a coin. Hence, the two of you are in a Nash equilibrium, though you are playing mixed rather than pure strategies.

In a game like this, the mixed-strategy equilibrium is easy to find. In other games it can be more tricky. Consider the battle of the sexes (Example 10.4). In order to find a mixed-strategy equilibrium in a game like this, there is one critical insight: in order for players to rationally play a mixed strategy, they must be indifferent between the pure strategies they are mixing. Why? If a player strictly preferred one over the other, the only rational thing to do would be to play the preferred strategy with probability one. Thus, you can find the mixed-strategy equilibrium in a game by setting up equations and solving for the probabilities with which the players play different strategies.

Example 10.9 Battle of the sexes, cont.   In order to find the mixed-strategy equilibrium in the battle of the sexes (Table 10.8), let us assume that Player I plays U with probability p and D with probability $(1 - p)$ and that Player II plays L with probability q and R with probability $(1 - q)$.

Consider Player I first. In order to play a mixed strategy, he must be indifferent between U and D, meaning that $u(U) = u(D)$. The utility of playing U will depend on what Player II does, that is, on what q is. When playing U, Player I has a probability of q of getting 2 utiles and a probability of $(1 - q)$ of getting 0. Consequently, $u(U) = q*2 + (1 - q)*0 = 2q$. When playing D, Player I has a probability of q of getting 0 utiles and a probability of $(1 - q)$ of getting 1. Thus, $u(D) = q*0 + (1 - q)*1 = 1 - q$. So $u(U) = u(D)$ entails that $2q = 1 - q$, meaning that $q = 1/3$.

Next, consider Player II. In order to play a mixed strategy, she needs to be indifferent between L and R, meaning that $u(L) = u(R)$. Now $u(L) = p*1 + (1 - p)*0 = p$ and $u(R) = p*0 + (1 - p)*2 = 2 - 2p$. So $u(L) = u(R)$ entails that $p = 2 - 2p$, meaning that $p = 2/3$.

Hence, there is a Nash equilibrium in mixed strategies in which Player I plays U with probability 2/3 and Player II plays L with probability 1/3. In the mixed-strategy equilibrium, Player I gets payoff $u(U) = u(D) = 2q = 2/3$ and Player II gets payoff $u(L) = u(R) = p = 2/3$.

As this example shows, games with pure-strategy equilibria may also have mixed equilibria.

Exercise 10.10 Mixed-strategy equilibrium   Find the mixed-strategy Nash equilibria in Tables 10.4(a) and (b).

In the mixed-strategy equilibrium in (a), notice that Player I is more likely to play D than U and that Player II is more likely to play R than L. This might seem strange, since you would perhaps expect the players to be more likely to play the strategy associated with the more desirable equilibrium $\langle U, L \rangle$. But assume for a proof by contradiction that the two players are in a mixed-strategy equilibrium in which

Table 10.8 An impure coordination game

	L	R
U	2,1	0,0
D	0,0	1,2

Player I plays U and Player II plays L with some high probability. If so, Player I would strictly prefer U to D and Player II would strictly prefer L to R. Thus, the two players would not be in equilibrium at all, contrary to the initial assumption. For the two players to want to mix, they must be indifferent between the two pure strategies, and this can happen only when Player I is more likely to play D than U and that Player II is more likely to play R than L.

Notice also that the probability p with which Player I plays U is a function not of Player I's own payoffs, but of Player II's payoffs. This might seem equally counterintuitive. Yet, it follows from the fact that p must be selected in such a manner as to make Player II indifferent between her pure strategies. Similarly, the probability q with which Player II plays L is determined not by her payoffs, but by her opponent Player I's payoffs. This is a fascinating feature of Nash equilibria in mixed strategies.

Exercise 10.11 Pure vs. mixed equilibria Find all Nash equilibria (in pure and mixed strategies) in the games depicted in Table 10.9.

Although a mixed-strategy equilibrium may at first blush seem like an artificial construct of mainly academic interest, mixed strategies are important and common in a wide variety of strategic interactions. Even if you are a tennis player with a killer cross-court shot, it would be unwise to hit the cross-court shot every time, or your opponent will learn to expect it. Every so often, you must hit the ball down the line. In games like these, in order to keep your opponent guessing, you must mix it up a bit. This analysis shows that it is not a mistake, but *necessary*, every so often to hit your weaker shot.

Example 10.12 Spousonomics According to the authors of the book *Spousonomics*: "Economics is the surest route to marital bliss" because "it offers dispassionate, logical solutions to what can often seem like thorny, illogical, and highly emotional domestic disputes." Suppose that you are stuck in an equilibrium where you do the dishes, make the bed, and empty the cat litter while your spouse sits back and relaxes. Spousonomics, apparently, teaches that you can turn your spouse into an acceptable (if not ideal) partner by playing a mixed strategy, by sometimes doing the laundry, sometimes not, sometimes making the bed, sometimes not, and so on.

Exercise 10.13 Rock-paper-scissors (a) Draw the payoff matrix for the game rock-paper-scissors. Suppose that a win gives you 1 utile, a tie 0, and a loss -1. (b) What is the unique Nash equilibrium in this game?

We already know that not all games have Nash equilibria in pure strategies. But now that we have access to the concept of a Nash equilibrium in mixed strategies it

Table 10.9 Mixed Nash equilibrium exercises

	L	R		L	R		L	R
U	5,2	1,1	U	4,1	2,0	U	1,1	0,0
D	1,1	2,5	D	5,1	1,2	D	0,0	0,0
	(a)			(b)			(c)	

is possible to prove a famous theorem originally due to John Nash. Simplified and expressed in words:

Theorem 10.14 Nash's theorem   *Every finite game – that is, every game in which all players have a finite number of pure strategies – has a Nash equilibrium.*

Proof. Omitted.   □

Given this theorem, the search for Nash equilibria is not futile. As long as the number of pure strategies available to each player is finite – and whether this condition is satisfied is fairly easy to determine – we know that the game has at least one Nash equilibrium in pure or mixed strategies. This is neat.

Example 10.15 Chess   Chess is a finite game. We know this because every player has a finite number of moves to choose from at any point in the game and because every game ends after a finite number of moves. Because it is a finite game, Nash's theorem establishes that it has an equilibrium.

This suggests that chess should be uninteresting, at least when played by experienced players. Assuming Player I plays the equilibrium strategy, Player II can do no better than playing the equilibrium strategy, and vice versa. Thus, we should expect experienced players to implement the equilibrium strategies every time, and the outcome to be familiar and predictable.

Yet Nash's theorem only establishes the existence of an equilibrium; it does not reveal what the equilibrium strategies are. As of yet, no computer is powerful enough to figure out what they are. And even if we knew what the strategies were, they might be too complex for human beings to implement. Thus, chess is likely to remain interesting for a good long time.

Before we move on, two more exercises.

Exercise 10.16 Chicken   The game **chicken** was popularized in the 1955 film *Rebel Without a Cause*, starring James Dean. The game is played by two people who drive cars straight at each other at high speed; the person who swerves first is called "chicken" and becomes an object of contempt. In this game, the British philosopher Bertrand Russell saw an analogy with Cold War policy:

> Since the nuclear stalemate became apparent, the Governments of East and West have adopted the policy which [US Secretary of State] Mr Dulles calls "brinkmanship". This is a policy adapted from a sport which, I am told, is practised by some youthful degenerates. This sport is called "Chicken!" ... As played by irresponsible boys, this game is considered decadent and immoral, though only the lives of the players are risked. But when the game is played by eminent statesmen, who risk not only their own lives but those of many hundreds of millions of human beings, it is thought on both sides that the statesmen on one side are displaying a high degree of wisdom and courage, and only the statesmen on the other side are reprehensible. This, of course, is absurd.

Imagine that each player has the choice between swerving (S) and not swerving (¬S), and that the payoff structure is that of Table 10.10. Find all Nash equilibria in this game.

Table 10.10   Chicken

	S	¬S
S	3,3	2,5
¬S	5,2	1,1

In a branch of game theory called **evolutionary game theory**, this game figures prominently under the heading of **hawk & dove**. Hawks are willing to fight to the death whereas doves easily give up. The best possible outcome for you results when you are a hawk and your opponent is a dove, the second best outcome when both of you are doves, the third best when you are a dove and your opponent is a hawk, and and the worst possible outcome when both of you are hawks. If doves "swerve" and hawks do not, the payoff structure of hawk & dove is the same as that of chicken. In evolutionary game theory, the mixed-strategy equilibrium is interpreted as describing a population in which hawks and doves coexist in given proportions – just as they do in the real world.

Exercise 10.17 The stag hunt   This game is due to Jean-Jacques Rousseau, the eighteenth-century French philosopher. Rousseau describes a scenario in which two individuals go hunting. The two can hunt hare or deer but not both. Anyone can catch a hare by himself, but the only way to bag a deer is for both hunters to pursue the deer. A deer is much more valuable than a hare. The **stag hunt**, which is thought to provide an important parable for social cooperation, is usually represented as in Table 10.11. What are the Nash equilibria (in pure and mixed strategies) of this game?

Table 10.11   The stag hunt

	D	H
D	3,3	0,1
H	1,0	1,1

Notice how superficially subtle differences in the payoff structure between the prisoners' dilemma (Table 10.5(b)), chicken (Table 10.10), and the stag hunt (Table 10.11) lead to radically different results.

10.4   Equilibrium refinements

The concept of a Nash equilibrium is associated with a number of controversial results. In this section, we consider two alternative equilibrium concepts, designed to deal with supposedly problematic cases.

Example 10.18 Trembling-hand perfection   Let us return to Table 10.9(c). As you know, ⟨U,L⟩ is a Nash equilibrium. ⟨D,L⟩ is *not* an equilibrium, since Player I can improve his payoff by playing U instead of D, and neither is ⟨U,R⟩. But consider ⟨D,R⟩. If Player II plays R, Player I can do no better than playing D; if Player I plays D, Player II can do no better than playing R. Thus, ⟨D,R⟩ is a Nash equilibrium.

There are no mixed equilibria. No matter what Player II does, Player I will never be indifferent between U and D, and no matter what Player I does, Player II will never be indifferent between L and R.

There is nothing wrong with the analysis here, but there is something odd about the second equilibrium $\langle D, R \rangle$. A strategy X is said to weakly dominate another strategy Y if choosing X is no worse than choosing Y no matter what the other player does, and choosing X is better than choosing Y for at least one strategy available to the other player. In Example 10.18, U weakly dominates D and L weakly dominates R. Thus, there seems to be no reason why rational individuals would ever play the second equilibrium $\langle D, R \rangle$. And the problem is not that (1,1) Pareto dominates (0,0) (see Section 10.2).

The concept of a **trembling-hand-perfect equilibrium** was designed to handle this kind of situation.

Definition 10.19 Trembling-hand-perfect equilibrium *A trembling-hand-perfect equilibrium is a Nash equilibrium that remains a best response for each player even when others have some minuscule probability of* **trembling***, that is, accidentally playing an out-of-equilibrium strategy.*

In Table 10.9(c), $\langle U, L \rangle$ is a trembling-hand-perfect equilibrium: even if there is a minuscule probability $\epsilon > 0$ that Player II plays R, she still plays L with probability $(1 - \epsilon)$ and U remains a best response for Player I. (And similarly for the other player.) By contrast, $\langle D, R \rangle$ is not trembling-hand perfect. If there is a minuscule probability $\epsilon > 0$ that Player II plays L, no matter how small, U is a strictly preferred strategy for Player I.

Exercise 10.20 Battle of the sexes, cont. Are the two pure-strategy equilibria in the battle of the sexes (Table 10.8) trembling-hand perfect?

Trembling-hand-perfect equilibrium is a **refinement** of Nash equilibrium. This means that every trembling-hand-perfect equilibrium is a Nash equilibrium, but not every Nash equilibrium is trembling-hand perfect.

Exercise 10.21 Trembling-hand perfection Find (a) all Nash equilibria in pure strategies in Table 10.12 and (b) identify which of them are trembling-hand perfect.

Substituting the concept of trembling-hand-perfect equilibrium for the concept of Nash equilibrium would eliminate some problematic implications of the

Table 10.12 Trembling-hand perfection, cont.

	L	M	R
U	1,4	0,0	0,0
M	0,0	4,1	0,0
D	0,0	0,0	0,0

Nash-equilibrium concept. The concept of trembling-hand equilibrium is, however, insufficient to deal with all problematic cases.

Example 10.22 Credible versus non-credible threats   Consider a game with two stages. In the first stage, Player I plays U or D. If Player I plays D, both players get a payoff of 2. If Player I plays U, it is Player II's turn. In the second stage, Player II plays L or R; if Player II plays L, Player I gets 5 and Player II gets 1. If Player II plays R, both get 0. What are the Nash equilibria of this game?

The game can be represented as in Table 10.13. There are two Nash equilibria: ⟨U,L⟩ and ⟨D,R⟩.

Table 10.13   Subgame perfection

	L	R
U	5,1	0,0
D	2,2	2,2

Yet there is something odd about the second of the two equilibria. The only thing preventing Player I from playing U is the threat of Player II playing R. But suppose that Player I did play U. Then, Player II would have the choice of playing L (for a payoff of 1) and R (for a payoff of 0). In the second stage, it is not in Player II's interest to play R. So while it is perfectly possible for Player II to threaten to play R if Player I plays U, she would have no interest in carrying out the threat. Knowing this, it appears that Player I should just go ahead and play U. Game theorists say that the problem is that Player II's threat is not **credible**. Many people think that it is problematic that a Nash equilibrium might involve a non-credible threat. And the problem is not that the Nash equilibrium is not trembling-hand perfect.

Games with multiple stages are called **sequential**. To analyze such games, it is often useful to use a tree-like representation called the **extensive form**. The game from Example 10.22 can, for example, be represented as in Figure 10.3. This representation affords another way to spell out the problem. Consider that part of the game which starts at the node where Player II moves (see the shaded area in the figure). We refer to it as a **subgame** of the original game. In the subgame, Player II has two strategies (L and R) and there is only one Nash equilibrium: to play L (for a payoff of 1) rather than R (for a payoff of 0). Yet the Nash equilibrium in the game requires Player II to play R in the subgame. One way to spell out the problem, then, is to say that the Nash equilibrium of the *game* requires Player II to play a strategy that is not a Nash equilibrium in the *subgame*.

Consistent with this analysis, game theorists have proposed another equilibrium concept: **subgame-perfect equilibrium**. As suggested in the previous paragraph, a subgame of a game is any part of that game which in itself constitutes a game. A game is always its own subgame, but in this case there is a proper subgame starting at the node where Player II moves.

Definition 10.23 Subgame-perfect equilibrium   *A subgame-perfect equilibrium is a strategy profile that constitutes a Nash equilibrium in each subgame.*

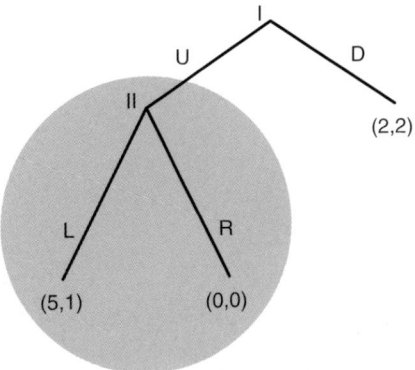

Figure 10.3 Subgame perfection

Like trembling-hand-perfect equilibrium, subgame-perfect equilibrium is a refinement of Nash equilibrium: all subgame-perfect equilibria are Nash equilibria, but not all Nash equilibria are subgame perfect.

One way to find subgame-perfect equilibria is to start at the end and use backward induction. Backward induction would tell you to start with the last subgame, that is, at the node where Player II moves (the shaded area of the figure). Since L would lead to a payoff of 1 and R would lead to a payoff of 0, L is the unique Nash equilibrium strategy. So, in subgame-perfect equilibrium, Player II will play L. Given that Player II will play L, what will Player I do at the first node? Player I has the choice between playing U for a payoff of 3, and playing D for a payoff of 2. Thus, Player I will play U. In brief, there is only one subgame-perfect equilibrium in this game, and it is $\langle U, L \rangle$.

Example 10.24 MAD   Mutually assured destruction (MAD) is a military doctrine according to which two superpowers (such as the US and the USSR) can maintain peace by threatening to annihilate the human race in the event of an enemy attack. Suppose that the US moves first in a game like that in Figure 10.3. The US can launch an attack (U) or not launch an attack (D). If it launches an attack, the USSR can refrain from retaliating (L) or annihilate the human race (R). Given the payoff structure of the game in the figure, $\langle D, R \rangle$ is a Nash equilibrium. The doctrine is flawed, however, in that the threat is not credible: the MAD Nash equilibrium presupposes that USSR forces are willing to annihilate the human race in the event of a US attack, which would obviously not be in their interest. Thus, the MAD Nash equilibrium is not subgame perfect.

In Stanley Kubrick's 1963 film *Dr Strangelove*, the USSR tries to circumvent the problem by building a **doomsday machine**: a machine that in the event of an enemy attack (or when tampered with) automatically launches an attack powerful enough to annihilate the human race. Such a machine would solve the strategic problem, because it guarantees retaliation to enemy attack and therefore makes the threat credible. As the film illustrates, however, such machines are associated with other problems. To begin with, you must not forget to tell your enemy that you have one.

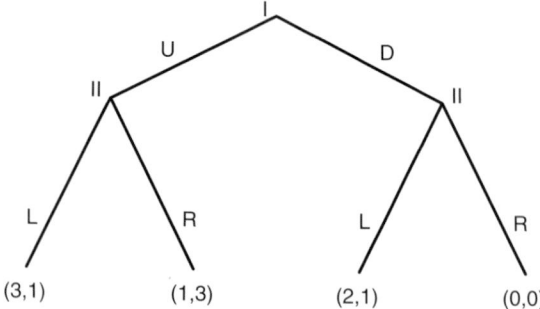

Figure 10.4 Subgame perfection exercise

Exercise 10.25 Subgame perfection Use backward induction to find the unique subgame-perfect equilibrium in the game in Figure 10.4. Recall that a strategy is a complete plan of action, which means that a strategy for Player II will have the form "L at the first node and L at the second (LL)," "R at the first node and L at the second (RL)," and the like. In this game, then, whereas Player I only has two strategies to choose from, Player II has four.

Finally, one more exercise:

Exercise 10.26 The centipede game The centipede game has four stages (see Figure 10.5). At each stage, a player can Take, thereby ending the game, or Pass, thereby increasing the total payoff and allowing the other player to move. (a) Use backward induction to find the unique subgame-perfect equilibrium. (b) Would the outcome of the game differ if it had 1000 stages instead of four?

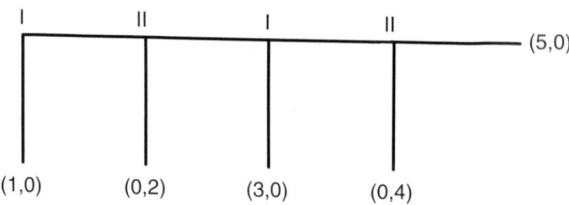

Figure 10.5 The centipede game

10.5 Discussion

Like the theories we came across earlier in this book, analytical game theory admits of descriptive and normative interpretations. According to the descriptive interpretation, game theory captures the manner in which people behave when they engage in strategic interactions. In this view, game theory predicts that people will jointly choose an equilibrium strategy profile. Specific predictions, of course, will depend not only on the game played, but on the equilibrium concept that is employed. According to the normative interpretation, game theory describes how rational agents should behave when they engage in strategic interaction. In this view, game theory says that players should jointly choose an equilibrium strategy profile. Again, the specific advice offered by the theory will depend on the game played and the equilibrium concept employed.

One thing to notice is that games do not necessarily have a unique equilibrium. And analytical game theory in itself does not contain the resources required to identify *which* equilibrium people will or should play. While the theory can be interpreted as predicting that the outcome of strategic interaction will or should be a Nash equilibrium, this is only to say that some Nash equilibrium will or should obtain. In this sense, then, the theory is indeterminate. And because some games (like the indefinitely repeated prisoners' dilemma) have an infinite number of equilibria, the theory is radically indeterminate.

If we want determinate predictions, we must augment the theory with additional resources. The most famous such effort is the theory of **focal points**, due to the 2005 Nobel laureate Thomas C. Schelling. According to this theory, some equilibria tend to stand out in the minds of the players. Schelling predicts that people will frequently succeed in selecting such equilibria. The precise feature of an equilibrium that makes it stand out in the minds of the players is far from obvious.

> Finding the key ... may depend on imagination more than on logic; it may depend on analogy, precedent, accidental arrangement, symmetry, aesthetic or geometric configuration, casuistic reasoning, and who the parties are and what they know about each other.

This theory can explain why people favor ⟨U, L⟩ over ⟨D, R⟩ in Table 10.9(c). When there is a unique Pareto-optimal outcome that also happens to be a Nash equilibrium, it seems plausible to assume that people will use Pareto optimality as a focal point. If so, we might be able to explain observed behavior without making the transition to trembling-hand-perfect equilibrium.

In the next chapter, we will explore behavioral economists' challenge to analytical game theory.

Additional exercises

Exercise 10.27 Paradoxes of rationality   Experimental economists have invited students with different majors to play prisoners'-dilemma games against each other. In an experiment pitching economics majors against economics majors, and non-majors against non-majors, who would you expect to do better?

Chapter 11 contains more game-theoretic exercises.

Further reading

There are many fine introductions to game theory, including Binmore (2007), Dixit et al. (2009), and Osborne and Rubinstein (1994). *Spousonomics* is Szuchman and Anderson (2011, pp. xii–xv, 294–8). Life in the state of nature is described in Hobbes (1994 [1651], xiii, 8–9, p. 76). Skyrms (1996) discusses the doctrine of mutually assured destruction (pp. 22–5) and the games of chicken and hawk & dove (pp. 65–7); Russell (1959, p. 30) examines the game of chicken. The theory of focal points is due to Schelling (1960, p. 57). Evidence about economics majors' performance in prisoner dilemma games can be found in Frank et al. (1993).

Behavioral Game Theory

11.1 Introduction

Analytical game theory is in many ways a huge success story: it is increasingly becoming the foundation of other sub disciplines of economics (including microeconomics) and it has migrated to philosophy, biology, political science, government, public policy, and elsewhere. But, as we will see in this chapter, its descriptive adequacy and normative correctness are controversial. **Behavioral game theory** aims to study the degree to which analytical game theory succeeds in capturing the behavior of real people engaging in strategic interaction, and proposes extensions of analytical game theory in the interest of capturing that behavior. Yet some of the proposed extensions to analytical game theory do not in fact constitute deviations from neoclassical orthodoxy. Thus, there is nothing distinctively behavioral about some of the models discussed under the heading "behavioral game theory." Other models, however, constitute real deviations from neoclassical orthodoxy.

11.2 Social preferences: Altruism, envy, fairness, and justice

Much of the literature on social preferences is driven by data from two games: the **ultimatum game** and the **dictator game**. Both are played by two agents: a **proposer** (Player I) and a **responder** (Player II). Here, these games are outlined as they are presented to participants in laboratory experiments, where outcomes are described in terms of dollars and cents rather than in terms of the utilities that players derive from them. In order to analyze the interaction, we need to transform the dollars and cents into utilities. Strictly speaking, you do not even know what game the players are playing until you have identified payoffs in utility terms. But doing so is far from obvious, as we will see.

The ultimatum game has two stages. At the outset, the proposer is given a fixed amount of money; for purposes of this discussion, let us suppose it is $10. In the first stage, Player I proposes a division of the dollar amount; that is, the proposer offers some share of the $10 to the other player. The proposer might propose to give it all away (leaving nothing for himself), to give none of it away (leaving all of it for himself), or to offer some fraction of the $10 to the other player (leaving the balance for himself). For example, the proposer might offer $4, leaving $6 for himself. In the second stage, the responder accepts or rejects the proposed division. If she accepts, both players receive their proposed share; if she rejects, neither player receives anything. The ultimatum game can be represented as in Figure 11.1. In this figure, I have omitted all branches corresponding to fractional amounts, and I have left out all but one set of branches representing Player II's decision in the second stage.

Example 11.1 Dividing the cake When two children have to divide a cake, they sometimes follow a procedure in which the first child splits the cake in two and the

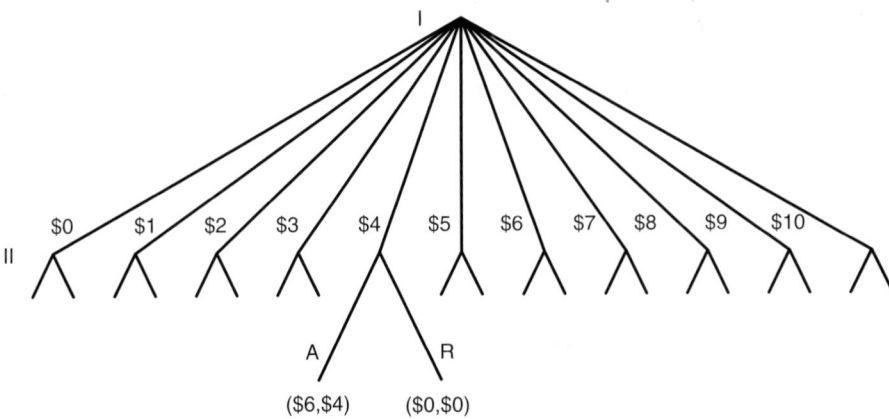

Figure 11.1 The ultimatum game (in dollar terms)

second chooses first. Given that Kid II will choose the largest piece, Kid I will want to divide the cake as evenly as possible, thereby guaranteeing a 50–50 split. We can easily imagine a variation of this procedure, in which Kid I proposes a division of the cake, and Kid II gets to approve (in which case each child gets the proposed piece) or disapprove (in which case the parents give the entire cake to the dog). The new procedure would constitute an example of the ultimatum game.

The ultimatum game has been extensively studied by experimental economists. According to Colin F. Camerer's survey of the results:

> The results . . . are very regular. Modal and median ultimatum offers are usually 40–50 per-cent and means are 30–40 percent. There are hardly any offers in the outlying categories 0, 1–10, and the hyper-fair category 51–100. Offers of 40–50 are rarely rejected. Offers below 20 percent or so are rejected about half the time.

Based on these results, we should expect responders to reject offers below $2 when playing the (one-shot, anonymous) game in Figure 11.1. But such low offers would be rare. By and large, we should expect offers in the $3–$5 range. Many people have drawn the conclusion that these results are inconsistent with analytical game theory.

The observed outcomes are quite consistent with Nash equilibrium predictions, however, even when players care about nothing but their own dollar payoffs. Let us assume that each individual is simply trying to maximize his or her dollar pay-offs, and that $u(x) = x$. Player I must choose an amount to offer the other player; suppose that he offers $4. Player II's strategy is a little more convoluted. Because a strategy must specify what a player will do under all possible circumstances (see Section 10.2), Player II's strategy must specify what she will do at each of the nodes where she might find herself. Suppose that Player II rejects all proposed divisions in which Player I offers less than $4 and accepts all others. If so, the two players are in equilibrium. If Player I decreased his offer, it would be rejected, and both would receive nothing; if he increased his offer, it would be accepted, but he would receive less. Given that Player I offers $4, Player II can do no better than accepting. In brief, data on the ultimatum game do not represent a puzzle from the point of view of the theory we learned in Section 10.2, since observed outcomes are consistent with Nash equilibrium predictions. (Given the many equilibria of this game, though, this is not saying much.)

Nevertheless, many people think the Nash equilibrium prediction is problematic, since it requires players to reject positive offers. One way to articulate the problem is to say that the Nash equilibrium in the game requires players to reject what is in effect a dominant strategy (namely, accepting) in the subgame that starts at the node where Player II moves. Another way to articulate the problem is to say that the equilibrium is not subgame perfect and that Player II's threat to reject a low offer is not credible (see Section 10.4). We might, therefore, restrict our analysis to subgame-perfect equilibria. Yet there is only one subgame-perfect equilibrium in this game. In this equilibrium, Player I offers nothing and Player II accepts all offers. This might be counterintuitive. But it is a Nash equilibrium because (a) given Player I's offer, Player II would be no better off if she rejected it, and (b) given that Player II accepts all offers, Player I can do no better than to keep all the money for himself. It is a subgame-perfect equilibrium, because Player II's strategy is also a Nash equilibrium strategy in all subgames: no matter what she has been offered, she cannot improve her payoff by rejecting the offer. A prediction based on the idea of subgame-perfect equilibrium, given our assumption about the two players' utility function, is in fact inconsistent with the experimental results.

The dictator game resembles the ultimatum game, except for the fact that the second stage has been eliminated. In dollar terms and assuming that the proposer starts out with $10, the dictator game can be represented as in Figure 11.2; again, I have left out all the branches representing fractional amounts. On the assumption that the players' utility function remains $u(x) = x$, there is only one Nash equilibrium and therefore only one subgame-perfect equilibrium: the case in which Player I offers nothing to the responder and keeps all the money for himself.

Example 11.2 Charitable donations   One example of a dictator game played in the real world involves a person's decision about whether to give money to charity. Whenever you walk by a beggar, for example, you are in effect playing a dictator game in which you must propose some allocation of the money in your pocket with the panhandler. If you walk on, you have in effect picked the maximally selfish, Nash-equilibrium allocation.

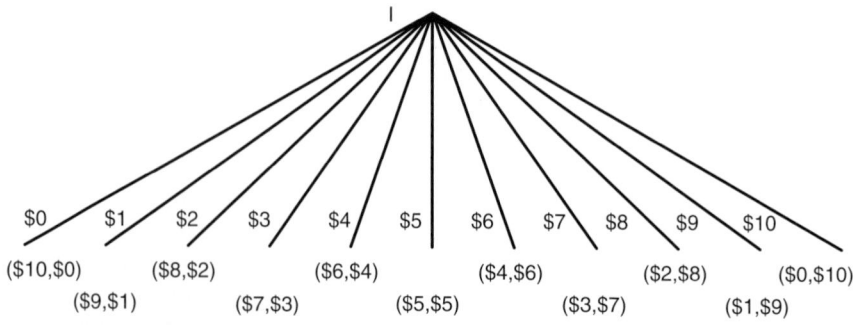

Figure 11.2   The dictator game (in dollar terms)

Experimental evidence suggests that proposers in the (one-shot, . nonymous) dictator game typically offer less than proposers in the (one-shot, anonymous) ultimatum game. That said, many proposers are nevertheless willing to share a substantial amount (10–30 percent) of their initial allocation. In the version of the game in Figure 11.2, this means that the proposer would be willing to share $1–$3 with the responder, even though the latter has no way to penalize proposers who offer nothing.

The literature on **social preference** grapples with these phenomena. This literature is based on the assumption that people sometimes care not only about their own attainment but about other people's attainment too. We can model this by assuming that a person P's utility function $u_P(\cdot)$ has two or more arguments. Thus, P's utility function may be given by $u_P(x,y)$, where x is P's attainment and y is the other person Q's attainment.

It is quite possible for P to derive positive utility from Q's attainment, so that $u_P(x,y)$ is an increasing function of y. For example, P's utility function may be $u_P(x,y) = 3/5\sqrt{x} + 2/5\sqrt{y}$. If so, P is said to be **altruistic** and to have **altruistic preferences**. Some parents, relatives, friends, and admirers are willing to make real sacrifices in order to improve other people's situation. This is easily explained if we assume that their utility is (in part) a function of the other person's attainment. Altruism in this sense might be what Adam Smith had in mind when he said: "[There] are evidently some principles in [man's] nature, which interest him in the fortune of others, and render their happiness necessary to him" (quoted in Section 1.2).

There is no requirement that P derive *positive* utility from Q's attainment. In fact, $u_P(x,y)$ may be a decreasing function of y. For example, P's utility function may be $u_P(x,y) = \sqrt{x} - \sqrt{y}$. This specification entails that P's utility goes up when Q's attainment goes down and *vice versa*. If so, P is said to be **envious**. Some Prius hybrid-car owners derive deep satisfaction from rising gasoline prices. This cannot be explained by reference to the financial effects of gasoline prices on the Prius owner: though fuel-efficient, a Prius remains a gasoline-powered car; so rising gasoline prices will hurt Prius owners too. But it can be explained if we assume that the disutility Prius owners derive from getting less gasoline for their dollar is outweighed by the utility they derive from knowing that SUV owners suffer even more.

There is no reason to restrict our analysis to these functional forms. According to a common interpretation of John Rawls's theory of justice (see Section 6.2), societies should be ordered with respect to justice based on the welfare of the least fortunate in each society. Thus, a person with **Rawlsian preferences** might try to maximize the minimum utility associated with the allocation. If each individual derives $\sqrt{x}$ utiles from his or her private consumption x, the Rawlsian P might maximize $u_P(x,y) = \min(\sqrt{x}, \sqrt{y})$. Rawls uses the term "justice as fairness" to describe his theory, so Rawlsian preferences could also be described as preferences for **fairness**.

Another agent might care about the degree of inequality among the relevant agents, so as to rank allocations based on the absolute difference between the best and worst off. Such an agent is said to be **inequality averse** and to have inequality-averse preferences. If each individual derives $\sqrt{x}$ utiles from his or her private consumption x, the inequality-averse P might maximize $u_P(x,y) = \min(|\sqrt{x} - \sqrt{y}|)$. Such agents care about equality for its own sake, unlike the Rawlsians who (given the definition above) care about equality only insofar as it benefits the least well off. Because the inequality-averse agent ends up assessing the outcomes of ultimatum and dictator games so similarly to the Rawlsian agent, I will not discuss this case further.

Utilitarians like Bentham, whom we came across in section 1.2, believe that we should pursue the greatest good for the greatest number. Thus, a utilitarian agent might try to maximize the total amount of utility derived from private consumption. If each individual derives $\sqrt{x}$ utiles from his or her private consumption x, the utilitarian P might maximize $u_P(x, y) = \sqrt{x} + \sqrt{y}$. So understood, **utilitarian preferences** constitute a special case of altruistic preferences. Obviously, this list is far from exhaustive: any agent who derives utility from another agent's private consumption counts as having social preferences.

To see how the shape of the proposer's utility function affects his assessment of the various outcomes in the ultimatum and dictator games, see Table 11.1. When the payoff is ($0, $0) all kinds of agent receive zero utility. Egoists and enviers prefer the outcome where they get all the money. Utilitarians and Rawlsians prefer outcomes where the dollar amount is split evenly. Finally, an altruist who gives a little more weight to her own private utility than does a utilitarian might prefer the outcome ($7, $3) to all others.

It goes without saying that certain kinds of social preference would go a long way toward explaining proposers' behavior in the ultimatum and dictator games. Altruists, Rawlsians, and utilitarians actually *prefer* more equal outcomes. For such agents, there is nothing mysterious about the fact that they voluntarily offer non-zero amounts to responders.

Exercise 11.3 Altruism and the ultimatum game Imagine the ultimatum game from Figure 11.1 played by two utilitarians with $u(x, y) = \sqrt{x} + \sqrt{y}$. Find the unique subgame-perfect equilibrium in this game.

One important insight underscored by the literature on social preferences is that the game people are playing depends on their utility functions. The following exercise illustrates how agents with different utility functions end up playing very different games, even when their interactions superficially might look identical.

Table 11.1 Dictator game utility payoffs (maxima in boldface)

Payoffs	Player P's utility function $u_P(x, y)$				
(x, y)	$\sqrt{x}$	$\sqrt{x} + \sqrt{y}$	$\sqrt{x} - \sqrt{y}$	$\min(\sqrt{x}, \sqrt{y})$	$\frac{3}{5}\sqrt{x} + \frac{2}{5}\sqrt{y}$
($10, $0)	**3.16**	3.16	**3.16**	0.00	1.90
($9, $1)	3	4.00	2.00	1.00	2.20
($8, $2)	2.83	4.24	1.41	1.41	2.26
($7, $3)	2.65	4.38	0.91	1.73	**2.28**
($6, $4)	2.45	4.45	0.45	2	2.27
($5, $5)	2.24	**4.47**	0.00	**2.24**	2.24
($4, $6)	2.00	4.45	−0.45	2	2.18
($3, $7)	1.73	4.38	−0.91	1.73	2.10
($2, $8)	1.41	4.24	−1.41	1.41	1.98
($1, $9)	1.00	4.00	−2.00	1.00	1.80
($0, $10)	0.00	3.16	−3.16	0.00	1.26

Table 11.2 Prisoners' dilemma (in dollar terms)

	C	D
C	$16,$16	$0,$25
D	$25,$0	$9,$9

Exercise 11.4 Social preferences and the prisoners' dilemma Find the Nash equilibria in pure strategies in Table 11.2, when played by (a) two egoists, for whom $u(x,y) = \sqrt{x}$; (b) two utilitarians, for whom $u(x,y) = \sqrt{x} + \sqrt{y}$; (c) two enviers, for whom $u(x,y) = \sqrt{x} - \sqrt{y}$; and (d) two Rawlsians, for which $u(x,y) = \min(\sqrt{x}, \sqrt{y})$. Notice that this game (in dollar terms) has the payoff structure of the prisoners' dilemma (Table 10.5 on page 179).

Social preferences are fascinating and important. Economists who do not allow for the possibility of social preferences run the risk of committing terrible mistakes, whether they are trying to explain or predict behavior or to design optimal incentives. If we are mistaken about the players' utility function, we will not even know what game they are playing. Consequently, our analysis of their interaction is likely to fail. Consider the game in Table 11.2. Superficially, when expressed in dollar terms, this looks like a prisoners' dilemma. But as Exercise 11.4 showed, the players may in fact be playing a very different game.

Notice, however, that the entire analysis in this section can be completed without departing from neoclassical orthodoxy. As we know from sections 1.1 and 2.6, the standard approach makes no assumptions about the nature of people's preferences. Consequently, it makes no assumptions about what can enter as an argument in people's utility function. It is sometimes argued that the results from the dictator and ultimatum games refute the "selfishness axiom" of neoclassical economics. But this charge is misguided: not only is there no such axiom in the calculus, but selfishness is not even entailed by the theory. Hence, there is nothing specifically behavioral about models of social preferences; if anything, the analysis shows the strength and power of the neoclassical framework.

11.3 Intentions, reciprocity, and trust

There is, however, something awkward about the account offered in the previous section. In order to accommodate the behavior of the proposer in the dictator game, we postulate that proposers are largely altruistic. But in order to accommodate the behavior of responders in the ultimatum game, this approach is inadequate. As you can tell from the third column of Table 11.1, an altruist with utility function $u(x,y) = \sqrt{x} + \sqrt{y}$ would prefer any outcome to ($0,$0). In a subgame-perfect equilibrium, therefore, an altruistic responder would accept all offers (see Exercise 11.3). But this is inconsistent with the observation that low offers frequently are rejected. Of all the agents described in the table, only the enviers prefer ($0,$0) to a sharply unfavorable division like ($8,$2). And it would be inconsistent to postulate that people are simultaneously altruistic (to explain their behavior in the dictator game) and envious (to accommodate their behavior in the ultimatum game).

There are other awkward results. In a variation of the ultimatum game, respon-ders were found to reject the uneven division ($8,$2) if the proposer had the choice between ($8,$2) and the even division ($5,$5), but accept it if the proposer had the choice between ($8,$2) and the maximally uneven division ($10,$0). This makes no sense from the point of view of a responder who evaluates final outcomes in accordance with either one of the social preference functions in the previous section. According to each of those models, either ($8,$2) is better than ($0,$0) or it is not; the choices available to the proposer do not matter at all.

To some analysts, these results suggest that responders do not base their deci-sions on the final outcome of the game alone, but are (at least in part) responsive to what they see as the proposer's **intentions**. In this view, people are willing to reward people who are perceived as having good intentions and to punish peo-ple who are perceived as having bad intentions. A proposer who offers $2 rather than $0 is interpreted as having good intentions, even if the resulting allocation is uneven, whereas a proposer who offers $2 rather than $5 is interpreted as hav-ing bad intentions. Sometimes, these results are discussed in terms of **reciprocity** or **reciprocal altruism**. Respondents are said to exhibit **positive reciprocity** when they reward players with good intentions and **negative reciprocity** when they punish proposers with bad intentions. Thus, a responder in the ultimatum game who rejects a small positive offer from the proposer is said to exhibit negative reciprocity.

Reciprocity is often invoked in discussions of the **trust game**. This game is played by two players: a **sender** (Player I) and a **receiver** (Player II). At the outset, both are awarded some initial amount, let us suppose $10. In the first stage, the sender sends some share x of his $10 to the receiver. The amount is sometimes called an "investment." Before the investment is received by the receiver, it is multiplied by some factor, let us say three. Thus, the receiver receives $3x$. In the second stage, the receiver returns to the sender some share y of her total allocation $10 + $3x$. The final outcome, then, is ($10 − $x + $y, $10 + $3x − $y). The game is called the trust game for the obvious reason that the sender might **trust** the receiver to return some of her gains to him. When both agents maximize $u(x) = x$, there is only one subgame-perfect equilibrium in this game. Since the receiver maximizes by keeping all her money, y will equal zero. Notice that the receiver is in effect playing a dictator game with the sender as a beneficiary. Given that none of the share x will be returned to him, the sender will keep all his money and x will equal zero. Notice that the resulting allocation ($10,$10) is Pareto inferior to many other attainable allocations. If $x = 10$ and $y = 20$, for example, the final outcome is ($20,$20).

Example 11.5 Investment decisions Suppose that you have the opportunity to invest in a promising business venture, but that you have no way to recover your expenses in case your business partner turns out to be unreliable. In order to cap-tures the gains from trade, you simply must trust the partner to do the job. If so, you and your business partner are playing a trust game against each other. If you play the subgame-perfect equilibrium strategy, you will never invest. But if you never invest, you will never capture any of the available surplus.

Experimental economists have found that senders in the (one-shot, anonymous) trust game on the mean send about half of their initial allocation, and that receivers return a little less than what was invested. Given the figures from the previous paragraph, we should expect senders to send about $5 and receivers to return somewhere between $4 and $5. Thus, Player II succeeds in capturing some, but not all, of the available surplus. (There is a great deal of variability across studies, however.)

Why would a responder care to return some of the sender's investment when the latter has no way to penalize a receiver who returns nothing? According to one frequent answer, the receiver feels like she must reciprocate the sender's investment. Thus, a receiver who returns some of the sender's investment is said to exhibit positive reciprocity. The receiver's behavior is also consistent with altruism and inequality aversion. Meanwhile, the sender's behavior is thought to reflect the expectation that his investment will be repaid in combination with some degree of altruism.

A similar analysis obtains in the case of prisoners' dilemma and **public-goods games**. We know the prisoners' dilemma from Section 10.2. In a typical public-goods game, there are n players. For purposes of this discussion, let us assume that there are three players. Each is given an initial allocation, say $10. The game has only one stage, in which all players move simultaneously. Each player has the option of transferring a share of their initial allocation to a public account. The money in the public account is multiplied by some factor between one and three, say two, and split evenly between the players.

Given the nature of the game, the Pareto optimal outcome results when all players transfer all their money to the public account. In this case, the payoff is ($20, $20, $20). But the Pareto optimal outcome is not a Nash equilibrium, for each player can improve his outcome by transferring less. Indeed, there is only one Nash equilibrium in this game, and it is when nobody transfers any money to the public account and the outcome is ($10, $10, $10). Public-goods games therefore have certain structural similarities with the prisoners' dilemma.

The nature of this interaction should be familiar. Perhaps a set of roommates all prefer the state in which all assist in washing the dishes to the state in which nobody washes the dishes, but no matter what the others do, each roommate prefers not to wash any dishes. Thus, nobody washes the dishes and all suffer the Pareto-inferior outcome. Or, all members in a neighborhood association prefer the state in which all members spend one day a year cleaning up the neighborhood to the state in which nobody spends any time cleaning up the neighborhood, but no matter what the others do, each member prefers not to clean the neighborhood. Thus, nobody cleans the neighborhood and all suffer the Pareto-inferior outcome.

Yet, in experimental studies, cooperation remains a remarkably stubborn phenomenon. In the prisoners' dilemma, the fraction of people playing the cooperative strategy is not 100 percent. But neither is it zero, even when people are playing the one-shot game anonymously. And in anonymous, one-shot public-goods games, Robyn M. Dawes and Richard H. Thaler report:

> While not everyone contributes, there is a substantial number of contributors, and the public good is typically provided at 40–60 percent of the optimal quantity. That is, on average, the subjects contribute 40–60 percent of their stake to the public good. In [one study], these results held in many conditions: for subjects playing the game for the first time, or after a previous experience; for subjects who believed they were playing in groups of 4 or 80; and for subjects playing for a range of monetary stakes.

Why do people cooperate in one-shot prisoners'-dilemma and public-goods games? The experimental results are consistent with a high level of trust in the other players and with a desire to reciprocate what they expect to be generous contributions from the others. Contrary to predictions in our discussion about cheap talk (see Section 10.2), pre-play communication actually increases cooperation in prisoners' dilemmas and contributions in public goods games. In this sense, talk – even when cheap – might serve to promote reciprocity. Other explanations are consistent with the experimental data. Players might, for example, be altruistic as well. It should be noted that when the game is repeated, the level of contributions tends to decline. Thus, repetition appears to bring the players in closer accord with subgame-perfect-equilibrium predictions.

Predictions based on egoistic utility functions in combination with game theoretic equilibrium concepts suggest that people will be unable to coordinate their actions even when it is in their interest to do so. Yet, this is a needlessly pessimistic vision of human nature. The economist Elinor Ostrom won the 2009 Nobel Prize for exploring ways in which people develop sophisticated mechanisms that allow them to reach beneficial outcomes in trust and public-goods style games. There is plenty of evidence from the field and from the lab suggesting that people do succeed in coordinating their behavior under a wide range of conditions. Some roommates do succeed in developing mutually acceptable arrangements to make sure the dishes get washed, and some neighborhood associations do succeed in getting their members to participate in neighborhood-cleanup operations. Bad social and political philosophy, and bad social and political institutions, might result from the false assumption that cooperation cannot emerge spontaneously.

Like social preferences, it is quite possible that a story about intentions, trust, and reciprocity can be incorporated into the traditional neoclassical model. There appears to be no principled reason why it cannot be done, and some game theorists have tried. Because the specifications are a little more complicated than those in the previous section, they have been left out of this discussion. That said, it might well be possible to fit the analysis of intentions, reciprocity, and trust into the traditional neoclassical framework. Or it might not.

11.4 Limited strategic thinking

John Maynard Keynes, one of the most influential economists of the twentieth century, drew an analogy between investing in the stock market and participating in a certain kind of newspaper contest. In *The General Theory of Employment, Interest and Money*, Keynes wrote:

> [Professional] investment may be likened to those newspaper competitions in which the competitors have to pick out the six prettiest faces from a hundred photographs, the prize being awarded to the competitor whose choice most nearly corresponds to the average preferences of the competitors as a whole; so that each competitor has to pick, not those faces which he himself finds prettiest, but those which he thinks likeliest to catch the fancy of the other competitors, all of whom are looking at the problem from the same point of view. It is not a case of choosing those which, to the best of one's judgment, are really the prettiest, nor even those which average opinion genuinely thinks the prettiest.

The basic structure of this strategic interaction is captured by the **beauty-contest game**. Here, n players simultaneously pick a number between zero and 100 inclusive. The person whose number is closer to seven-tenths of the average number wins a fixed price. (The fraction does not have to be seven-tenths, but it must be common knowledge among the players.)

There is only one Nash equilibrium in this game. In this equilibrium, every player picks the number zero and everyone ties for first place. Suppose everyone picked 100, the highest number available. If so, the winning number would be 70. Thus, no rational person would ever pick a number greater than 70. But if no one picks a number greater than 70, the winning number cannot be greater than 49. Yet, if nobody picks a number greater than 49, the winning number cannot be greater than about 34. And so on, all the way down to zero.

Real people, however, do not play the Nash equilibrium strategy in the one-shot game. When played for the first time, answers might fall in the 20–40 range. Interesting things happen when the game is repeated with feedback about the average number in the previous round. During subsequent rounds, the average number will decrease and eventually approach zero. This suggests that, over time, real people converge to the Nash equilibrium prediction.

The favored explanation of the result in the one-shot game is based on the idea that people have different degrees of sophistication. "Level-0" players just pick a number between zero and 100 randomly. "Level-1" players believe that all the other players are level-0 players. Level-1 players, therefore, predict that the mean number will be 50, and therefore pick $0.7 * 50 = 35$. Level-2 players believe that all other players are level-1 players and that the average will be 35, and therefore pick $0.7 * 35 \approx 25$, and so on. Using statistical techniques, behavioral game theorists can estimate what proportion of each sample is level 0, level 1, and so on. The results suggest that most humans are level-1 or level-2 players.

One fascinating feature of this game is that, even if you know the unique Nash equilibrium strategy, you may not want to play it. As long as you expect other players to play out-of-equilibrium strategies and choose a positive number, you will want to do so too. And as long as other players expect you to expect them to pick a positive number, they will want to pick a positive number. And so on. Thus, everyone plays a positive number and an out-of equilibrium strategy. But, although you want to pick a number greater than zero, the number must not be too high: the aim is to stay one step ahead of the other players.

In keeping with Keynes's analogy, it has been suggested that this kind of game captures the dynamics of real markets and can explain bubbles in stock and real-estate markets. Even if all investors know that the market will ultimately crash, and that the unique Nash equilibrium strategy is to exit the market, they might assume that others will continue to buy for just a little while longer. As long as individual investors think that they can stay one step ahead of the competition and exit the market just before everybody else does, they will want to continue to buy. In the process, of course, they will drive prices even higher.

Example 11.6 Rock-paper-scissors, cont. The game rock-paper-scissors has a unique Nash equilibrium, in which both players randomize with probability 1/3, 1/3, and 1/3, and in which both players have an equal probability of winning (see Exercise 10.13 on page 184). So it might surprise you to hear that there is a World Rock-Paper-Scissor Association and a World Championship competition. According to the Association website, rock-paper-scissor is a game of skill, not chance: "Humans, try as they might, are terrible at trying to be random [and] in trying to approximate randomness become quite predictable."

Here is one piece of advice. The pros will tell you that "rock is for rookies," because inexperienced males tend to open with rock. Thus, if your opponent is one, open with paper. If your opponent is slightly more sophisticated and may be thinking you will open with rock and therefore opens with paper, open with scissors. If you are playing against an even more sophisticated agent, who will for the reason just identified open with scissors, open with rock.

Here is another piece of advice. Inexperienced players will not expect you to call your throw ahead of time. Thus, if you announce that you are throwing rock next, an inexperienced opponent will assume that you will not and instead will choose something other than paper. So you will want to throw rock. If you play against a slightly more sophisticated agent, though, they will expect you to throw rock after announcing that you will throw rock; so what you need to do is to throw scissors.

As in the beauty-contest game, the goal is to stay exactly one step ahead of your opponent. A similar analysis might apply to people's performance in the centipede game (see Exercise 10.26 on page 190). The typical finding is that people Pass until a few stages from the end, when they Take. This outcome would be expected if neither player thinks the other will play the unique subgame-perfect equilibrium, and that both attempt to Take one stage before the other one does.

Unlike models of social preferences, in this case there is little hope of capturing observed behavior in the one-shot game within the traditional neoclassical model. Things are quite different in the repeated version of the game. As the same group plays the game again and again, they approximate equilibrium predictions.

11.5 Discussion

According to the great Austrian economist Friedrich A. Hayek, the existence of spontaneous coordination constitutes the central problem of economic science. Hayek wrote:

> From the time of Hume and Adam Smith, the effect of every attempt to understand economic phenomena – that is to say, of every theoretical analysis – has been to show that, in large part, the co-ordination of individual efforts in society is not the product of deliberate planning, but has been brought about, and in many cases could only have been brought about, by means which nobody wanted or understood.

In this view, economists have never seriously doubted *that* coordination takes place; the question is *how* it emerges and is sustained. Much of the behavioral game theory literature on social preferences, trust, and reciprocity was developed in large part to answer this question. Obviously, this chapter does not contain a complete account of strategic interaction that fails to fit the picture painted by analytical game theory, or of the models behavioral game theorists have offered to capture the way in which people really interact with each other.

To what extent is the work presented under the heading "behavioral game theory" compatible with the traditional neoclassical framework? As we have seen, much of what goes under the heading is in fact consistent with analytical game theory. Models of social preferences are clearly consistent, since they proceed by allowing a person P's utility function to reflect another person Q's attainment. The degree to which ideas of intentions, reciprocity, and trust can be incorporated into neoclassical theory remains unclear, though game theorists have tried. Models that try to capture people's limited ability to think strategically, by contrast, are more clearly inconsistent with any model that relies on Nash or subgame-perfect equilibrium concepts.

In defense of analytical game theory, it has been argued that neoclassical theory is only intended to apply under sharply circumscribed conditions. Thus, the prominent game theorist Ken Binmore writes:

> [Neoclassical] economic theory should only be expected to predict in the laboratory if the following three criteria are satisfied:
> ▶ The problem the subjects face is not only "reasonably" simple in itself, but is framed so it seems simple to the subjects;
> ▶ The incentives provided are "adequate";
> ▶ The time allowed for trial-and-error adjustment is "sufficient".

Binmore recognizes that he is also denying the predictive power of neoclassical economics in the field, and adds: "But have we not got ourselves into enough trouble already by claiming vastly more than we can deliver?" Binmore's view is nicely illustrated by the beauty-contest game (see Section 11.4). Here, real people's behavior differs dramatically from Nash equilibrium predictions during the first round, but converges to it as the game is repeated and players learn the outcome of previous rounds. The same thing might be true for public-goods and other games. Binmore's defense of analytical game theory does not constitute an argument against behavioral game theory, however, provided behavioral game theory is intended to apply when the three conditions are not satisfied.

Additional exercises

Problem 11.7 Equilibrium concepts *We know from Section 10.4 that some game theorists think the Nash equilibrium concept is problematic, and that the concept of subgame-perfect equilibrium better captures the behavior of rational agents. But as the single subgame-perfect equilibrium in the ultimatum game suggests (see Section 11.2), there is something funny about subgame-perfect equilibrium too. For one thing, the subgame-perfect equilibrium requires the responder to accept an offer of $0. And in most Nash equilibria, the responder does better than this. In your view, which equilibrium concept offers the best prediction of the behavior of rational agents: Nash or subgame-perfect equilibrium?*

Further reading

The most well-known and thorough treatment of behavioral game theory is Camerer (2003), which includes the quote summarizing results from the ultimatum game (p. 49). Kagel and Roth, eds (1995) contains thorough treatments of experimental methods and results; Durlauf and Blume (2010) offers

Further reading cont'd

more concise and up-to-date treatments. A good review of cooperation in laboratory experiments is Dawes and Thaler (1988), which among other things summarizes the results of public-goods experiments (p. 189). The World Rock-Paper-Scissor Association (2011) will tell you how to beat anyone at rock-paper-scissors. The two historical quotes are from Keynes (1936, p. 156) and Hayek (1933, p. 129); for more on Hayek's take on information and cooperation, see Angner (2007). The Binmore quote is from Binmore (1999, p. F17).

Part VI

Concluding Remarks

Chapter 12

General Discussion

Introduction

At the turn of the century, as we saw in Chapter 1, behavioral economics was already firmly established as a subdiscipline of economics. But the enterprise appears to have received an additional boost from the economic crisis that struck during the first decade of the new century. As David Brooks put it in the *New York Times*: "My sense is that this financial crisis is going to amount to a coming-out party for behavioral economists and others who are bringing sophisticated psychology to the realm of public policy."

While Brooks is frequently described as a conservative, commentators across the political spectrum have blamed the crisis in part on the use of inadequate economic models. The former chairman of the Federal Reserve, Alan Greenspan, is known as a follower of Ayn Rand's objectivism, which celebrates the value of rational self-interest. Yet, in 2008, Congressional testimony, Greenspan said: "I made a mistake in presuming that the self-interests of organizations, specifically banks and others, were such as that they were best capable of protecting their own shareholders and their equity in the firms." Similarly, the Nobel laureate and liberal economic commentator Paul Krugman argues:

> [Economists] need to abandon the neat but wrong solution of assuming that everyone is rational and markets work perfectly. The vision that emerges as the profession rethinks its foundations may not be all that clear; it certainly won't be neat; but we can hope that it will have the virtue of being at least partly right.

Implicit in this line of thinking is the thesis that economic theories can have a real impact on worldly events. The thesis was wholeheartedly endorsed by Keynes, who wrote:

> [The] ideas of economists and political philosophers, both when they are right and when they are wrong, are more powerful than is commonly understood. Indeed the world is ruled by little else. Practical men, who believe themselves to be quite exempt from any intellectual influences, are usually the slaves of some defunct economist. Madmen in authority, who hear voices in the air, are distilling their frenzy from some academic scribbler of a few years back. I am sure that the power of vested interests is vastly exaggerated compared with the gradual encroachment of ideas . . . it is ideas, not vested interests, which are dangerous for good or evil.

Once we realize that economic theory (for better or for worse) can have a real impact on the world in which we live, we will want to ask how it is used to formulate policy.

Behavioral welfare economics

Like their neoclassical counterparts, behavioral economists frequently wish not only to understand but also to change the world in which they live. As Hayek put it in 1933:

> It is probably true that economic analysis has never been the product of detached intellectual curiosity about the *why* of social phenomena, but of an intense urge to reconstruct a

world which gives rise to profound dissatisfaction. This is as true of the phylogenesis of economics as the ontogenesis of probably every economist.

Since behavioral (like neoclassical) economists take their central normative concern to be welfare, and perhaps its distribution, this work is often discussed under the heading of **behavioral welfare economics**. Behavioral welfare economics subsumes **behavioral law and economics**, which incorporates behavioral economic theories into law and economics (see Section 6.3), as well as **behavioral public economics**, which relies on behavioral economics to describe and evaluate the effects of public policies. If you believe, like the writers named in Section 12.1, that neoclassical economics was a contributing cause to the financial crisis, this development might be a source of hope; if you do not, it may be a cause for concern.

Behavioral welfare economists have proposed a number of specific interventions, which are thought to be welfare-enhancing, and which were motivated by theoretical developments in behavioral economics. Here is a sample:

- **Default options** are options that will be selected in case the decision-maker fails to make an active choice. Insofar as people are prone to the status quo bias, they will exhibit a tendency to stick with the default even when it would be virtually costless to make an active decision. By having a **choice architect** carefully determine what option should be the default, in light of people's own interests, behavioral economists believe that more people will end up with the option that is best for them.
- The **Save More Tomorrow (SMarT) Program** encourages workers to save more for retirement by giving them the option of committing in advance to allocating a portion of their future raises toward savings. Because committing a future raise feels like a foregone gain whereas committing money in the pocket feels like a loss, prospect theory predicts that workers will find it easier to save future salary increases than money in the pocket. The SMarT program is designed to increase savings rates by leveraging this effect.
- **Cooling-off periods** are periods of time following a decision during which decision-makers have the option to reverse their choices. Cooling-off periods are based on the idea that people in a transient "hot" emotional state sometimes make suboptimal decisions. Behavioral economists argue that cooling-off periods offer people the opportunity to reevaluate their decisions from the perspective of a "cool" state, which is likely to lead to a better decision.

Many policy prescriptions offered by behavioral economists are presented under headings such as **libertarian** or **light paternalism**. All these policies are thought to help people make better decisions, by their own lights, without imposing any substantial costs. In particular, libertarian or light paternalism assumes that it is possible to help people make better decisions without preventing those who already are rational and well informed from choosing whatever option they prefer.

Exercise 12.1 Apples or fries?   US hamburger chains have started serving apple slices instead of French fries with their "meal" options. Fries are still available, but the customer has to ask to have fries substituted for apples. Preliminary reports suggest that as a result, customers end up eating more apples and less fries. What kind of intervention is this?

Meanwhile, it is important to note that behavioral economists do not deny that people respond to incentives, or that the most effective way to accomplish a certain goal might be to change the incentives facing the relevant actors.

Any argument to the effect that some intervention is or is not welfare enhancing presupposes a **welfare criterion**: a rule that (at least in principle) allows us to determine who is well off and who is not. Neoclassical economics relies on a preference-based criterion, according to which people are well off to the extent that their preferences are satisfied. Given our understanding of "utility" (see Section 2.7), this is equivalent to saying that people are well off to the extent that their utility is high. It has been argued that behavioral economics entails that this criterion is inadequate and that we must instead accept a happiness-based criterion, according to which people are well off to the extent that they are happy. Notice that these criteria are substantially different, since it is possible to have satisfied preferences without being happy and vice versa. Others maintain that it is possible to maintain the preference-based criterion by assuming (as some neoclassical economists already do) that the preferences that count are not the preferences actually revealed in people's choices, but the preferences that they would have if they were perfectly rational, ideally informed, and so on.

12.3 Assessing behavioral economics

If the upshot of the previous section is correct, there may be little difference in the normative foundations of neoclassical and behavioral economics; the difference when it comes to policy proposals by and large reflect differences in descriptive theory. This, then, brings us to the question of how to assess the relative merits of neoclassical and behavioral economics. It is not my intention to try to settle the argument here. A proper assessment would require a thorough discussion of experimental and other methods, statistical methodology, and interpretation of a wide range of empirical results. All this is beyond the scope of this book, which (as explained in the Preface) is primarily an exercise in exposition. Yet, in the preceding chapters, the aim has been to offer some indication of what is at stake in the debate between behavioral and neoclassical economists, as well as what a proper assessment would look like.

One important insight is that neoclassical economics is not as silly as some of its critics make it out to be, and that many of the objections against the enterprise are misguided. As we saw in Section 11.2, for example, observed behavior in the ultimatum game is perfectly consistent with Nash equilibrium predictions. And Sections 2.6 and 11.2 have shown that neoclassical economics does not say that people are selfish, materialistic, greedy, or anything of the sort. Thus, attacks on what some critics have called the "selfishness axiom" of neoclassical economics are misguided not just in the sense that selfishness is not an axiom in the calculus, but in the sense that selfishness is not implied by the theory. Relatedly, standard theory does not say that people relentlessly pursue their own happiness or pleasure, meaning that criticism assuming that they do is flawed. Moreover, as Sections 4.7 and 6.6 indicate, the standard approach does not say that people (consciously or not) perform any sort of calculations in their head. Thus, any criticism premised on the notion that most people are unable, for example, to apply Bayes's theorem in their head is misguided.

For practical purposes, economists have no choice but to use additional assumptions, often called **auxiliary assumptions**, in conjunction with their theories. In order to make substantive predictions, for example, the theorist might need to make more specific assumptions about what, exactly, people have preferences over, and how, exactly, these preferences order the available options. Depending on context, auxiliary assumptions might say that people only care about their own payoffs in dollar terms. The auxiliary assumptions need to be justified on independent grounds, and the justification may or may not be convincing. Such auxiliary assumptions, though, form no essential part of the neoclassical enterprise and can easily be replaced by others.

A no less important insight, however, is that anecdotal, experimental, and field evidence all suggest that people's observed behavior deviates from neoclassical theory in predictable fashion. There is little doubt that people (sometimes) do things such as honoring sunk costs, relying on adaptive but imperfect heuristics, violating the sure-thing principle, acting impulsively, and exhibiting limited strategic thinking. If deviations were random and unsystematic, they would (for many purposes) be theoretically uninteresting. In fact, however, deviations are frequently substantial and systematic which means that they are predictable and can be captured by using a descriptive, scientific theory. At a fundamental level, behavioral economics is the result of this insight. The fact that people's behavior is irrational does not mean that it is unpredictable, nor that it cannot be described using scientific means.

The models developed by behavioral economists can be challenged on various grounds. We have seen that some of the empirical results invoked by behavioral economists might be possible to accommodate within the standard framework, either by redescribing the choices available to the agent or by admitting additional arguments into the utility function. And it is important not to attribute irrationality to people when their behavior is better described as consistent with standard theory. That said, neoclassical economists frequently bend over backwards to accommodate empirical results in a manner that is both artificial and ad hoc. It is often both simpler and more plausible to infer that people sometimes are in violation of standard theory.

Some neoclassical economists, as we have seen, are happy to admit that this is so. In defense of analytical game theory, as we know from Section 11.5, it has been argued that neoclassical theory is only intended to apply under sharply circumscribed conditions. Of course, this defense of neoclassical economics does not constitute an argument against behavioral economics. Instead, this response might offers a way to reconcile neoclassical and behavioral economics. Many behavioral economists are happy to admit that observed behavior sometimes approaches or coincides with neoclassical predictions under certain conditions. But if those conditions do not hold, neoclassical economists should be able to agree that a non-neoclassical theory is required to explain and predict behavior. This is the domain of behavioral economics.

12.4 Conclusion

Science progresses in fits and starts. Rather than a steady progression of darkness to light, science tends to offer a series of increasingly complex models that capture to a greater or a lesser extent empirical phenomena that for whatever reason attract scientists' interest. The "final" theory is likely to remain out of reach. The same is true of economics. In *Worstward Ho*, Samuel Beckett wrote: "Ever tried. Ever failed. No matter. Try again. Fail again. Fail better." To use Beckett's phrase, progress in science in general and economics in particular can be thought of as a matter of failing better. Incidentally, Beckett might just as well have been describing the study of science, which is never finished, or the writing of textbooks, which can always be improved. To what extent do behavioral economists fail better than neoclassical economists? I do not pretend to have the answer. But I do hope to have shed some light on the nature of both neoclassical and behavioral economics, and to have underscored some of the power and promise of economic analysis of social phenomena.

Further reading

Worstward Ho, first published in 1983, is included in *Nohow On* (Beckett, 1989); the quote appears on p. 101. The quotes in the introductory section are from Brooks (2008), which contains the Greenspan quote, and Krugman (2009, p. 43). The passage from Keynes appears in *The General Theory of Employment, Interest and Money* (Keynes, 1936, pp. 383–384). The Hayek quote is from Hayek (1933, pp. 122–3). For a variety of perspectives on behavioral welfare economics, see Thaler and Sunstein (2008) as well as Caplin and Schotter, eds (2008); happiness economics and its welfare criteria are discussed in Angner (2009). For a deeper discussion about the nature of behavioral economics, its strengths and weaknesses, see Davis (2011) and Ross (2005). For a more advanced textbook, see Wilkinson and Klaes (2012).

Appendix: Answer Key

Appendix: Answer Key

Chapter 1

Exercise 1.1 (a) Descriptive. (b) Normative. (c) Descriptive.

Exercise 1.3 (a) 100. (b) $400,000. (c) $242 (see Section 8.2 on interest rates).

Chapter 2

Exercise 2.1 (a) fBn. (b) nBf. (c) nBn.

Exercise 2.2 {Afghanistan, Albania, Algeria, Andorra, Angola, ..., Zimbabwe}. Any order is fine, but the curly brackets are part of a correct answer. Notice that if you were to spell it out, this would be a pretty long list.

Exercise 2.3 (a) In all likelihood: $d \succcurlyeq r$. (b) In all likelihood: $r \succcurlyeq d$.

Exercise 2.7 (a) Intransitive, incomplete. (b) Transitive, incomplete. (c) Transitivity depends on whether we consider half-siblings; either way, it is incomplete. (d) Intransitive, incomplete. (e) Transitive, incomplete. (f) Transitive, incomplete. (g) Transitive, incomplete.

Exercise 2.8 (a) Transitive, complete. (b) Transitive, incomplete. (c) Transitive, incomplete. (d) Transitive, incomplete.

Exercise 2.9 (a) Transitivity implies that if apples are at least as good as bananas, and bananas are at least as good as starvation, then apples are at least as good as starvation; that if starvation is at least as good as bananas, and bananas are at least as good as apples, then starvation is at least as good as apples; and so on. (b) Completeness implies that either apples are at least as good as bananas or bananas are at least as good as apples, but also that apples are at least as good as apples, and that bananas are at least as good as bananas.

Exercise 2.12 Assume that $x \succcurlyeq y \ \& \ y \sim z$. The fact that $y \sim z$ implies that $y \succcurlyeq z$. Given that $x \succcurlyeq y \ \& \ y \succcurlyeq z$, it follows that $x \succcurlyeq z$.

Exercise 2.15 After assuming that $x \succ y \ \& \ y \succ z$, use the definition of strict preference (twice) and the transitivity of weak preference (once) to get the answer.

Exercise 2.16 After assuming that there is an x such that $x \succ x$, apply the definition of strict preference and the contradiction is right there.

Exercise 2.17 Here is the complete proof:

1. $x \succ y \,\&\, y \succcurlyeq z$ by assumption
2. $x \succcurlyeq y \,\&\, \neg y \succcurlyeq x$ from (1), by Definition 2.13
3. $x \succcurlyeq z$ from (1) and (2), by Axiom 2.5
4. $z \succcurlyeq x$ by assumption, for proof by contradiction
5. $y \succcurlyeq x$ from (1) and (4), by Axiom 2.5
6. $\bot$ from (2) and (5)
7. $\neg z \succcurlyeq x$ from (4)–(6), by contradiction
8. $x \succ z$ from (3) and (7), by Definition 2.13
$\therefore x \succ y \,\&\, y \succcurlyeq z \rightarrow x \succ z$ QED

Exercise 2.18 (a) Assume that $x \succ y$. Apply the definition of strict preference and rely on the principles of logic to derive the claim that $x \succcurlyeq y$. (b)–(h) Omitted.

Exercise 2.19 Begin by assuming what is to the left of the arrow, in this case $x \sim y \,\&\, y \sim z$. Then, on a separate line, assume (for a proof by contradiction) the opposite of what you are trying to prove; that is, assume that $x \succ z$. Finally, derive a contradiction.

Exercise 2.20 (a) Begin by assuming that $\neg x \succcurlyeq y$ and that $\neg y \succcurlyeq z$. Apply Proposition 2.18(f) twice to get $y \succ x$ and $z \succ y$. Transitivity will yield $z \succ x$, which by Proposition 2.18(i) gives you the result $\neg x \succcurlyeq z$. (b) Begin by assuming that $\neg x \succ y$ and that $\neg y \succ z$. Proposition 2.18(d) applied twice, transitivity, and 2.18(e) will give you the result.

Exercise 2.21 The answer is, of course, that $f^+ \succ c$. Begin by assuming that $f \sim c \,\&\, f^+ \succ f$. You need to prove two things: that $f^+ \succcurlyeq c$ and that not $\neg c \succcurlyeq f^+$. After using the definitions of indifference and strict preference, the first part follows by transitivity of weak preference. For the second part, assume (for a proof by contradiction) that $c \succcurlyeq f^+$.

Exercise 2.22 A rational person is indifferent. Because $c_1 \sim c_2 \,\&\, c_2 \sim c_3$, Proposition 2.11 implies that $c_1 \sim c_3$. Because, in addition, $c_3 \sim c_4$, the same proposition implies that $c_1 \sim c_4$ and so on. Ultimately, you will find that $c_1 \sim c_{1000}$. QED.

Exercise 2.23 Assume that $x \succ y \,\&\, y \succ z \,\&\, z \succ x$. Apply the definition of strict preference a few times, and a contradiction is immediate.

Exercise 2.24 Assume that $x \succcurlyeq y \,\&\, y \succcurlyeq z \,\&\, z \succcurlyeq x$, Use the transitivity of weak preference and the definition of indifference to establish that $x \sim y \,\&\, y \sim z \,\&\, z \sim x$.

Exercise 2.25 See Figure A.1.

Exercise 2.27 The new menu would be {nothing at all, soup, salad, chicken, beef, soup-and-chicken, soup-and-beef, salad-and-chicken, salad-and-beef}.

Exercise 2.28 See Figure A.2.

Exercise 2.32 In order to prove this proposition, you need to do two things. First, assume that $x \sim y$ and prove that $u(x) = u(y)$. Second, assume that $u(x) = u(y)$ and prove that $x \sim y$. Here is the complete proof:

1. $x \sim y$ by assumption
2. $x \succcurlyeq y \ \& \ y \succcurlyeq x$ from (1), by Definition 2.13
3. $u(x) \geqslant u(y) \ \& \ u(y) \geqslant u(x)$.   from (2), by Definition 2.29 (twice)
4. $u(x) = u(y)$ from (3), by math
5. $u(x) = u(y)$ by assumption
6. $u(x) \geqslant u(y) \ \& \ u(y) \geqslant u(x)$ from (5), by math
7. $x \succcurlyeq y \ \& \ y \succcurlyeq x$ from (6), by Definition 2.29 (twice)
8. $x \sim y$ from (4) and (8), by Definition 2.13
$\therefore x \sim y \Leftrightarrow u(x) = u(y)$ QED

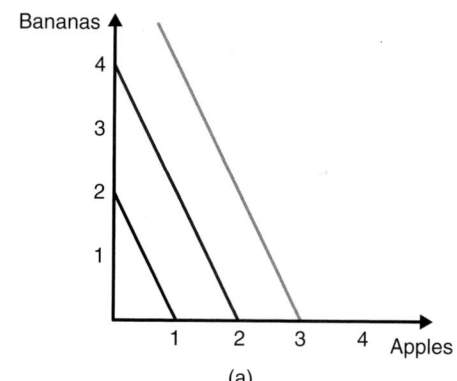

(a)

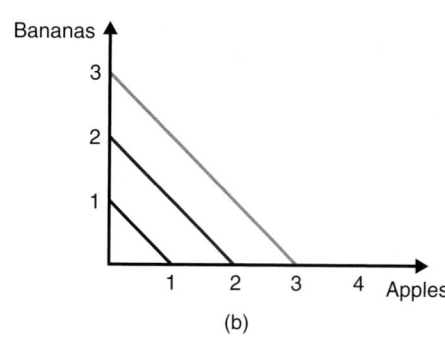

(b)

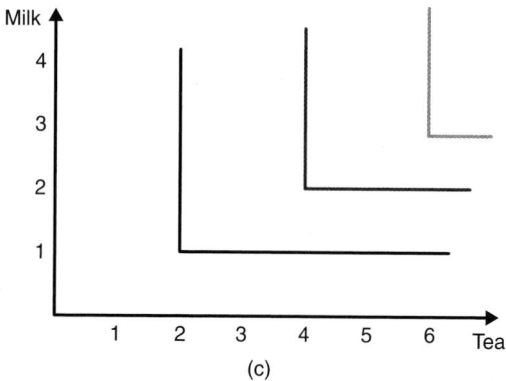

(c)

Figure A.1   Indifference curves

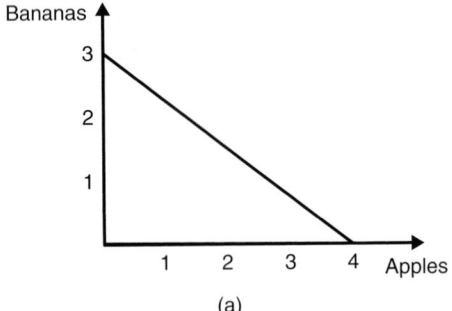

(a)

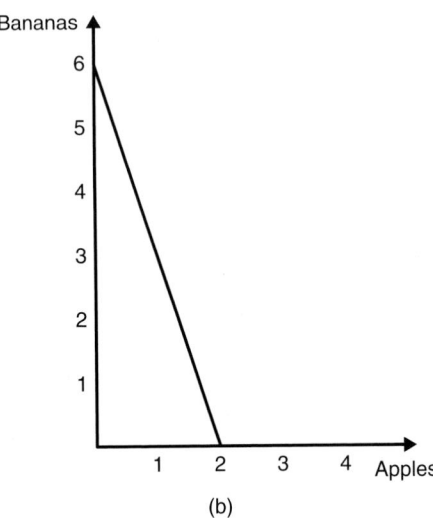

(b)

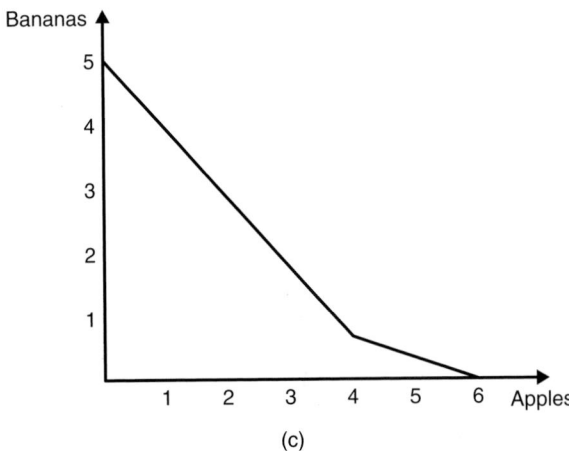

(c)

Figure A.2   Budget lines

Exercise 2.33 See Table A.1.

Table A.1 Properties of weak preference, indifference, and strong preference

	Property	Definition	≽	~	≻
(a)	Transitivity	$xRy \,\&\, yRz \rightarrow xRz$ (for all x, y, z)	✓	✓	✓
(b)	Completeness	$xRy \vee yRx$ (for all x, y)	✓		
(c)	Reflexivity	xRx (for all x)	✓	✓	
(d)	Irreflexivity	$\neg xRx$ (for all x)			✓
(e)	Symmetry	$xRy \rightarrow yRx$ (for all x, y)		✓	
(f)	Anti-symmetry	$xRy \rightarrow \neg yRx$ (for all x, y)			✓

Exercise 2.34 Omitted.

Exercise 2.35 (a) She violates completeness. (b) He violates transitivity.

Chapter 3

Exercise 3.1 (a). See Figure A.3. (b) $1000. (c) $1000.

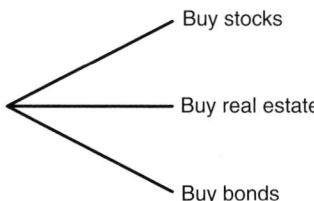

- Buy stocks
- Buy real estate
- Buy bonds

Figure A.3 Investment problem

Exercise 3.3 See Figure A.4.

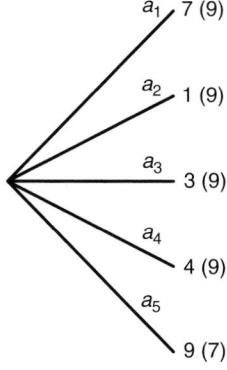

a_1 , 7 (9)

a_2 , 1 (9)

a_3 3 (9)

a_4 4 (9)

a_5 9 (7)

Figure A.4 Opportunity costs

Exercise 3.5 For highly paid people, the opportunity cost of mowing lawns, etc., is greater.

Exercise 3.7 Not necessarily: if another, even more successful campaign to boost revenue were available to you at the time, it would have been irrational to invest in the advertising campaign.

Exercise 3.10 See Figure A.5.

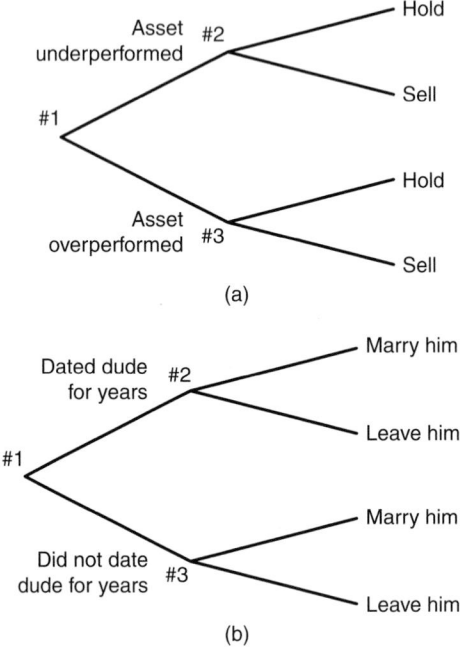

(a)

(b)

Figure A.5 Sunk costs, again

Exercise 3.11 Sign up for the course at the public university. The tuition already paid to the liberal arts college is a sunk cost.

Exercise 3.15 (a) You would want to put it in area B. (b) Before.

Exercise 3.16 (a) Show a property that is not in as good shape as and even farther from the office than the first property, but which is still in better shape than the second property. (b) Show a property that is in even worse shape and slightly farther from the office than the second property, but which is still closer to the office than the first property.

Exercise 3.17 (a) Choose a wingman or wingwoman who is less desirable than you are along all relevant dimensions, but who beats each competitor along at least one dimension. (b) You want your wingman or wingwoman to fall in the 8–9 range (exclusive) both with respect to attractiveness and intelligence. (c) He or she thinks you are less desirable than he or she is along all relevant dimensions.

Exercise 3.20 (a) Alex thought of the $2 as a foregone gain, so for him the absolute value of the $2 was 1. Mathematically, the change in value can be computed as

$v(0) - v(+2) = 0 - 2/2 = -1$. (b) Bob thought of the \$2 as a loss, so for him the absolute value of the \$2 was 4. Mathematically, the change in value can be computed as $v(-2) - v(0) = -4 - 0 = -4$. (c) Bob.

Exercise 3.21   The answer is given by the expression $v(+1) + v(-1) = 1/2 - 2 = -3/2$.

Exercise 3.22   See Figure A.6.

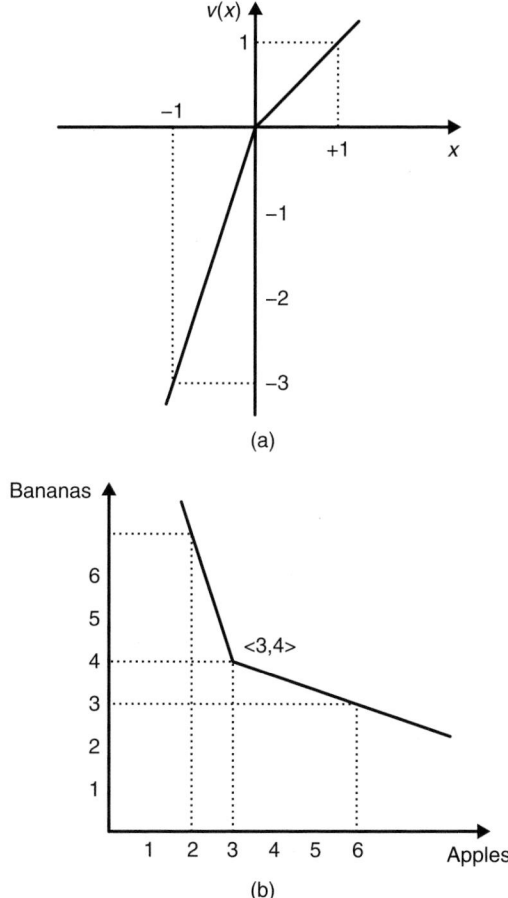

Figure A.6   Value function and indifference curve

Exercise 3.23   (a) Status quo bias would entail that Europeans would tend to favor the European system while Americans would tend to favor the American system. The bias is driven by loss aversion. For Europeans, the loss of government-provided health care would not be outweighed by the gain in disposable income; for Americans, the loss of disposable income would not be outweighed by the gain in government-provided health care. (b) See Figure A.7. (c) Loss aversion suggests that after adaptation has occurred, Americans would be unwilling to give up the new system, and the opposition party would find it difficult to engineer a return to the old one.

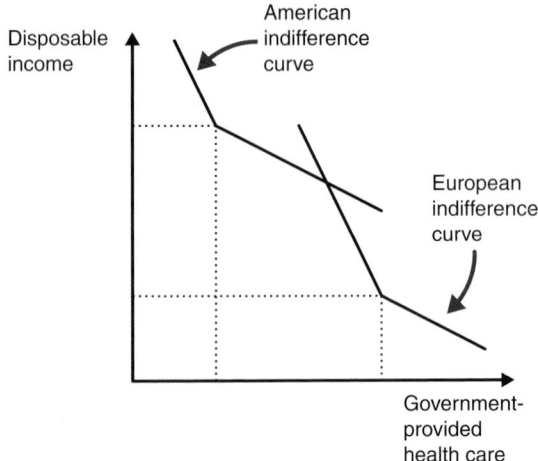

Figure A.7 Health care systems

Exercise 3.24 A person who does not expect a raise would experience $v(+5)$. A person who does expect a raise would experience $v(-5)$. See Figure A.8 for a graphical representation of the difference.

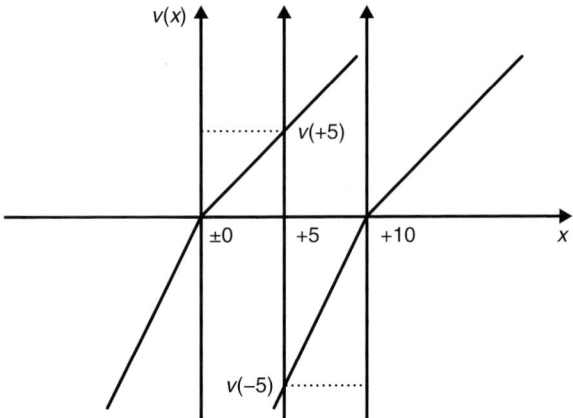

Figure A.8 The raise

Exercise 3.25 (a) $v(+93-75)=v(+18)=9$. (b) $v(+67-75)=v(-8)=-16$. (c) The theory would suggest that you should set low expectations and perform well.

Exercise 3.26 The theory would suggest that you should surround yourself with low-paying people and make a lot of money.

Exercise 3.30 Assume that the emperor computed the number of grains of rice that he would owe the inventor during the first n days, where n is a number considerably less than 64, used that number as an anchor, and insufficiently adjusted the number upwards.

Exercise 3.31   The answer is (b) $10. The answer is the value to you of going to the Dylan concert ($50) minus what you would have to pay to go ($40). Only 21.6 percent of the professional economists in the study got the answer right, which is particularly embarrassing if you reflect on the fact that they could have done better had they simply picked their answers randomly.

Exercise 3.32   The sunk-cost fallacy.

Exercise 3.33   See Figure A.9.

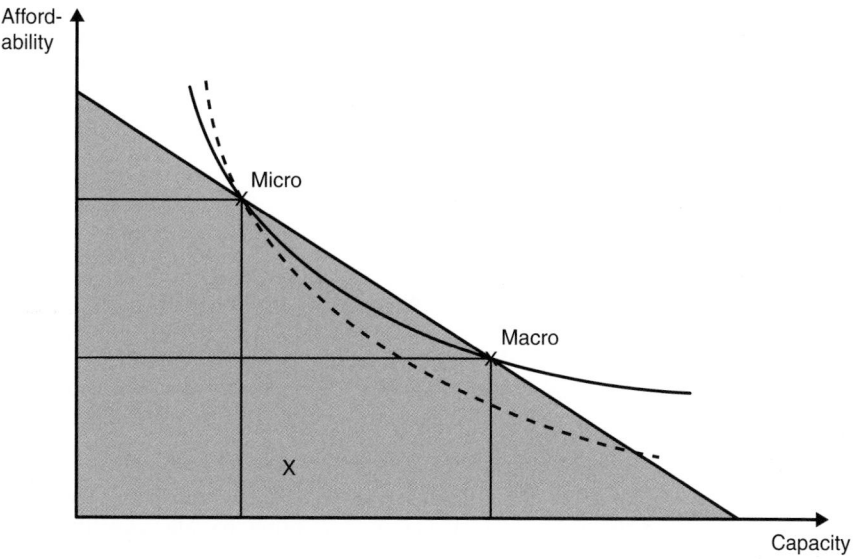

Figure A.9   Pear Corporation hijinks

Exercise 3.34   (a) Sunk-cost fallacy. (b) Anchoring and adjustment. (c) Loss aversion. (d) Sunk-cost fallacy. (e) Failure to consider opportunity costs. (f) The compromise effect.

Chapter 4

Exercise 4.8   1/52.

Exercise 4.9   The outcome space is reduced to $\{GB, GG\}$ and the probability is 1/2.

Exercise 4.10   (a) $\{BBB, GGG, BBG, GGB, BGB, GBG, BGG, GBB\}$.
(b) $\{GGG, BBG, GGB, BGB, GBG, BGG, GBB\}$. (c) 1/7. (d) $\{GGG, GGB, GBG, BGG\}$. (e) 1/4.

Exercise 4.11   (a) $\{W/W, W/W, R/R, R/R, W/R, R/W\}$. (b) $\{W/W, W/W, W/R\}$. (c) 1/3.

Exercise 4.12   (a) $\{W/W, W/W, B/B, B/B, R/R, R/R, R/W, W/R\}$. (b) $\{B/B, B/B\}$. (c) 1. (d) $\{R/R, R/R, R/W\}$. (e) 1/3.

Exercise 4.13   The analysis of this problem is not completely uncontroversial, but it is fairly widely agreed that the probability is 1/3.

Exercise 4.15   (c) and (d).

Exercise 4.16 $4/52 = 1/13$.

Exercise 4.20 It is equally likely: the probability is $1/36$ either way.

Exercise 4.21 (d).

Exercise 4.22 Not independent.

Exercise 4.23 Because there are two (mutually exclusive) ways for the dots to add up to eleven, the answer is $1/36 + 1/36 = 1/18$.

Exercise 4.24 (a) $1/52 * 1/52 = 1/2,704$. (b) $1/13 * 1/13 = 1/169$.

Exercise 4.25 (a) $1/6 * 1/6 = 1/36$. (b) $(1 - 1/6) * (1 - 1/6) = 25/36$. (c) $1/6 * (1 - 1/6) + (1 - 1/6) * 1/6 = 10/36$. (d) $1 - (1 - 1/6) * (1 - 1/6) = 11/36$.

Exercise 4.26 It would be a mistake because you would be applying the OR rule to two outcomes that are not mutually exclusive.

Exercise 4.27 The answer is:

$$\frac{6}{49} * \frac{5}{48} * \frac{4}{47} * \frac{3}{46} * \frac{2}{45} * \frac{1}{44} = \frac{1}{13,983,816}.$$

This amounts to about $0.000,000,07$. So, if you were to play once a year, on the average you would win once every $13,983,816$ years. If you played once per day, given that there are 364.25 days in a year, on the average you would win once every $268,920$ years.

Exercise 4.29 If people assess the value of the ticket by using the amount that can be won as an anchor and adjusting downwards, insufficient adjustment would imply that they overestimate the value of the ticket. If, in addition, people assess the probability of winning by using the probability of picking the first number correctly as an anchor and adjusting downwards, insufficient adjustment would imply that they overestimate the probability of winning.

Exercise 4.30 (a) $\Pr(H|T)$ means "The probability that the patient has a headache given that he or she has a tumor," whereas $\Pr(T|H)$ means "The probability that the patient has a tumor given that he or she has a headache." (b) The probabilities are clearly different. In general, we should expect that $\Pr(H|T) > \Pr(T|H)$.

Exercise 4.33 $\Pr(AS_1 \& AS_2) = \Pr(AS_1) * \Pr(AS_2 | AS_1) = 1/52 * 0 = 0$.

Exercise 4.36 (a) Assume that $\Pr(A|B) = \Pr(A)$, then use Proposition 4.34 to derive $\Pr(B|A) = \Pr(B)$. (b) Assume that $\Pr(B|A) = \Pr(B)$, then use Proposition 4.32 to derive $\Pr(A\&B) = \Pr(A) * \Pr(B)$. (c) Assume that $\Pr(A\&B) = \Pr(A) * \Pr(B)$, then use Proposition 4.32 to derive $\Pr(A|B) = \Pr(A)$.

Exercise 4.38 (a) See Figure A.10. (b) $\Pr(D) = 2/5$.

Exercise 4.40 The answer is $2/3$.

Exercise 4.41 (a) $1/4 * 1/6 = 1/24$. (b) $3/4 * 2/3 = 6/12 = 12/24$. (c) $1/24 + 12/24 = 13/24$. (d) $(1/24)/(13/24) = 1/13$. Good news!

Exercise 4.42 (a) The probability assigned to the hypothesis goes from $1/2$ to $2/3$ after the first trial. (b) It goes from $2/3$ to $4/5$ after the second trial.

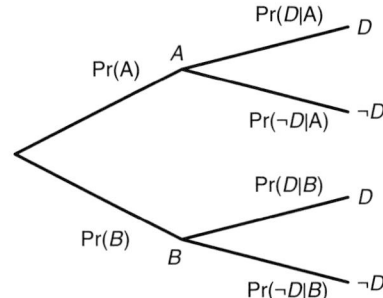

Figure A.10 Cancers A and B

Exercise 4.43 Given the way we have defined H and E for the purposes of this exercise, $\Pr(E \mid H)$ is now zero, since a coin with two heads cannot come up tails. Therefore, the posterior probability will equal 0 no matter the prior:

$$\Pr(H \mid E) = \frac{0 * \Pr(H)}{0 * \Pr(H) + 0.5 * \Pr(\neg H)} = 0.$$

Exercise 4.44 The outcomes are dependent, but not mutually exclusive.

Exercise 4.45 The answer is $(1/25,000)^3 = 1/15,625,000,000,000$. So if Langford gambles on undoctored machines three times a year, he could expect to win once every $15,625,000,000,000$ years. Notice, though, that the probability that the machines were doctored given that he won does not necessarily equal the probability that he would win given that the machines were not doctored.

Exercise 4.46 (a) Because there are 26 letters in the alphabet, the probability is $(1/26)^8 = 1/208,827,064,576 \approx 0.000,000,000,005$. (b) The probability that any one letter will *not* spell out the vulgarity is $1 - 1/208,827,064,576 = 208,827,064,575/208,827,064,576$. So the probability that at least one of the letters will spell out the vulgarity is $1 - (208,827,064,575/208,827,064,576)^{100} \approx 0.000,000,000,5$. That is a little higher, but not much.

Exercise 4.47 Note that there are $2^{10} = 1024$ different ways to answer ten true/false questions. So: (a) 1/1024. (b) 1/1024. (c) 1/1024. (d) 10/1024. (e) 11/1024.

Exercise 4.48 (a) 1/2. (b) 1/2. (c) $(1/2)^{10} = 1/1,024$. (d) $1 - (1/1,024) = 1023/1024$.

Chapter 5

Exercise 5.1 (a) 1/256. (b) 1/2.

Exercise 5.2 (a) 1/10,000. (b) 1/100.

Exercise 5.3 1/25,000.

Exercise 5.6 The answer to all these questions are given by the expression $1 - (7/10)^t$, where t is the number of hours. So: (a) 0.51. (b) Approximately 0.66. (c) Approximately 0.97. Notice that under these circumstances, it is highly likely that you will come across at least one tornado during a 10-hour hike.

Exercise 5.7 The probability of a flood in any given year is $1/10$. So: (a) 0.81. (b) 0.18. (c) 0.19. (d) Approximately 0.65.

Exercise 5.8 The probability of having no attack on any given day is $1 - 0.000, 1 = 0.999, 9$. There are $365.25 * 10 = 3652.5$ days in ten years. So the probability of at least one attack in ten years is $1 - (0.999, 9)^{3652.5} \approx 0.306 = 30.6$ percent.

Exercise 5.9 (a) Approximately 0.08. (b) Approximately 0.15. (c) Approximately 0.55. (d) Approximately 0.98.

Exercise 5.10 Imagine that you line up the 30 students in a row. The first student can be born on any day of the year, and the probability of this happening is $365/365$; the probability that the second student does not share a birthday with the first is $364/365$; the probability that the third student does not share a birthday with either of the first two is $363/365$; and so on, until you get to the 30th student: the probability that this student will not share a birthday with any of the other 29 students is $336/365$. So the probability you are looking for is $365/365 * 364/365 * \ldots 336/365 \approx 29.4$ percent. Thus, in a class this size, the probability that at least two students share a birthday is quite high: about 70.6 percent.

Exercise 5.11 (a) Approximately 0.634. (b) Approximately 0.999, 96.

Exercise 5.12 (a) The probability of a catastrophic engine failure is p. (b) The probability of a catastrophic engine failure is $1 - (1-p)^2 = 2p - p^2$. To see why this is so, refer to Figure A.11. (c) The single-engine plane. Notice that when p is small, p^2 will be so small as to be negligible. If so, the twin-engine plan is virtually twice as likely to experience a catastrophic engine failure as the single-engine plane! (d) Now, the probability of a catastrophic engine failure is p^2.

	Non-Failure	Failure
Non-Failure	$(1-p)^2$	$(1-p)*p$
Failure	$p*(1-p)$	

Figure A.11 The private jets

Exercise 5.14 Because the base rate in men is extremely low, the test would not be diagnostic.

Exercise 5.15 Let B mean "The cab is blue," and let P mean "The witness says that the cab is blue." Here is the equation that produces the right answer:

$$\Pr(B \mid P) = \frac{8/10 * 15/100}{8/10 * 15/100 + 2/10 * 85/100} \approx 41\%$$

Notice that, in spite of the fact that the witness is relatively reliable, the cab that was involved in the accident is more likely to be green than blue

Exercise 5.16   The answer is given by this equation:

$$\frac{75/100 * 20/100}{75/100 * 20/10 + 25/100 * 80/100} \approx 43\%$$

Exercise 5.17   The answer is given by this equation:

$$\frac{1/1000 * 90/100}{1/1000 * 90/100 + 10/1000 * 10/100} \approx 47\%$$

Exercise 5.18   The probability is:

$$\frac{\frac{10}{10,000,000} * \frac{999}{1000}}{\frac{10}{10,000,000} * \frac{999}{1000} + \frac{9,999,990}{10,000,000} * \frac{1}{1000}} \approx 0.001 = 0.1\%$$

Exercise 5.19   (a) 98/1,000,000,000. (b) 19,999,998/1,000,000,000. (c) $98/20,000,096 \approx 0.000,005 = 0.000,5$ percent. (d) No.

Exercise 5.20   In Kabul the base rate is likely to be higher, and this might make the test diagnostic.

Exercise 5.21   The correct answer is C.

Exercise 5.24   The answers are given by:

$$(a)\ \frac{1/10,000 * 99/100}{1/10,000 * 99/100 + 9999/10,000 * 10/100} = 1/1000$$

$$(b)\ \frac{1/1000 * 99/10,000}{1/1000 * 99/10,000 + 999/1000 * 9999/10,000} = 1/10,000$$

Exercise 5.25   Given that the optometrist mainly sees contact users without problems, an image of a healthy user is most available to her. Given that the ophthalmologist mainly sees users with problems, an image of an unhealthy user is most available to him. Insofar as the two are prone to the availability bias, the optometrist is likely to underestimate, and the ophthalmologist to overestimate, the probability of developing serious problems as a results of wearing contacts.

Exercise 5.26 $Pr(HHH) = (2/3)^3 = 8/27$ whereas $Pr(HHT) = (2/3)^2(1/3) = 4/27$. It is best to bet on HHH.

Exercise 5.27   (a) 0.04. (b) 0.64. (c) 0.36. (d) Approximately 0.67.

Exercise 5.28   (a) 0.072. (b) 0.092. (c) 0.164. (d) Approximately 0.439. (e) The base-rate fallacy.

Exercise 5.29   This problem is in effect the same as Exercise 5.15, so the answer is the same: approximately 41 percent.

Exercise 5.30 (a) Let T mean that a person is a terrorist and M mean that a person is Muslim. Based on the figures provided, I assume that $\Pr(T) = 10/300,000,000$; that $\Pr(M \mid T) = 9/10$; and that $\Pr(M \mid \neg T) = 2/300$. If so:

$$\Pr(T \mid M) = \frac{\dfrac{10}{300,000,000} * \dfrac{9}{10}}{\dfrac{10}{300,000,000} * \dfrac{9}{10} + \dfrac{299,999,990}{300,000,000} * \dfrac{2}{300}} \approx 0.000,005 = 0.000,5\%$$

(b) Obviously, there are many more dangerous things for Juan Williams to worry about. But if the image of a Muslim terrorist is particularly available to him, he would be prone to exaggerating the probability that a random Muslim would fall in that category.

Exercise 5.31 (a) Confirmation bias. (b) Disjunction fallacy. (c) Availability bias. (d) Base-rate neglect. (e) Availability bias. (f) Conjunction fallacy. (g) Hindsight bias. (h) Availability bias.

Chapter 6

Exercise 6.1 (a) C. (b) A. (c) B. The risk-payoff matrix is Table A.2.

Table A.2 Risk-payoff matrix

	S_1	S_2
A	2	0
B	1	1
C	0	4

Exercise 6.4 See Figure A.12.

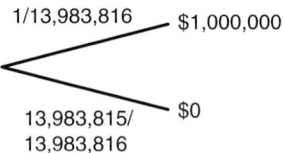

Figure A.12 Lotto 6/49 Tree

Exercise 6.7 (a) $EV(A) = 1/2 * 10 + 1/2 * 0 = 5$. (b) $EV(R) = 4$.

Exercise 6.9 See Table A.3.

Exercise 6.10 (a) The expected value is $1/5 * (-\$30) = -\$6$. (b) Yes.

Exercise 6.12 $3.50.

Table A.3 Roulette payoffs

Bet	Description	Payout	Pr(win)	Expected Value
Straight Up	One number	$36	1/38	$36/38
Split	Two numbers	$18	2/38	$36/38
Street	Three numbers	$12	3/38	$36/38
Corner	Four numbers	$9	4/38	$36/38
First Five	0, 00, 1, 2, 3	$7	5/38	$35/38
Sixline	Six numbers	$6	6/38	$36/38
First 12	1–12	$3	12/38	$36/38
Second 12	13–24	$3	12/38	$36/38
Third 12	25–36	$3	12/38	$36/38
Red		$2	18/38	$36/38
Black		$2	18/38	$36/38
Even		$2	18/38	$36/38
Odd		$2	18/38	$36/38
Low	1–18	$2	18/38	$36/38
High	19–36	$2	18/38	$36/38

Exercise 6.13 (a) $400,020. (b) Open the boxes. (c) $150,030. (d) Take the sure amount.

Exercise 6.15 (a) $-5/-100 = 1/20$. (b) $-5/-10 = 1/2$.

Exercise 6.17 The answer is $1/1,000,000$.

Exercise 6.18 $p = -79/-325 \approx 0.24$

Exercise 6.22 (a) $EU(R) = u(4) = 4^2 = 16$. (b) $EU(A) = 1/2 * u(10) + 1/2 * u(0) = 1/2 * 10^2 + 1/2 * 0^2 = 50$. (c) You should accept the gamble.

Exercise 6.23 (a) About $0.000,7$ cents. (b) $1. (c) The dollar.

Exercise 6.24 (a) (i) $EV(G) = 1/4 * 25 + 3/4 * 1 = 7$. (ii) $EU(G) = 1/4 * \sqrt{25} + 3/4 * \sqrt{1} = 2$. (b) (i) $EV(G^*) = 2/3 * 7 + 1/3 * 4 = 6$. (ii) $EU(G^*) = 2/3 * \sqrt{7} + 1/3 * \sqrt{4} \approx 2.43$.

Exercise 6.25 (a) See Figure A.13(a). (b) See Figure A.13(b). (c) $EU(\neg S) = 0$. (d) $EU(S) = 0.85 * 10 + 0.10 * (-2) + 0.05 * (-10) = 7.8$. (e) Have the operation.

Exercise 6.26 (a) See Figure A.14. (b) The expected utility of going home is $3/4 * 12 + 1/4 * (-2) = 8.5$. The expected utility of staying put is $2/3 * 9 + 1/3 * 3 = 7$. Thus, you should go home, in spite of the possibility that your aunt might show up.

Exercise 6.27 There are many ways to complete this exercise, but the important result is that B is the rational choice no matter what.

Exercise 6.29 (a) $p = 1/2$. (b) $p = 3/4$. (c) $p = 2/3$.

Exercise 6.31 In this case, $EU(A) = 1/2 * 3^2 + 1/2 * 1^2 = 5$, whereas $EU(R) = 2^2 = 4$. So you should definitely accept the gamble.

Exercise 6.32 (a) Risk prone. (b) Risk averse. (c) Risk prone. (d) Risk averse. (e) Risk prone. (f) Risk neutral. (g) Risk prone.

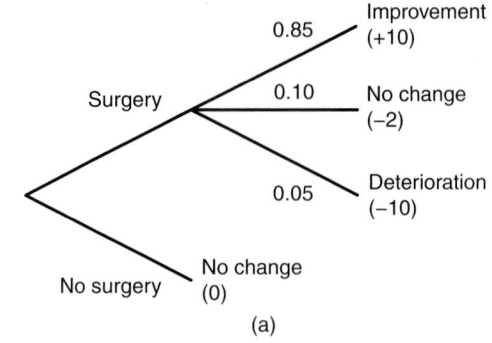

	Improvement	No change	Deterioration
S	10	-2	-10
¬S	0	0	0

(b)

Figure A.13 Hearing loss

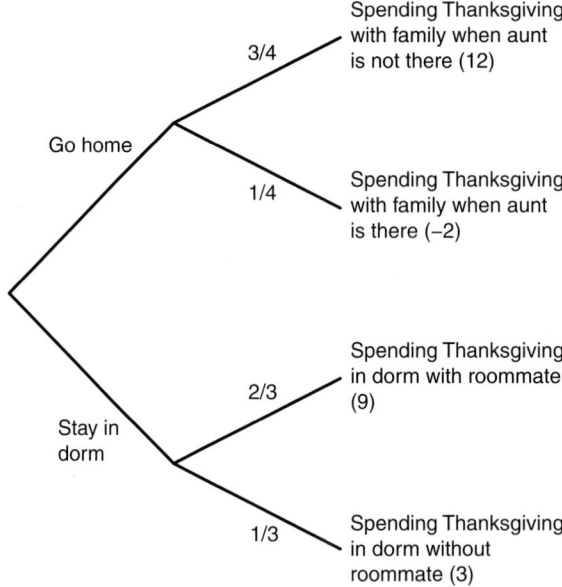

Figure A.14 Thanksgiving indecision

Exercise 6.34 See Figure A.15.

Exercise 6.36 $\sqrt{5}$.

Exercise 6.37 (a) The utility of $4 is 2. The expected utility of G is 3/2. The certainty equivalent is 9/4. Choose $4. (b) The utility of $4 is 16. The expected utility of G is 21. The certainty equivalent is $\sqrt{21}$. Choose G.

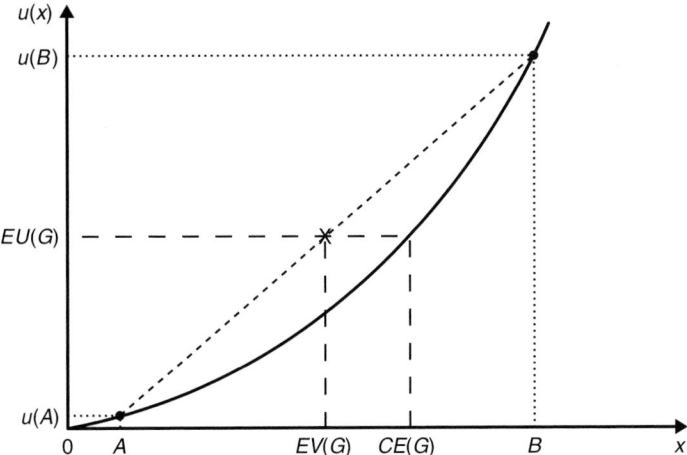

Figure A.15 Finding the certainty equivalent, cont.

Exercise 6.38   (a) The expected value of the gamble is 1.75. (b) The expected utility is 5/4. (c) The certainty equivalent is 25/16. (d) $p = 1/2$.

Exercise 6.39   (a) The expected utility is 5/2. (b) The certainty equivalent is 25/4. (c) The probability is 1/8. (d) You are risk averse.

Exercise 6.40   Approximately 0.000,000,49 cents.

Exercise 6.41   (a) The boxes. (b) The fixed amount. (c) $118,976.

Exercise 6.42   (a) EU (B) $= 3$. (b) EU (R) $= 4$. (c) Press the red button.

Chapter 7

Exercise 7.4   This problem can be analyzed using Figure 7.3 on page 127. Jen is risk averse because she takes "no animals saved" to be her reference point. Joe is risk prone because he takes "no animals lost" to be his reference point.

Exercise 7.6   (a) v (A) $= 1/2 * \sqrt{1000/2} \approx 11.18$. (b) v (B) $= \sqrt{500/2} \approx 15.81$. (c) v (C) $= 1/2 * (-2)\sqrt{1000} \approx -31.62$. (d) v (D) $= -2\sqrt{500} \approx -44.72$.

Exercise 7.7   (a) $v(-4) = -4$ whereas $v(+4) \approx 1.41$. (b) (i) $v(+2) = \sqrt{2/2} = 1$. (ii) $1/2 * v(0) + 1/2 * v(+4) = 1/2 * \sqrt{4/2} \approx 0.71$. She would prefer the sure amount. (b) (i) $v(-2) = -2\sqrt{2} = -2.83$. (ii) $1/2 * v(0) + 1/2 * v(-4) = 1/2 * (-2)\sqrt{4} = -2$. She would prefer the gamble.

Exercise 7.8   (a) $v(+48 + 27) = v(+75) = \sqrt{75/3} = 5$. (b) $v(+48) + v(+27) = \sqrt{48/3} + \sqrt{27/3} = 7$. (c) It is better to segregate.

Exercise 7.9   (a) $v(-144 - 25) = v(-169) = -3\sqrt{169} = -39$. (b) $v(-144) + v(-25) = -3\sqrt{144} + (-3)\sqrt{25} = -51$. (c) It is better to integrate.

Exercise 7.10   (a) $v(-9 + 2) = v(-7) \approx -5.29$. (b) $v(-9) + v(+2) = -5$. (c) It is better to segregate.

Exercise 7.12 The choice pattern (1a) and (2a) is excluded, as is the choice pattern (1b) and (2b).

Exercise 7.14 A strict preference for A over B entails that $EU(A) > EU(B)$, which means that $1 * u(30) > 0.80 * u(45)$. Divide each side by four, and you get $0.25 * u(30) > 0.20 * u(45)$. A strict preference for D over C entails that $EU(D) > EU(C)$, which means that $0.20 * u(45) > 0.25 * u(30)$. But this is inconsistent.

Exercise 7.16 Since the probabilities are *most* ambiguous in game 3, you would be *least* likely to bet on that game.

Exercise 7.19 (a) 1000. (b) 1018. (c) 1030. (d) Invest in stocks. (e) Invest in bonds.

Exercise 7.20 (a) Silver lining. (b) Mental accounting. (c) Competence hypothesis. (d) Certainty effect. (e) Ambiguity aversion.

Chapter 8

Exercise 8.3 See Table A.4.

Table A.4 Cost of credit

Credit-card offer	$1,000	$100	$10,000
Silver Axxess Visa Card	$247.20	$67.92	$2,040.00
Finance Gold MasterCard	$387.50	$263.75	$1,625.00
Continental Platinum MasterCard	$248.20	$68.92	$2,041.00
Gold Image Visa Card	$213.50	$53.75	$1,811.00
Archer Gold American Express	$296.50	$118.75	$2,074.00
Total Tribute American Express	$332.50	$168.25	$1,975.00
Splendid Credit Eurocard	$294.50	$94.25	$2,297.00

Exercise 8.5 $r = 0.20 = 20$ percent.

Exercise 8.8 (a) $105. (b) $162.89. (c) $1146.74.

Exercise 8.9 (a) $8664.62. (b) 8603.62. (c) $14,104$ percent. (d) Just don't do it.

Exercise 8.12 (a) 1, 0.3, 0.04, and 1.34. (b) Choose **d**. (c) Choose **a**.

Exercise 8.13 (a) Low. (b) High. (c) High. (d) Low. (e). High.

Exercise 8.16 (a) $\delta = 1/3$. (b) $\delta = 3/4$. (c) $\delta = 1/2$. (d) $\delta = 3/4$.

Exercise 8.15 (a) The curve would be steeper. (b) The curve would be flatter.

Exercise 8.17 (a) 2/3. (b) 1. (c) 1/2.

Exercise 8.19 The table would look like Table A.5, and $\delta = 80/609$.

Exercise 8.20 (a) $\delta = 1/(1+i)$, meaning that $r = i$. (b) $\delta = 1/\sqrt{(1+i)}$.

Table A.5 Time discounting

	$t=0$	$t=1$
a	81	16
b	1	625

Chapter 9

Exercise 9.3 (a) $U^{Thu}(\mathbf{a}) = 8$ and $U^{Thu}(\mathbf{b}) = 10$; on Thursday, you would choose **b**. $U^{Wed}(\mathbf{a}) = 6.67$ and $U^{Wed}(\mathbf{b}) = 8.33$; on Wednesday, you would choose **b**. (b) $U^{Thu}(\mathbf{a}) = 8$ and $U^{Thu}(\mathbf{b}) = 2$; on Thursday, you would choose **a**. $U^{Wed}(\mathbf{a}) = 1.33$ and $U^{Wed}(\mathbf{b}) = 0.33$; on Wednesday, you would choose **a**. (c) $U^{Thu}(\mathbf{a}) = 8$ and $U^{Thu}(\mathbf{b}) = 6$; on Thursday, you would choose **a**. $U^{Wed}(\mathbf{a}) = 4$ and $U^{Wed}(\mathbf{b}) = 6$; on Wednesday, you would choose **b**. (d) $U^{Thu}(\mathbf{a}) = 8$ and $U^{Thu}(\mathbf{b}) = 4$; on Thursday, you would choose **a**. $U^{Wed}(\mathbf{a}) = 2.67$ and $U^{Wed}(\mathbf{b}) = 2.67$; on Wednesday, you would be indifferent between **a** and **b**.

Exercise 9.4 (a) 8 and 4. (b) 12 and 6. (c) 3 and 1. (d) 3 and 6. (e) Benny. (f) Benny.

Exercise 9.5 (a) 2/3. (b) 3/4.

Exercise 9.6 (a) $\beta = 3/4$ and $\delta = 2/3$. (b) $x = 4.5$.

Exercise 9.7 $\beta = 4/5$ and $\delta = 1/2$.

Exercise 9.9 (a) If you are an exponential discounter, from the point of view of $t = 0$, you choose between $U^0(\mathbf{a}) = 3$, $U^0(\mathbf{b}) = 5$, $U^0(\mathbf{c}) = 8$, and $U^0(\mathbf{d}) = 13$. Obviously you prefer **d**, and because you are time consistent, that is the movie you will watch. (b) If you are a naive hyperbolic discounter, from the point of view of $t = 0$, you choose between $U^0(\mathbf{a}) = 3$, $U^0(\mathbf{b}) = 1/2 * 5 = 2.5$, $U^0(\mathbf{c}) = 1/2 * 8 = 4$, and $U^0(\mathbf{d}) = 1/2 * 13 = 6.5$. Thus, you will skip the mediocre movie and plan to see the fantastic one. From the point of view of $t = 1$, you choose between $U^1(\mathbf{b}) = 5$, $U^1(\mathbf{c}) = 1/2 * 8 = 4$, and $U^1(\mathbf{d}) = 1/2 * 13 = 6.5$. You will skip the good movie, still planning to see the fantastic one. From the point of view of $t = 2$, you choose between $U^2(\mathbf{c}) = 8$, and $U^2(\mathbf{d}) = 1/2 * 13 = 6.5$. You watch the great movie, foregoing the opportunity to see the fantastic one. (c) If you are a sophisticated hyperbolic discounter, you know that you would be unable to skip the great movie at $t = 2$ and that you consequently will not get to watch the fantastic movie. You also know that from the point of view of $t = 1$, your only realistic options would be $U^1(\mathbf{b}) = 5$ and $U^1(\mathbf{c}) = 1/2 * 8 = 4$. Consequently, you would watch the good movie. From the point of view of $t = 0$, then, your only realistic options are $U^0(\mathbf{a}) = 3$ and $U^0(\mathbf{b}) = 1/2 * 5 = 2.5$, meaning that you will watch the mediocre movie.

Exercise 9.10 (a) 8. (b) 13. (c) 4. (d) 12.33.

Exercise 9.12 Less pleasant.

Exercise 9.13 Given that the episode represented by a solid line has higher peak utility than the episode represented by a dashed line, and that the two have the same end utility, the person would favor the former over the latter.

Exercise 9.14 (a) 16/3 and 4. (b) 8 and 6. (c) 4 and 2. (d) 4 and 6. (e) Yves. (f) Ximena.

Exercise 9.15 (a) Hyperbolic discounting. (b) Choosing not to choose. (c) Preference over profiles. (d) Hyperbolic discounting. (e) Preference over profiles.

Chapter 10

Exercise 10.5 (a) $\langle U, L \rangle$ and $\langle D, R \rangle$. (b) $\langle U, L \rangle$. (c) $\langle U, R \rangle$.

Exercise 10.10 Suppose that Player I plays U with probability p and Player II plays L with probability q. (a) There is an equilibrium in which $p = q = 1/3$. (b) There is an equilibrium in which $p = 1/2$ and $q = 1$.

Exercise 10.11 Suppose that Player I plays U with probability p and Player II plays L with probability q. (a) There are two equilibria in pure strategies, $\langle U, L \rangle$ and $\langle D, R \rangle$, and a mixed equilibrium in which $p = 4/5$ and $q = 1/5$. (b) There are no equilibria in pure strategies but a mixed equilibrium in which $p = q = 1/2$. (c) There are two equilibria in pure strategies, $\langle U, L \rangle$ and $\langle D, R \rangle$, but no equilibria in mixed strategies.

Exercise 10.13 (a) The payoff matrix is given in Table A.6. (b) In the unique Nash equilibrium, both players randomize with probability 1/3, 1/3, and 1/3 (cf. Example 11.6 on pages 201–202).

Table A.6 Rock-paper-scissor payoff matrix

	R	P	S
R	0,0	0,1	1,0
P	1,0	0,0	0,1
S	0,1	1,0	0,0

Exercise 10.16 This game has two Nash equilibria in pure strategies, $\langle S, \neg S \rangle$ and $\langle \neg S, S \rangle$, and a mixed equilibrium in which each player plays S with probability 1/3.

Exercise 10.17 This game has two Nash equilibria in pure strategies, $\langle D, D \rangle$ and $\langle H, H \rangle$, and a mixed equilibrium in which each player plays D with probability 1/3.

Exercise 10.20 Yes.

Exercise 10.21 (a) This game has three Nash equilibria in pure strategies: $\langle U, L \rangle$, $\langle M, M \rangle$, and $\langle D, R \rangle$. (b) $\langle U, L \rangle$ and $\langle M, M \rangle$, but not $\langle D, R \rangle$, are trembling-hand perfect.

Exercise 10.25 The unique subgame-perfect equilibrium is $\langle D, RL \rangle$. That is, Player II plays R at the left node and L and the right node, and (anticipating this) Player I plays D.

Exercise 10.26 (a) In the unique subgame-perfect equilibrium, players always Take. (b) No.

Exercise 10.27 You would predict that economics majors would defect more frequently than non-majors, and that the economics majors therefore would do worse when playing against each other than non-majors would. Empirical evidence supports the prediction.

Chapter 11

Exercise 11.3 In a subgame-perfect equilibrium, a utilitarian Player II will accept any offer, since to her any division is better than ($0,$0). Because a utilitarian Player I would actually prefer ($5,$5) to any other outcome, that is the division that he will propose.

Exercise 11.4 See Table A.7 for the actual games played by (a) egoists, (b) utilitarians, (c) enviers, and (d) Rawlsians. The answers are: (a) ⟨D,D⟩, (b) ⟨C,C⟩ and ⟨D,D⟩, (c) ⟨D,D⟩, and (d) ⟨C,C⟩ and ⟨D,D⟩.

Table A.7 Social preferences

	C	D		C	D
C	4,4	0,5	C	8,8	5,5
D	5,0	3,3	D	5,5	6,6
	(a) Egoists			(b) Utilitarians	

	C	D		C	D
C	0,0	−5,5	C	4,4	0,0
D	5,−5	0,0	D	0,0	3,3
	(c) Enviers			(d) Rawlsians	

Chapter 12

Exercise 12.1 The intervention simply changes the default option from French fries to apple slices.

Bibliography

Ainslie, George (1975), "Specious reward: A behavioral theory of impulsiveness and impulse control," *Psychological Bulletin, 82* (4), 463–496.

Allais, Maurice (1953), "Le comportement de l'homme rationnel devant le risque: critique des postulats et axiomes de l'école américaine," *Econometrica, 21* (4), 503–6.

Allingham, Michael (2002), *Choice Theory: A Very Short Introduction*, Oxford: Oxford University Press.

Anand, Easha (2008), "Payday lenders back measures to unwind state restrictions," *Wall Street Journal*, October 28, p. A6.

Angner, Erik (2006), "Economists as experts: Overconfidence in theory and practice," *Journal of Economic Methodology, 13* (1), 1–24.

—— (2007), *Hayek and Natural Law*, London: Routledge.

—— (2009), "The politics of happiness: Subjective vs. economic measures as measures of social well-being," in Lisa Bortolotti, ed., *Philosophy and Happiness*, New York, NY: Palgrave Macmillan, pp. 149–66.

—— and George Loewenstein (2012), "Behavioral economics," in Uskali Mäki, ed., *Handbook of the Philosophy of Science: Philosophy of Economics*, Amsterdam: Elsevier, pp. 641–90.

Ariely, Dan (2008), *Predictably Irrational: The Hidden Forces that Shape our Decisions*, New York, NY: Harper.

——, George Loewenstein, and Drazen Prelec (2003), "'Coherent arbitrariness': Stable demand curves without stable preferences," *The Quarterly Journal of Economics, 118* (1), 73–105.

Arkes, Hal R. and Catherine Blumer (1985), "The psychology of sunk cost," *Organizational Behavior and Human Decision Processes, 35* (1), 124–40.

Associated Press (2007), "Ireland: Another metric system fault," *New York Times*, November 1.

Bar-Hillel, Maya (1980), "The base-rate fallacy in probability judgments," *Acta Psychologica, 44* (3), 211–33.

Becker, Gary S. (1976), *The Economic Approach to Human Behavior*, Chicago, IL: University of Chicago Press.

Beckett, Samuel (1989), *Nohow On*, London: Calder.

Bentham, Jeremy (1996 [1789]), *An Introduction to the Principles of Morals and Legislation*, Oxford: Clarendon Press.

Binmore, Ken (1999), "Why experiment in economics?," *The Economic Journal, 109* (453), F16–24.

—— (2007), *Game Theory: A Very Short Introduction*, New York, NY: Oxford University Press.

Brooks, David (2008), "The behavioral revolution," *New York Times*, October 28, p. A31.

Buehler, Roger, Dale Griffin, and Michael Ross (1994), "Exploring the 'planning fallacy': Why people underestimate their task completion times," *Journal of Personality and Social Psychology, 67* (3), 366–81.

Burroughs, William S. (1977 [1953]), *Junky*, Harmondsworth, Middlesex: Penguin Books.

Camerer, Colin F. (2003), *Behavioral Game Theory: Experiments in Strategic Interaction*, New York, NY: Russell Sage Foundation.

——, George Loewenstein, and Drazen Prelec (2005), "Neuroeconomics: How neuroscience can inform economics," *Journal of Economic Literature, 43* (1), 9–64.

——, Linda Babcock, George Loewenstein, and Richard H. Thaler (1997), "Labor supply of New York City cabdrivers: One day at a time," *The Quarterly Journal of Economics, 112* (2), 407–41.

Caplin, Andrew and Andrew Schotter, eds (2008), *The Foundations of Positive and Normative Economics: A Handbook*, New York, NY: Oxford University Press.

Consumer Federation of America (2006), "Press Release: How Americans view personal wealth vs. how financial planners view this wealth," January 9.

Davis, John B. (2011), *Individuals and Identity in Economics*, Cambridge: Cambridge University Press.

Dawes, Robyn M. and Richard H. Thaler (1988), "Anomalies: Cooperation," *The Journal of Economic Perspectives*, 2 (3), 187–97.

Dixit, Avinash K., Susan Skeath, and David Reiley (2009), *Games of Strategy*, 3rd ed., New York, NY: W. W. Norton & Co.

Durlauf, Steven N. and Lawrence Blume (2010), *Behavioural and Experimental Economics*, New York, NY: Palgrave Macmillan.

Earman, John and Wesley C. Salmon (1992), "The confirmation of scientific hypotheses," in Merrilee H. Salmon, John Earman, Clark Glymour, James G. Lennox, Peter Machamer, J. E. McGuire, John D. Norton, Wesley C. Salmon, and Kenneth F. Schaffner, eds., *Introduction to the Philosophy of Science*, Englewood Cliffs, NJ: Prentice Hall, pp. 7–41.

Ellsberg, Daniel (1961), "Risk, ambiguity, and the Savage axioms," *The Quarterly Journal of Economics*, 75 (4), 643–69.

Farhi, Paul (2010), "Juan Williams at odds with NPR over dismissal," *The Washington Post*, October 22, p. C1.

Fischhoff, Baruch (1975), "Hindsight is not equal to foresight: The effect of outcome knowledge on judgment under uncertainty," *Journal of Experimental Psychology: Human Perception and Performance*, 1 (3), 288–99.

FOX6 WBRC (2009), "Tension builds around courthouses' reopening," October 08.

Frank, Robert H. (2005), "The opportunity cost of economics education," *New York Times*, September 1, p. C2.

——, Thomas Gilovich, and Dennis T. Regan (1993), "Does studying economics inhibit cooperation?," *The Journal of Economic Perspectives*, 7 (2), 159–71.

Frank, Thomas (2007), "Security arsenal adds behavior detection," *USA Today*, September 25, p. B1.

Frederick, Shane, George Loewenstein, and Ted O'Donoghue (2002), "Time discounting and time preference: A critical review," *Journal of Economic Literature*, 40 (2), 351–401.

Harsanyi, John C. (1975), "Can the maximin principle serve as a basis for morality? A critique of John Rawls's theory," *The American Political Science Review*, 69 (2), 594–606.

Hastie, Reid and Robyn M. Dawes (2010), *Rational Choice in an Uncertain World: The Psychology of Judgment and Decision Making*, 2nd ed., Los Angeles, CA: Sage Publications.

Hayek, Friedrich A. (1933), "The trend of economic thinking," *Economica*, (40), 121–37.

Heath, Chip and Amos Tversky (1991), "Preference and belief: Ambiguity and competence in choice under uncertainty," *Journal of Risk and Uncertainty*, 4, 5–28.

Heuer, Richards J. (1999), *Psychology of Intelligence Analysis*, Washington, DC: Central Intelligence Agency Center for the Study of Intelligence.

Hobbes, Thomas (1994 [1651]), *Leviathan: With Selected Variants from the Latin Edition of 1668*, Indianapolis, IN: Hackett Pub. Co.

Huber, Joel, John W. Payne, and Christopher Puto (1982), "Adding asymmetrically dominated alternatives: Violations of regularity and the similarity hypothesis," *The Journal of Consumer Research*, 9 (1), 90–8.

Jevons, W. Stanley (1965 [1871]), *The Theory of Political Economy*, 5th ed., New York, NY: A. M. Kelley.

Kagel, John H. and Alvin E. Roth, eds (1995), *The Handbook of Experimental Economics*, Princeton, NJ: Princeton University Press.

Kahneman, Daniel and Amos Tversky (1979), "Prospect theory: An analysis of decision under risk," *Econometrica*, 47 (2), 263–91.

____, **Jack L. Knetsch, and Richard H. Thaler** (1991), "Anomalies: The endowment effect, loss aversion, and status quo bias," *The Journal of Economic Perspectives*, 5 (1), 193–206.

____, **Peter P. Wakker, and Rakesh Sarin** (1997), "Back to Bentham? Explorations of experienced utility," *The Quarterly Journal of Economics*, 112 (2), 375–405.

Keynes, John Maynard (1936), *The General Theory of Employment, Interest and Money*, New York, NY: Harcourt, Brace.

Knoch, Daria, Alvaro Pascual-Leone, Kaspar Meyer, Valerie Treyer, and Ernst Fehr (2006), "Diminishing reciprocal fairness by disrupting the right prefrontal cortex," *Science, 314* (5800), 829–32.

Krugman, Paul (2009), "How did economists get it so wrong?," *New York Times Magazine*, September 6, pp. 36–43.

Levitt, Steven D. and Stephen J. Dubner (2005), *Freakonomics: A Rogue Economist Explores the Hidden Side of Everything*, New York, NY: William Morrow.

Lichtenstein, Sarah and Paul Slovic (1973), "Response-induced reversals of preference in gambling: An extended replication in Las Vegas," *Journal of Experimental Psychology, 101* (1), 16–20.

Loewenstein, George and Erik Angner (2003), "Predicting and indulging changing preferences," in George Loewenstein, Daniel Read, and Roy F. Baumeister, eds., *Time and Decision: Economic and Psychological Perspectives on Intertemporal Choice*, New York, NY: Russell Sage Foundation, pp. 351–91.

____ **and Nachum Sicherman** (1991), "Do workers prefer increasing wage profiles?," *Journal of Labor Economics, 9* (1), 67–84.

____, **Daniel Read, and Roy F. Baumeister, eds** (2003), *Time and Decision: Economic and Psychological Perspectives on Intertemporal Choice*, New York, NY: Russell Sage Foundation.

Lord, Charles G., Lee Ross, and Mark R. Lepper (1979), "Biased assimilation and attitude polarization: The effects of prior theories on subsequently considered evidence," *Journal of Personality and Social Psychology*, 37 (11), 2098–109.

Luce, R. Duncan and Howard Raiffa (1957), *Games and Decisions: Introduction and Critical Survey*, New York, NY: Wiley.

McKinley, Jesse (2009), "Schwarzenegger statement contains not-so-secret message," *New York Times*, October 29, p. A16.

Mas-Colell, Andreu, Michael D. Whinston, and Jerry R. Green (1995), *Microeconomic Theory*, New York, NY: Oxford University Press.

Myers, David G. (1992), *The Pursuit of Happiness: Who Is Happy—and Why*, New York, NY: W. Morrow.

Nickerson, Raymond S. (1998), "Confirmation bias: A ubiquitous phenomenon in many guises," *Review of General Psychology*, 2 (2), 175–220.

O'Donoghue, Ted and Matthew Rabin (2000), "The economics of immediate gratification," *Journal of Behavioral Decision Making*, 13 (2), 233–50.

Osborne, Martin J. and Ariel Rubinstein (1994), *A Course in Game Theory*, Cambridge, MA: MIT Press.

Peterson, Martin (2009), *An Introduction to Decision Theory*, New York, NY: Cambridge University Press.

Pigou, Arthur C. (1952 [1920]), *The Economics of Welfare*, 4th ed., London: Macmillan.

Proust, Marcel (2002), *The Fugitive*, Vol. 5 of *In Search of Lost Time*, New York, NY: Allen Lane. Originally published in 1925.

Ramsey, Frank P. (1928), "A mathematical theory of saving," *The Economic Journal*, 38 (152), 543–59.

Rawls, John (1971), *A Theory of Justice*, Cambridge, MA: Belknap Press.

Redelmeier, Donald A. and Daniel Kahneman (1996), "Patients' memories of painful medical treatments: Real-time and retrospective evaluations of two minimally invasive procedures," *Pain, 66* (1), 3–8.

Ross, Don (2005), *Economic Theory and Cognitive Science: Microexplanation*, Cambridge, MA: MIT Press.

Russell, Bertrand (1959), *Common Sense and Nuclear Warfare*, New York, NY: Simon and Schuster.

de Sade, Donatien Alphonse François, Marquis (1889 [1791]), *Opus Sadicum: A Philosophical Romance* (Paris: Isidore Liseux). Originally published as *Justine*.

Schelling, Thomas C. (1960), *The Strategy of Conflict*, Cambridge, MA: Harvard University Press.

Schwartz, Barry (2004), *The Paradox of Choice: Why More Is Less*, New York, NY: Ecco.

Shafir, Eldar, Itamar Simonson, and Amos Tversky (1993), "Reason-based choice," *Cognition*, 49 (1–2), 11–36.

Skyrms, Brian (1996), *Evolution of the Social Contract*, Cambridge: Cambridge University Press.

Smith, Adam (1976 [1776]), *An Inquiry into the Nature and Causes of the Wealth of Nations*, 5th ed., Chicago, IL: University of Chicago Press.

—— (2002 [1759]), *The Theory of Moral Sentiments*, 6th ed., Cambridge: Cambridge University Press.

Smith, James P., John J. McArdle, and Robert Willis (2010), "Financial decision making and cognition in a family context," *The Economic Journal*, 120 (548), F363–80.

Staw, Barry M. and Jerry Ross (1989), "Understanding behavior in escalation situations," *Science*, 246 (4927), 216–20.

Szuchman, Paula and Jenny Anderson (2011), *Spousonomics: Using Economics to Master Love, Marriage and Dirty Dishes*, New York, NY: Random House.

Thaler, Richard H. (1980), "Toward a positive theory of consumer choice," *Journal of Economic Behavior & Organization*, 1 (1), 39–60.

—— (1985), "Mental accounting and consumer choice," *Marketing Science*, 4 (3), 199–214.

—— and Cass R. Sunstein (2008), *Nudge: Improving Decisions About Health, Wealth, and Happiness*, New Haven, CT: Yale University Press.

—— and Eric J. Johnson (1990), "Gambling with the house money and trying to break even: The effects of prior outcomes on risky choice," *Management Science*, 36 (6), 643–60.

Tomberlin, Michael (2009), "3rd lawsuit claims rigged jackpot," *The Birmingham News*, October 8, p. B1.

Tversky, Amos and Daniel Kahneman (1971), "Belief in the law of small numbers.," *Psychological Bulletin*, 76 (2), 105–10.

—— and —— (1974), "Judgment under uncertainty: Heuristics and biases," *Science*, 185 (4157), 1124–31.

—— and —— (1981), "The framing of decisions and the psychology of choice," *Science*, 211 (4481), 453–8.

—— and —— (1983), "Extensional versus intuitive reasoning: The conjunction fallacy in probability judgment," *Psychological Review*, 90 (4), 293–315.

—— and —— (1986), "Rational choice and the framing of decisions," *The Journal of Business*, 59 (4), S251–78.

—— and Eldar Shafir (1992), "The disjunction effect in choice under uncertainty," *Psychological Science*, 3 (5), 305–9.

Wilkinson, Nick and Matthias Klaes (2012), *An Introduction to Behavioral Economics*, 2nd ed., New York, NY: Palgrave Macmillan.

World RPS Society (2011), "How to beat anyone at rock paper scissors," http://www.worldrps.com/how-to-beat-anyone-at-rock-paper-scissors/.

Index

Printed in China